To my precious wife, Donna—Every day with you just keeps getting better!

Contents at a Glance

Contents

About the Author

Mark Collins has been developing software solutions for over 30 years. Some of the key technology areas of his career include COM, .NET, SQL Server, and SharePoint. He currently supports a large non-profit organization, serving as data architect and back office automation and integration specialist. You can see more info on his web site, www.TheCreativePeople.com. For questions and comments, contact Mark at markc@thecreativepeople.com.

About the Technical Reviewer

Damien Foggon is a developer, writer, and technical reviewer in cutting-edge technologies and has contributed to more than 50 books on .NET, C#, Visual Basic, and ASP.NET. He is the co-founder of the Newcastle based user-group NEBytes (online at http://www.nebytes.net), is a multiple MCPD in .NET 2.0 and .NET 3.5 and can be found online at http://blog.fasm.co.uk.

Acknowledgments

First and foremost, I acknowledge my Lord and Savior, Jesus Christ. The divine and eternal perspective on life, which can only be found in You, is an anchor, steadfast and sure. I humbly conclude that Your hand has guided me, often carrying me, through every endeavor, great and small. I submit that nothing of any value or significance is possible without You.

I want to say a very big thank you to my beautiful wife, Donna. I can honestly say that I would not be who I am if it were not for what you have sown into my life. I am truly blessed to be able to share my life with you. Thank you for your loving support and for making life fun!

Also, I want to thank Kevin Belknap for your help on this project. You have a keen eye and a seemingly innate ability to design great user experiences. I appreciate your friendship and willingness to jump in and help.

Next, I'd like to thank all the people at Apress who made this book possible and for all their hard work that turned it into the finished product you see now; this is truly a team effort. Jonathan, thank you for another opportunity; Ana, thanks for being a cheerleader, helper, and taskmaster all at the same time; Damien, thank you for your input and critique, helping to improve the quality and accuracy of this book; Douglass, Lori, and all the other contributors at Apress, thanks for overseeing the details. Everyone at Apress has made writing this book a pleasure.

Introduction

HTML5 is such an exciting opportunity for software developers. For a long time, the web has been the favorite platform for providing software applications to both external and internal users because of its reach and ease of deployment and maintenance. The primary limitation has been the client-side support, which can severely limit the user experience. With the lack of cross-browser standardization, using any of the advanced features often meant broken pages on older browsers or difficult polyfills.

HTML5 is a game-changer. Not only does it bring browser vendors together with a common set of specifications, but the features included in HTML5 enable web applications to provide a user experience that rivals even client applications. With mobile devices rapidly jumping on the HTML5 bandwagon, the number of HTML5 devices is expected to exceed 1 billion in the next year. I have seen the rise of many technologies and standards that promised to change the future of software development, but the momentum and support for HTML5 seems unprecedented.

Having said that, we are not quite there yet. Many of the specifications are still in draft and browsers, even current releases of them, do not all support the features that have been agreed upon. However, there are already enough features that are generally supported by browser vendors to make the switch to HTML5 very attractive. And the future is even more promising.

Who This Book Is For

HTML5 consists of changes in the markup, CSS improvements, and JavaScript enhancements and can be used with any implementation platform. However, this book presents these new features with the professional Visual Studio developer in mind. My goal is to answer the question "What would most ASP.NET developers need to know to incorporate the benefits of HTML5?" The sample applications are written using Visual Studio 2012 and many of the examples are specific to the ASP.NET platform, including web forms and MVC 4.

How This Book Is Structured

I've split the book into four parts, each going a bit deeper into the more advanced features.

Part 1 provides a quick introduction into web application technologies. This explains the operating environment that web developers find themselves in and where the HTML5 umbrella fits in.

Part 2 covers the basics of HTML5, including form development with both traditional web forms as well as the MVC model. Chapter 4 provides a really good overview of CSS with a focus on the new features available in CSS3. This part also demonstrates some of the scripting enhancements in Visual Studio 2012 and includes a discussion of how to support mobile devices with HTML5.

Part 3 takes this further and demonstrates some of the really cool features, including the new audio and video elements. I then demonstrate the graphics support available using both SVG and Canvas. This part also includes a discussion of how to use polyfills to deal with older browsers.

Part 4 explains some of the more advanced features such as Indexed DB, which provides for a persistent, client-side data store. This section includes a demonstration of geolocation and mapping using Bing Maps. It also explains how web sockets and drag-and-drop can be used for advanced applications.

Downloading the code

The code for the examples shown in this book is available on the Apress web site, `www.apress.com`. A link can be found on the book's information page under the Source Code/Downloads tab. This tab is located underneath the Related Titles section of the page.

Contacting the Author

Should you have any questions or comments—or even spot a mistake you think I should know about—you can contact the author at `markc@thecreativepeople.com`.

■ ■ ■

PART 1

What is HTML5?

HTML5 promises to change the way web applications are developed by providing cross-browser standardization. The term HTML5 has come to mean far more than just HTML, however. The HTML5 umbrella includes almost anything related to client-side functionality, including cascading style sheets and a host of new browser-provided standard features.

Before I get into demonstrating all of this great capability, Chapter 1 will provide a quick overview of the web environment. I'll then show you how HTML5 fits in. I'll give a high-level overview of the new features included in the HTML5 umbrella and briefly describe the current browser support for HTML5. This is rapidly changing but I'll provide some tips to show you how to determine what features are supported.

This book is intended primarily for the professional Visual Studio developer. However, in this chapter I will demonstrate some free alternatives including Web Matrix and Visual Studio Express for Web. These provide a great alternative, especially for those wanting to learn HTML5 who don't have access to Visual Studio.

CHAPTER 1

■ ■ ■

Before You Begin

Throughout this book I will be demonstrating how you can take advantage of the really cool new features known as HTML5. It will be very hands-on with lots of code samples and working web pages. Before we get started however, I wanted to set the stage and provide some context for where we will be going. What is generally referred to as HTML5 includes many technologies and HTML is just the tip of the iceberg.

In this chapter I will briefly review the operating environments that host web sites, currently and historically. I will also describe the development tools that are available. While this book is specifically focused on Visual Studio 2012, there are some free alternatives that will enable you to work through most of these exercises. Finally, I'll take a quick inventory of the HTML5 support in current and future browsers.

Reviewing Web Environment

To better understand where HTML5 sits from the web developer's view I will first review the web environment that we find ourselves in. This will be a very basic overview and quite familiar to most readers. However, I often find it useful to step back, once in a while, and get a better perspective.

The Basic HTTP Page

In the early days of the web, the model was quite simple. It included a web server that was responsible for serving up web pages and a browser that would render them on the client. In the Microsoft stack, Internet Information Services (IIS) provided the server component and Internet Explorer was the de facto browser. There were other browsers, of course, such as Netscape. The browser would request a page from the web server by passing the address (URL) in an HTTP GET request. The server would respond by providing an HTML document as illustrated in Figure 1-1.

Figure 1-1. *A simple page-centric web model*

If the web page included a form with input fields, the browser would provide for this data to be entered. When the page was submitted, this data was sent to the web server through an HTTP POST request. The web application would do something with this data and then return an updated web page. The browser would then render the entire page on the client.

There are two key aspects that I want to focus on here, that still have a significant influence even with today's web environment:

- The model is very page-centric.

- There are both server and client aspects to web development.

Page Centric Web

As I mentioned, web sites are predominantly focused on web pages. A page is requested, returned, and rendered. Data on a page is posted to the server, processed, and an updated page is returned and rendered. Because the web server is stateless, it has no knowledge of previous pages that were returned. This is why the entire page must be submitted and returned. Current and future technology is helping to move away from this paradigm and I'll demonstrate many of these techniques throughout this book. However, page-centric designs are still prevalent and will likely to continue to be so for some time.

Client/Server Model

There are both a server and client components to consider when building a web application. On the server, IIS responds to the HTTP requests as I mentioned. For static content, the HTML files can be simply stored in a virtual folder within IIS and no programming is required. For dynamic content, a web application is needed to generate HTML. Enter ASP.NET.

ASP.NET allows you to write code to dynamically create HTML. For example, the page can query a database and populate a grid using the data returned from the database. Likewise, the data presented in an HTTP Post request can be written to a database. Also, while a web application is generally considered stateless, ASP.NET provides several techniques for saving information between requests.

On the client side, the browser is responsible for rendering the content. This content is provided as HTML, which is essentially text with embedded formatting tags. In addition, cascading style sheets (CSS) are provided which instruct the browser how to format the content. The support for these HTML tags and CSS constructs will vary, however, between the available browsers and herein lies some of the biggest challenges of web development.

Improving the Web Experience

The page-centric approach is a major obstacle in raising the bar of the overall user experience. Refreshing an entire page is not very efficient. To address this issue, two key improvements were introduced:

- Client-side scripting
- AJAX

Using Client-side Scripting

All browsers now provide the ability to run client-side scripts, which are predominantly written in JavaScript, although others such as VBScript are also possible in some browsers. The ability to run scripts in the browser is a huge improvement. For example, a script can hide or show a section or modify the format of the content based on the user input. Since this happens on the client, no round-trip to the server is necessary. This makes the web site seem much more responsive.

■ **Caution**   JavaScript can be disabled on the client and you should consider, and test, how your page will function with scripting disabled.

Using AJAX

AJAX is an acronym for asynchronous JavaScript and XML. While a bit of a misnomer since it doesn't have to be asynchronous, use JavaScript, or XML, the term refers to a collection of technologies that enable client-side scripting to communicate with the web server outside of the typical page refresh scenario. In a nutshell, AJAX uses JavaScript to request data from the web server. It then updates the page content using the Document Object Model (DOM). This allows portions of the web page to be updated as needed without a complete refresh.

AJAX can also be used to call web services independently from the web server that is hosting the web page. You can use this to access data provided by a third party such as stock quotes or currency conversion. You can also call your own web services to perform real-time updates or load data based on user input. For example, you can provide a product search feature and use AJAX to call a web service that returns the matching products. Again, this is all independent of the standard page refresh paradigm.

Figure 1-2 illustrates the more robust model that most web sites use today.

Figure 1-2. *A more robust web environment*

With the inclusion of client-side scripting and AJAX requests we can now create much more interactive and responsive web-based solutions. Of course, this requires more complex web applications and a broad set of technologies to work with on both the server and the client.

Reviewing Web Technologies

Let's quickly review the various technologies that you will likely need to use when building great-looking interactive web applications.

- HTML – HyperText Markup Language (HTML) is the primary means for delivering content to the browser. In addition to the actual text that is displayed, HTML contains embedded tags that control how the content is formatted. Tags are used to align the content in sections and tables, modify text attributes, and include non-textual content including links and graphics.

- CSS – Cascading Style Sheets (CSS) are used as a central place for controlling visual aspects of the web pages such as fonts, colors, background images and margins. They are called cascading because you normally define site-level styles in one style sheet and then provide additional style sheets as necessary to either further define or override these for specific pages, sections, or classes.

- DOM – The HTML that is rendered by the browser is similar to an XML document and the Document Object Model (DOM) defines the structure of this document. This is used for programmatically accessing and modifying the document's content.

- ECMAScript – Client-side scripts are interpreted and executed by the browser. To improve cross-browser compatibility, the ECMAScript standard defines the syntax and features of the scripting language. JavaScript is a dialect of the ECMAScript standard.

■ **Note**   Historically, JavaScript and JScript were two implementations of the same scripting language. Microsoft named their implementation JScript to avoid trademark issues with Sun but they are essentially the same and follow the evolving ECMAScript standards. With IE 10, Microsoft is moving away from this distinction and referring to their scripting language as JavaScript. And just to keep things interesting, Microsoft still provides a JScript language, which provides access to .NET and is very different from JavaScript. I will refer to JavaScript throughout this book as the standard ECMAScript compliant scripting language.

Exploring HTML5

So where does HTML5 fit in to this equation? Just about everywhere! What is generally classified as HTML5 is actually a broad set of specifications related to web browser standardization, many of which having nothing to do with HTML. I will briefly summarize these here and then demonstrate these features in detail throughout the rest of this book. There are a few things that you should keep in mind:

- Many of the specifications have not been finalized yet. Much of the core specifications are completed but some of the advanced features are still subject to change.

- Browser-support for these features will vary. Browser vendors are aggressively incorporating new features in each subsequent release.

- The specifications leave room for each browser vendor to decide how each feature is implemented. For example, all compliant browsers will provide a date picker control for entering dates, but each browser may implement this in a different way.

The general trend with HTML5 is to provide more native support in the browser. As you will see throughout this book, browsers are providing an increasingly impressive set of features. This will enable you to build better web applications with less work.

Reviewing Markup Changes

As you would expect, HTML5 includes some important improvements in the markup elements. There is a sizeable list of new markup elements and I will demonstrate many of these in Chapters 2, 3, and 4.

The generic `<div>` element is still supported but new, more context-specific elements are also provided. I will explain and demonstrate this in Chapter 4. The new content tags are:

- `<article>`
- `<aside>`
- `<footer>`
- `<header>`
- `<hgroup>`
- `<nav>`
- `<section>`

Several new input type elements are provided that allow native formatting and validation capabilities. These will be explained in Chapters 2 and 3. The new types are:

- `color`
- `datetime` (as well as `datetime-local`, `date`, `time`, `month`, and `week`)
- `email`
- `number`
- `range`
- `search`
- `tel`
- `url`

There are also some new elements that enable you to use browser-implemented controls such as:

- `<audio>`
- `<figcaption>`
- `<figure>`
- `<meter>`
- `<output>`
- `<progress>`
- `<video>`

There are a few other elements introduced with HTML5 that I will describe in more detail later. I will demonstrate the `<audio>` and `<video>` tags in Chapter 8. The new `<canvas>` element provides some significant graphics capabilities and I will demonstrate this in Chapter 10.

Understanding Cascading Style Sheets

Like HTML, CSS capabilities are defined by an evolving set of specifications. The current published *recommendation* is CSS 2.1 and the next version being drafted is referred to as CSS3. However, it has been broken down into over 50 "modules" with a separate specification for each. As of this writing, only a few of these modules have become official W3C Recommendations (REC) and several more are at W3C Candidate Recommendation (CR) status.

At the time of this writing the W3C Recommendations are:

- Color
- Namespaces
- Selectors Level 3

The candidate recommendations are:

- Backgrounds and Borders
- Marquee
- Media Queries

- Mobile Profile

- Multi-column Layout

- Paged Media

- Ruby

- Speech

- Style Attribute Syntax

■ **Tip**   Since the status of each CSS module is ever changing, for complete information about the current status of each, see the article at `http://www.w3.org/Style/CSS/specs`.

So the actual CSS3 "specification" is very much a moving target at the moment and browser support for these specifications will also vary. For example, Microsoft lists the CSS features that they will support in IE 10 in the article at `http://msdn.microsoft.com/en-us/library/ie/hh673536(v=vs.85).aspx`. However, there are already a number of cool features that are generally available and I will demonstrate some of these in Chapter 4.

Reviewing Other HTML Functionality

The actual scripting syntax is defined by the ECMAScript specification as I mentioned earlier. The current version, 5.1 was published in June, 2011. While not actually part of the HTML5 specifications, HTML5 compliant browsers are expected to support the ECMAScript 5.1 standard. As I said, however, this specification describes the language syntax and some built-in functions such as element selectors.

In addition to the language specification, there are quite a few other specifications that are loosely included under the HTML5 umbrella that define specific client-side functionality. I will demonstrate many of these in Chapter 5 and the rest will be covered in later chapters. The new functionality includes:

- Offline Cache – you can specify the pages that are required for offline support, including CSS and JavaScript files. The specification also includes an API and event handlers that allow you to monitor and control the local cache.

- Drag and Drop – provides the ability to select an item and drop it on another item on the web page. This will be demonstrated in Chapter 14.

- Web workers – allow you to execute a script on a separate thread. This includes mechanisms to communicate with workers and the ability to share workers between multiple web pages.

- Web storage – includes both `sessionStorage` for isolating session data between multiple tabs connected to the same site as well as `localStorage` for storing data on the client. The IndexedDB implementation will be covered in detail in Chapter 11.

- Geolocation – This is not part of the official specifications but has been generally included when discussing HTML5 features. Geolocation defines an API that can be called from JavaScript to determine the current geographic location. How the browser implements this is determined by the available hardware. On a GPS-enabled device it will use a GPS satellite. If GPS support is not available, it will use Wi-Fi, if possible to determine the location. Mobile devices can use cell tower triangulation. If all else fails, the IP address can at least provide some estimate of location. Obviously, the accuracy will vary greatly and the API handles this. I will demonstrate geolocation in Chapter 12.

- Web sockets – provides asynchronous communication between the web page (browser) and the server. Once the connection is established, the server can send real-time updates to the client. This will be demonstrated in Chapter 13.

Choosing a Development Tool

There are several development environments that you can use to create ASP.NET applications that take advantage of the HTML5 features. I will present them here briefly and cover them in a little more detail in subsequent chapters. The key thing to know is that there are some free alternatives to Visual Studio.

Using Visual Studio 2012

Visual Studio 2012 is the premier development environment for building ASP.NET applications. I won't say much about it here as I will be using it predominantly throughout this book to demonstrate HTML5 implementations. However, if acquiring Visual Studio is cost prohibitive, there are some free alternatives that will still allow you to work most of the exercises in this book.

■ **Tip** You can also use Visual Studio 2010 for most of the exercises. Make sure you have installed Visual Studio SP1 and then install MVC 4, which is available as a separate, free download. There are improvements in Visual Studio 2012 that will be helpful, but you can still accomplish much of the work using a properly configured 2010 environment.

Using Microsoft's Web Matrix

Microsoft's Web Matrix is a lightweight IDE that is specifically targeted for building web sites. While not limited to just ASP.NET pages you can build full-fledged ASP.NET applications. It includes SQL Server Compact, which is a file-based version of SQL Server. It also uses IIS Express to host a local web site for debugging. This is the same hosting environment provided in Visual Studio 2012, which replaces the ASP.NET Development Server used in previous versions of Visual Studio.

The ASP pages are based on ASP.NET MVC version 3 and use the Razor view engine. Consequently the file extensions are .cshtml (or .vbhtml if you're using VB). The classic ASP model with an .aspx markup file and separate .cs code-behind file is not supported, however. You can create .aspx files but adding a code behind file is not a practical option. Also, as of this writing, it uses .NET version 4.0 and does not support version 4.5.

You can download and install Web Matrix, version 2 from this site: http://www.microsoft.com/web/webmatrix/next.

■ **Note** As of this writing Version 2 was still in Beta. For a description of the Version 2 features see the article at http://www.microsoft.com/web/webmatrix/betafeatures.aspx.

When creating a new site, if you use the Starter template, it will create a familiar default ASP web application shown in Figure 1-3.

Figure 1-3. *The default ASP application*

The IDE is shown in Figure 1-4. Notice the .cshtml extensions and the Razor syntax for the page implementation.

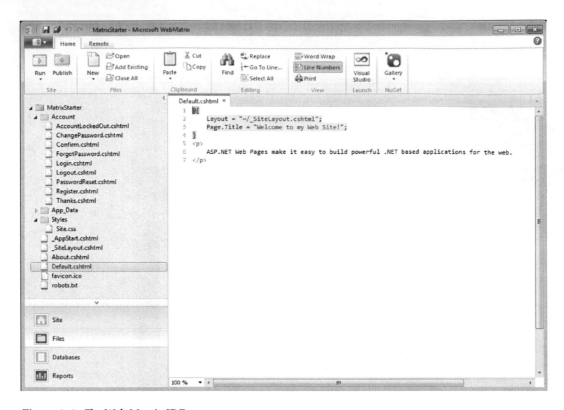

Figure 1-4. *The Web Matrix IDE*

The Web Matrix IDE includes the ability to manage SQL databases. You can create new databases or connect to existing SQL Server database. You can create and alter tables and view and edit data. You can also run SQL queries as shown in Figure 1-5.

Figure 1-5. *Web Matrix Database IDE*

For more information on using Web Matrix, I suggest starting with the tutorial found at:
`http://www.asp.net/web-pages/tutorials/basics/1-getting-started-with-webmatrix-and-asp-net-web-pages`.

Using Visual Studio Express for Web

Visual Studio Express for Web is essentially a free version of Visual Studio. It looks and functions just like the full retail version of Visual Studio with the non-web features removed. It also has the Team Foundation Server (TFS) integration removed. You can download Visual Studio Express for Web at
`http://www.microsoft.com/visualstudio/11/en-us/downloads#express-web`.

The IDE is identical to the retail version of Visual Studio and is shown in Figure 1-6.

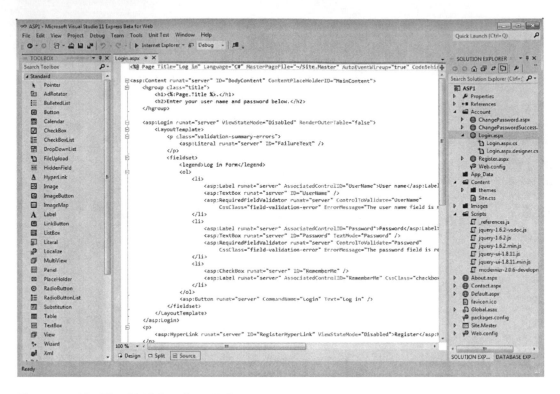

Figure 1-6. *The Visual Web Developer IDE*

The standard ASP.NET web project will create a basic ASP application shown in Figure 1-7. As you can see, one of the things that has changed with Visual Studio 2012 is the standard template generates a much more visually appealing web site.

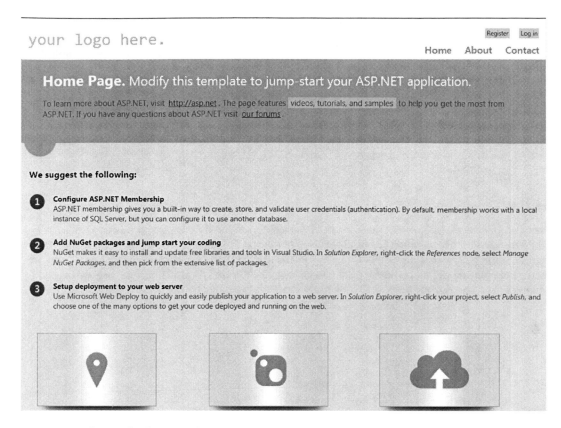

Figure 1-7. *The standard ASP application*

Visual Studio Express has some improvements over the Web Matrix application:

- If you're used to working with Visual Studio, this will be very familiar.

- Visual Studio Express includes all the debugging and IntelliSense capabilities of Visual Studio.

- You can build classic .aspx pages with code-behind files.

- There are more project templates available including web services, AJAX controls, and MVC applications.

- The solutions created with Visual Studio Express are compatible with Visual Studio.

Deciphering Browser Support for HTML5

All of the work to move applications to HTML5 is based on the assumption that the majority of browsers will be HTML5 compatible. This requires that the browser vendors step up to the plate and provide HTML5 compatible browsers and that the public at-large will adopt them. This also includes mobile devices, which are a key part of the push for HTML5 compliance. The general consensus is that we are moving in that direction at a pretty good clip.

As I mentioned earlier, the actual HTML5 specifications are still being defined. Initial estimates were as late as 2022 before the final recommendation was complete, according to HTML5 editor, Ian Hickson. More recently, dates as early as 2014 have been proposed. However, as parts of the specification are being finalized, vendors are implementing them so much is already available in browsers that are currently in use. As web developers, we should focus on the features that are generally available now or expect to be soon, and these are the features that I will cover in this book.

There is a really good web site at `http://html5test.com` that provides a summary of the browsers that are currently available and those that are still in development. Each browser is awarded points based on the HTML5 features that it supports. In addition to an overall score that allows you to compare browsers, the scores are also broken down by functional area so you can see which areas have good support from most browsers.

Summary

HTML5 covers a broad set of technologies that include improvements to the HTML markup, cascading style sheets, and client-side scripting. In addition, there are some significant enhancements to browsers that make it easier to provide some great web applications. While the official specifications are still a work-in-progress and the browser vendors are playing catch-up, there is quite a bit of functionality already available. Also, as you'll see in the next few chapters, Visual Studio and the ASP.NET platform has been expanded to leverage the HTML feature set.

PART 2

■ ■ ■

Using the New HTML5 Features

In this part you'll start using HTML5 to build basic forms and web pages. This will explore the three primary facets of the HTML5 specifications:

- Markup
- Cascading Style Sheets (CSS)
- Scripting

In Chapters 2 and 3 you'll use the new input elements to provide a better user experience with forms; first with a traditional .aspx web form and then using MVC4. Each of these frameworks provide HTML5 support but the approaches are significantly different.

In Chapter 4, you'll take a crash course on CSS, focusing primarily on the new features included with CSS3. The sample web page that you'll create will take advantage of the new structural elements such as aside, nav, and footer. Chapter 5 then demonstrates some of the basic scripting enhancements provided by HTML5 and Visual Studio. This includes using web workers to employ background threads on the client. You'll also try out the new JavaScript query selectors and demonstrate the bundling and minification support in Visual Studio 2012.

Finally, Chapter 6 rounds out this section by explaining how you can build mobile-friendly web applications. I will demonstrate many of the emulators that are available for testing your application on a variety of HTML5 compatible devices. You'll also use media queries to dynamically address different screen resolutions.

CHAPTER 2

■ ■ ■

ASP.NET Web Forms

In this chapter I will demonstrate some of the new input types defined by HTML5 and show you how to use these in an ASP.NET web form. Typically, the TextBox control is used when data needs to be entered on a form. Users can enter all kinds of data in a TextBox including strings, numbers, dates, and so on. To ensure valid data, the form would need to supply either server-side or client-side validation logic. The HTML5 specification provides several new input types that can provide much of this for you.

The following input types are defined (however, not all browsers support all of them yet):

- `select`
- `color`
- `datetime` (including `datetime-local`, `date`, `time`, `month`, and `week`)
- `email`
- `number`
- `range`
- `tel`
- `url`

When you build a web form using ASP.NET, the actual HTML that is sent to the browser is generated by .NET. I'll show you the ASP.NET way of inserting the new input types. Also, using some of the new HTML elements requires a little extra manipulation and I'll demonstrate how to handle that as well.

Introducing the New Input Types

I'll start out with a fairly simple example to demonstrate how to use the new email control combined with the placeholder attribute to quickly provide client-side instructions and validation. You'll start by creating a standard ASP project using the Visual Studio template and then modify the registration page. Then I'll introduce the new Page Inspector and explain the database support in Visual Studio 2012.

Creating an ASP.NET Project

In this chapter you'll create an ASP.NET project using the standard Web Forms template in Visual Studio 2012. Start Visual Studio 2012 (or the free version, Visual Studio Express for Web). From the Start Page, click the New Project link. In the New Project dialog box select the Web category and select the "ASP.NET Web Forms Application" template, enter **Chapter2** for the project name, and select an appropriate location as shown in Figure 2-1.

Figure 2-1. *Create an ASP Web Forms project*

Using the Email Control

For the first exercise, you'll modify the registration form to require a valid email address be used as the user name. You'll also use the `placeholder` attribute to let the users know that an email address is needed.

EXERCISE 2-1. MODIFYING THE REGISTRATION PAGE

1. In the `Chapter2` project, open the `Register.aspx` page, which you'll find in the `Account` folder.

2. There are several `li` elements in the `fieldset` node that define the input fields. The first one is for the User Name. Change this as follows by entering the attributes shown in bold:

   ```
   <asp:Label runat="server" AssociatedControlID="UserName">User name</asp:Label>
   <asp:TextBox runat="server" ID="UserName"
       TextMode="Email" placeholder="use your email address" Width="200" />
   <asp:RequiredFieldValidator runat="server" ControlToValidate="UserName"
       CssClass="field-validation-error"
       ErrorMessage="The user name field is required." />
   ```

3. Start the application by pressing F5. Using the Chrome browser, the Register page will look like Figure 2-2. Notice the text in the User name field.

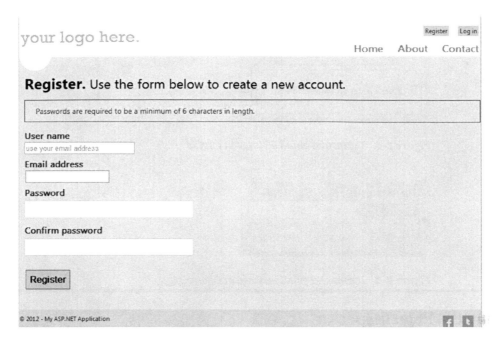

Figure 2-2. *The initial Register page*

4. If you enter an invalid email address you should see the error message shown in Figure 2-3 when the page is submitted.

Figure 2-3. *The invalid email error message*

5. Close the browser and stop debugging.

6. Try viewing this page with several different browsers. Notice that the email validation message looks different in each. In Firefox this will look like Figure 2-4 and in Opera it looks like Figure 2-5.

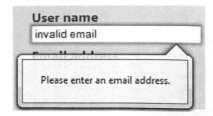

Figure 2-4. The invalid email message in Firefox

Figure 2-5. The invalid email message in Opera

Using the Page Inspector

For this example, I used Google Chrome as my browser. If you want to use a different browser, you can select it from the dropdown list in the menu as shown in Figure 2-6.

Figure 2-6. Selecting the browser to use for debugging

■ **Tip** This dropdown list automatically includes all of the browsers that are currently installed. You don't have to do anything to add them. If you install a new browser, you will need to restart Visual Studio before it will be included in the list. If you use Internet Explorer the browser will be more integrated with the debugger. For example, when you close the browser, Visual Studio will automatically stop debugging. However, when testing HTML5 support you'll need to use other browsers in addition to IE.

Notice that there is also an option for the Page Inspector. This is a new tool that is introduced with Visual Studio 2012. Select this option and then press F5 to debug your application. The first time you use the Page Inspector you'll need to enable it in the web.config file. The dialog box shown in Figure 2-7 explains this. Just click the Yes button to continue.

Figure 2-7. *Enabling the Page Inspector*

In addition to the browser window there are several other windows that provide useful information about the current web page. At the bottom, the HTML tab shows the actual HTML that is generated by ASP.NET. Select the User Name control in the page view and the relevant markup is highlighted as shown in Figure 2-8.

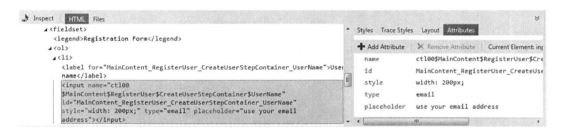

Figure 2-8. *The HTML generated for the user name control*

Except for the rather cryptic control name and id, this is standard HTML5 syntax. In particular, notice the following attributes; the email type value and the placeholder attribute are new in HTML5:

```
type="email"
placeholder="use your email address"
```

The placeholder attribute that you entered in the .aspx page is not an ASP.NET attribute. It was not processed by .NET but passed directly to the generated HTML.

Notice also the pane to the right that provides several tabs for viewing the CSS styles. I've selected the Attributes tab, which shows the values for all of the element's attributes. The other tabs show you the styles that are applied. Stop the debugger to close the page inspector.

Viewing the Default Database

When you create an ASP.NET project with Visual Studio 2012 (or Express for Web), it will use SQL Server 2012 for the default database. You don't need to install SQL Server; the necessary components are included with Visual Studio. The database is actually created the first time it is needed so you'll need to start the application and login or register. If you have SQL Server installed, you can view and modify the data using SQL Server Management Studio.

■ **Tip**　You can download and install SQL Server 2012 Express from this site:
`http://msdn.microsoft.com/en-us/evalcenter/hh230763.aspx`.

When connecting to the database, select "(LocalDb)\v11.0" for the server name and use Windows authentication as shown in Figure 2-9.

Figure 2-9.　*Connecting to the local DB*

Once you have connected, select the appropriate database. Visual Studio creates a new database for each project and the database name will be `aspnet-<project name>-<date/time>`. You can expand the database to see the tables that are included, which will be the standard ASP membership tables, as shown in Figure 2-10.

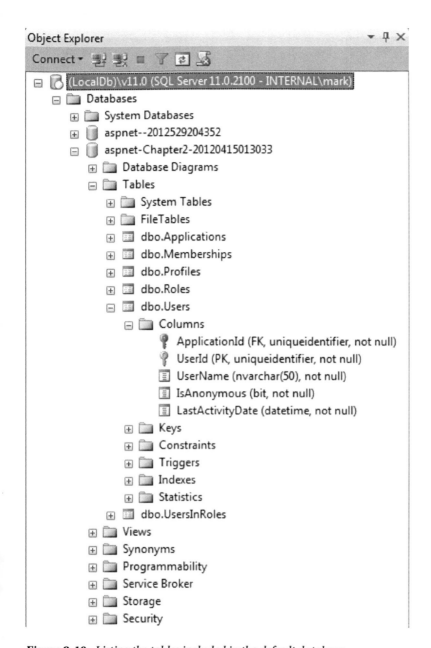

Figure 2-10. *Listing the tables included in the default database*

If you don't have SQL Server Management Studio installed, you can also use Visual Studio to view the database. From the menu select View ➤ Server Explorer. Expand the Data Connections node and then select "DefaultConnection (Chapter 2)". You can expand the tables, as shown in Figure 2-11.

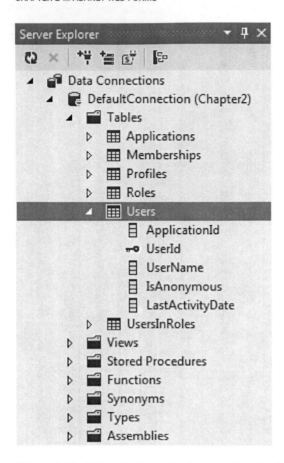

Figure 2-11. *Using the Server Explorer to view the database*

To execute a query, right-click any of the database nodes and select the "New Query" link. Type in a standard Transact-SQL command and click the Execute icon to run it. The query window will look similar to Figure 2-12.

Figure 2-12. *The Query window*

Exploring the Other Input Types

HTML5 introduces several other input types. To demonstrate them, you'll add a feedback form with some rather contrived questions. These will implement the other types that are available to you.

■ **Tip**   To get a detailed explanation of each of the input elements, check out the actual HTML5 specification. This address will take you to the section on input elements: `http://www.whatwg.org/specs/web-apps/current-work/multipage/the-input-element.html#the-input-element`

Implementing a Feedback Form

In the next exercise, you'll create a new form and add several input controls; one of each type. After you have created the form I'll discuss each of the controls.

EXERCISE 2-2. ADDING A FEEDBACK FORM

1. Open the `Chapter2` project in Visual Studio if not already open.

2. In the Solution Explorer, right-click the `Chapter2` project and select the Add ➤ Webform links. Enter **Feedback** when prompted for the form name.

3. This will create a new form with a single `div` as shown in Listing 2-1.

    Listing 2-1. The blank form implementation

    ```
    <%@ Page Language="C#" AutoEventWireup="true" CodeBehind="Feedback.aspx.cs"
        Inherits="Chapter2.Feedback" %>

    <!DOCTYPE html>

    <html xmlns="http://www.w3.org/1999/xhtml">
    <head runat="server">
        <title></title>
    </head>
    <body>
        <form id="form1" runat="server">
        <div>

        </div>
        </form>
    </body>
    </html>
    ```

4. Within the empty `div`, enter the code shown in Listing 2-2. This will add several fields that each demonstrate one of the new input types.

Listing 2-2. Adding feedback fields

```
<fieldset>
    <legend>Feedback Form</legend>
    <ol>
        <li>
            <asp:Label ID="lblURL" runat="server"
                AssociatedControlID="URL">Default home page</asp:Label>
            <asp:textbox runat="server" ID="URL" TextMode="Url"></asp:textbox>
        </li>
        <li>
            <asp:Label ID="lblOptions" runat="server"
                AssociatedControlID="Options">Default browser</asp:Label>
            <asp:DropDownList ID="Options" runat="server">
                <asp:ListItem Text="Internet Explorer" Value="1"></asp:ListItem>
                 <asp:ListItem Text="Google Chrome" Value="2" Selected></asp:ListItem>
                <asp:ListItem Text="Firefox" Value="3"></asp:ListItem>
                <asp:ListItem Text="Opera" Value="4"></asp:ListItem>
            </asp:DropDownList>
        </li>
        <li>
            <asp:Label ID="lblBirthday" runat="server"
                AssociatedControlID="Birthday">Birthday</asp:Label>
            <asp:TextBox runat="server" ID="Birthday" TextMode="Date"></asp:TextBox>
        </li>
        <li>
            <asp:Label ID="lblMonth" runat="server"
                AssociatedControlID="Month">Favorite Month</asp:Label>
            <asp:TextBox runat="server" ID="Month" TextMode="Month"></asp:TextBox>
        </li>
        <li>
            <asp:Label ID="lblWeek" runat="server"
                AssociatedControlID="Week">Busiest Week</asp:Label>
            <asp:TextBox runat="server" ID="Week" TextMode="Week"></asp:TextBox>
        </li>
        <li>
            <asp:Label ID="lblStart" runat="server"
                AssociatedControlID="DateTime">Start Date/Time</asp:Label>
            <asp:TextBox runat="server" ID="DateTime"
                TextMode="DateTime"></asp:TextBox>
        </li>
        <li>
            <asp:Label ID="lblTime" runat="server"
                AssociatedControlID="Time">Current Time</asp:Label>
            <asp:TextBox runat="server" ID="Time" TextMode="Time" ></asp:TextBox>
        </li>
        <li>
            <asp:Label ID="lblPhone" runat="server"
                AssociatedControlID="Phone">Phone</asp:Label>
            <asp:TextBox runat="server" ID="Phone" TextMode="Phone"></asp:TextBox>
        </li>
        <li>
```

```
            <asp:Label ID="lblRange" runat="server"
                AssociatedControlID="Range">Overall satisfaction</asp:Label>
            <asp:TextBox runat="server" ID="Range" TextMode="Range"
                Width="200" Height="30"></asp:TextBox>
    </li>
    <li>
            <asp:Label ID="lblColor" runat="server"
                AssociatedControlID="Color">Preferred color</asp:Label>
            <asp:TextBox runat="server" ID="Color" TextMode="Color"></asp:TextBox>
    </li>
    <li>
            <asp:Label ID="lblScore" runat="server"
                AssociatedControlID="Score">Overall Rating</asp:Label>
            <asp:TextBox ID="Score" runat="server" TextMode="Number"
                MaxLength="1"></asp:TextBox>
    </li>
    <li>
            <asp:Label ID="lblComments" runat="server"
                AssociatedControlID="Multi">Comments</asp:Label>
            <asp:TextBox runat="server" ID="Multi" TextMode="Multiline"
                Rows="5" Columns="30"></asp:TextBox>
    </li>
    </ol>
    <asp:Button ID="Submit" runat="server" CommandName="Submit" Text="Submit" />
</fieldset>
```

5. Save the changes and press F5 to display the new page in the browser. The feedback form as rendered by the Opera browser is shown in Figure 2-13.

Figure 2-13. The initial feedback form

■ **Note**   I'm using the Opera browser to render the feedback form because it has the best support for the new input types, as of this writing. I'll explain that more, later in this chapter. You can download Opera from www.opera.com.

Reviewing the New Input Types

Now let's look at each of the new input types and see how they have been implemented in Opera. Keep in mind that different browsers may present the control differently.

URL

The first field uses the `url` input type, which expects a valid web address. If you enter an invalid address, when the page is submitted you'll see the validation error shown in Figure 2-14.

1. Default home page
2. Default browse
3. Birthday

Figure 2-14. *The URL field*

■ **Note**   The Opera implementation automatically adds the `http://` prefix if the protocol is not included in the url. For example, if you enter www.apress.com and tab off the field, the address is changed to `http://www.apress.com`.

Selection List

The next field provides a dropdown list of available browsers. In ASP.NET this is coded as a `DropDownList` that contains a number of `ListItem` elements. The generated HTML uses a `select` element that contains `option` elements like this:

```
<select name="Options" id="Options">
  <option value="1">Internet Explorer</option>
  <option selected value="2">Google Chrome</option>
  <option value="3">Firefox</option>
  <option value="4">Opera</option>
</select>
```

Notice that the selected item is indicated with the selected attribute. This is a boolean and doesn't need a value so simply adding the selected attribute with no value is sufficient, although Visual Studio will show a warning.

Date/Time Fields

The feedback form contains the following date/time fields that demonstrate the browser-support for various date-type fields:

- Birthday – (Date) a single date (no time portion)

- Favorite Month – (Month) an entire month

- Busiest Week – (Week) an entire week

- Start Date/Time – (DateTime) a single date including the time portion

- Current Time – (Time) the time without any date

The date fields are text boxes where you can key the desired value. However, there is also an icon that displays a date picker control. The different formats of this control (date, month, and week) are shown in Figures 2-15, 2-16, and 2-17, respectively. These controls are essentially the same except that the month and week versions will only allow you to select the entire month or week. Notice that the week format also displays the week number (from 1 to 52).

Figure 2-15. *The date picker control*

Figure 2-16. *The date picker selecting an entire month*

◄		April			►	2012	⇕
Week	Mon	Tue	Wed	Thu	Fri	Sat	Sun
13	26	27	28	29	30	31	1
14	2	3	4	5	6	7	8
15	9	10	11	12	13	14	15
16	16	17	18	19	20	21	22
17	23	24	25	26	27	28	29
18	30	1	2	3	4	5	6
					Today		

Figure 2-17. The date picker selecting an entire week

Both the Start Date/Time and Current Time fields include a time control that allows the hour and minute to be entered separately. You can also use the up/down arrows to increment the hour or minute portion depending on which is currently in focus.

Phone

The feedback form includes a Phone field that uses the new tel input type. At the time of this writing, none of the desktop browsers support this type. I included it in the exercise with the hope that by the time you read this you'll have a browser that will support it. As with all non-supported types, the browser treats this as a standard textbox control.

Range

The next control uses the new range input type. This allows you to slide the indicator across the extent of the control, providing a relative value. This is similar to a fuel gauge in a car where the specific value is not as important as the relative value such as ¾ full. I defined this with a width of 300 and height of 30 so the control was generated to slide horizontally. If the height was greater than the width, the slider would move vertically, like a thermometer.

There are some other attributes of the range control that you can manipulate in HTML that are not supported in ASP.NET. You could still specify these in the .aspx page and they would be passed to the generated HTML just like the placeholder attribute. However, I will show you another way to configure the range control later in this chapter.

Color

The color control includes a small square that displays the selected color. If you click the dropdown icon, you can select a color from the default pallet as shown in Figure 2-18.

Figure 2-18. *Selecting a color from the default pallet*

If you click the Other button, the full-featured color-picker shown in Figure 2-19 is displayed.

Figure 2-19. *The color-picker control*

Number

The Overall Rating field uses the number input type. The Opera and Chrome implementation include up and down arrows that allows you to increment and decrement the current value. Alpha and alpha-numeric values are ignored (deleted). With Chrome, an invalid entry is cleared out as soon as you tab off the field. With Opera, this does not happen until the form is submitted. In both cases, no error is displayed but the entire input is simply deleted.

Text Area

The last field uses the text area input type. I specified this to use 5 rows and 30 columns. This only affects how the field is displayed on the page. The text is stored as a single string and carriage returns that are entered in the field are stored as 
. The text will be wrapped to fit into the allotted size on the page but it can contain any number of rows.

Reviewing the Form

A completed form is shown in Figure 2-20.

Figure 2-20. *The completed feedback form*

After entering values for each of the fields, click the Submit button and then view the page's source. Each of the fields will now have a value attribute that contains the value that was included when the page was submitted. This is what the server-side code would use to store and/or process the submitted data. I extracted a portion of this, which is shown in Listing 2-3. I particularly want you to see how the various date/time field values are formatted. Also notice that the color is stored as a hexadecimal representation of the selected RGB values.

Listing 2-3. The source with submitted values

```
<li>
    <label for="Birthday" id="lblBirthday">Birthday</label>
    <input name="Birthday" type="date" value="2012-04-17" id="Birthday" />
</li>
<li>
    <label for="Month" id="lblMonth">Favorite Month</label>
    <input name="Month" type="month" value="2012-04" id="Month" />
</li>
```

```
<li>
    <label for="Week" id="lblWeek">Busiest Week</label>
    <input name="Week" type="week" value="2012-W16" id="Week" />
</li>
<li>
    <label for="DateTime" id="lblStart">Start Date/Time</label>
    <input name="DateTime" type="datetime"
        value="2012-04-17T09:15Z" id="DateTime" />
</li>
<li>
    <label for="Time" id="lblTime">Current Time</label>
    <input name="Time" type="time" value="15:05:00" id="Time" />
</li>
<li>
    <label for="Phone" id="lblPhone">Phone</label>
    <input name="Phone" type="tel" value="8005551212" id="Phone" />
</li>
<li>
    <label for="Range" id="lblRange">Overall satisfaction</label>
    <input name="Range" type="range" value="79" id="Range"
        style="height:30px;width:200px;" />
</li>
<li>
    <label for="Color" id="lblColor">Preferred color</label>
    <input name="Color" type="color" value="#b4a8e8" id="Color" />
</li>
```

Using the HTML5Test Web Site

I mentioned that I am using Opera for this exercise. Each browser may implement a different subset of HTML5 features. The HTML5Test.com web site that I mentioned in the previous chapter is a really useful tool for figuring out which browser works best for a specific set of features.

If you go to the Compare tab you can select up to three different browsers to see a side-by-side comparison for each feature. For example, I selected Google Chrome 18, IE 10, and Opera 11.60 to see how they stack up for the form features. The results are displayed in Figure 2-21. While Google Chrome has a higher overall score, Opera is the clear winner when it comes to supporting forms.

Forms

Field types	74	55	99
▸ input type=text	Yes ✓	Partial ○	Partial ○
▸ input type=search	Yes ✓	Yes ✓	Yes ✓
▸ input type=tel	Yes ✓	Yes ✓	Yes ✓
▸ input type=url	Yes ✓	Yes ✓	Yes ✓
▸ input type=email	Yes ✓	Yes ✓	Yes ✓
▸ input type=datetime	No ✗	No ✗	Yes ✓
▸ input type=date	No ✗	No ✗	Yes ✓
▸ input type=month	No ✗	No ✗	Yes ✓
▸ input type=week	No ✗	No ✗	Yes ✓
▸ input type=time	No ✗	No ✗	Yes ✓
▸ input type=datetime-local	No ✗	No ✗	Yes ✓
▸ input type=number	Yes ✓	Partial ○	Yes ✓
▸ input type=range	Yes ✓	Yes ✓	Yes ✓
▸ input type=color	No ✗	No ✗	Partial ○
▸ input type=checkbox	Yes ✓	Yes ✓	Yes ✓
▸ input type=image	Partial ○	Yes ✓	Partial ○
▸ input type=file	Yes ✓	Yes ✓	Yes ✓
▸ textarea	Yes ✓	Yes ✓	Yes ✓
▸ select	Yes ✓	Yes ✓	Yes ✓
▸ fieldset	Partial ○	Partial ○	Yes ✓
▸ datalist	No ✗	Yes ✓	Yes ✓
▸ keygen	Yes ✓	No ✗	Yes ✓
▸ output	Yes ✓	No ✗	Yes ✓
▸ progress	Yes ✓	Yes ✓	Yes ✓
▸ meter	Yes ✓	No ✗	Yes ✓

Figure 2-21. *A side-by-side comparison of Chrome, IE, and Opera*

Another way to use this site is to see how all browsers support a specific feature. From the Features sub-tab (in the Compare tab), you can select up to three specific features to see which browsers support it. I selected three features related to the range input type and you can see from Figure 2-22 that Opera has the only current desktop browser that supports these features.

browsers | features

features

Select up to three features and immediately see how well it is supported by each browser

	Minimal element support	step attribute	max attribute
Desktop browsers			
Chrome 6 »	Yes ✓	Yes ✓	Yes ✓
Chrome 10 »	Yes ✓	Yes ✓	Yes ✓
Chrome 14 »	Yes ✓	Yes ✓	Yes ✓
Chrome 16 »	Yes ✓	No ✗	Yes ✓
Chrome 18 »	Yes ✓	No ✗	Yes ✓
Chrome Canary »	Yes ✓	No ✗	Yes ✓
Firefox 3.0 »	No ✗	No ✗	No ✗
Firefox 3.6 »	No ✗	No ✗	No ✗
Firefox 4 »	No ✗	No ✗	No ✗
Firefox 8 »	No ✗	No ✗	No ✗
Firefox 10 »	No ✗	No ✗	No ✗
Firefox 11 »	No ✗	No ✗	No ✗
Internet Explorer 6 »	No ✗	No ✗	No ✗
Internet Explorer 7 »	No ✗	No ✗	No ✗
Internet Explorer 8 »	No ✗	No ✗	No ✗
Internet Explorer 9 »	No ✗	No ✗	No ✗
Internet Explorer 10 »	Yes ✓	No ✗	Yes ✓
Maxthon 3.3 »	Yes ✓	No ✗	Yes ✓
Opera 10.00 »	Yes ✓	Yes ✓	Yes ✓
Opera 10.50 »	Yes ✓	Yes ✓	Yes ✓
Opera 10.60 »	Yes ✓	Yes ✓	Yes ✓
Opera 11.10 »	Yes ✓	Yes ✓	Yes ✓
Opera 11.50 »	Yes ✓	Yes ✓	Yes ✓
Opera 11.60 »	Yes ✓	Yes ✓	Yes ✓
Opera 12.00 »	Yes ✓	Yes ✓	Yes ✓
Safari 5.1 »	Yes ✓	Yes ✓	Yes ✓
Safari 5.2 »	Yes ✓	No ✗	Yes ✓

Figure 2-22. Viewing how all browsers support the range control

■ **Caution** These comparisons and analysis are provided only for demonstration purposes. Browser support is changing at a pretty rapid pace and by the time you're reading this you may have very different results. The method for comparing browser support will still be valid however.

Using the Range Control

The range control supports attributes that allow you to configure its behavior. For example, you can specify the min and max attributes that define the value of the field when the slider is at each end of the control. You can also indicate the step attribute that controls stops along the scale where the slider can stop at. For example if the min is 0, the max is 100, and the step is 20, the control will only allow you to stop at increments of 20 (e.g. 0, 20, 40, 60, 80, and 100).

You would code this in HTML like this:

```
<!DOCTYPE html>

<input name="Range" type="range" id="Range"
    min="0" max="200" step="20"
    style="height:30px;width:200px;" />
```

Even though IntelliSense does not support these attributes, you could specify them and they would be included in the final HTML. Another way to do this is to modify the control when the page is loaded using JavaScript.

Modifying the Step Attribute

Now you'll write a simple script to configure the range attributes.

EXERCISE 2-3. MODIFYING THE RANGE CONTROL

1. Load the Chapter2 project in Visual Studio and open the Feedback.aspx page.

2. Inside the head tag add the following code shown in bold:

   ```
   <head runat="server">
       <title></title>

       <script type="text/javascript">
           function configureRange() {
               var range = document.getElementById("Range");
               range.min = 0;
               range.max = 200;
               range.step = 20;
           }
       </script>

   </head>
   ```

3. This simple JavaScript function modifies the attributes of the range control. The document property represents the HTML document of the current page. The getElementById() function is a selector that returns the specified element, the range control in this case. (I will cover selectors in JavaScript in more detail in Chapter 5.)

4. Now that the function has been implemented, you need to tell the page to execute it. To do that, add the following code in bold to the body tag:

```
<body onload="configureRange()">
    <form id="form1" runat="server">
```

5. This instructs the page to call the configureRange() function when the OnLoad event occurs.

6. Save your changes and press F5 to load the page.

7. The range control will look just like it did before but when you move the slider it will only stop where the tick marks are.

■ **Tip**   By default, tick marks are displayed at 10% increments along the range control. Since the total range is 200 and the step is 20, the steps are also at 10% increments so they coincide with the tick marks. Try changing the step to 5 and you should also have three stops between each tick mark.

Displaying the Range Value

While you're working on the range control I want to show you a simple trick to display its value. You'll add a TextBox control next to the range control and then use JavaScript to update its value when the range control is modified.

EXERCISE 2-4. DISPLAYING THE RANGE VALUE

1. In the Feedback.aspx page, add the following code in bold to the range item:

```
<li>
    <asp:Label ID="lblRange" runat="server"
        AssociatedControlID="Range">Overall satisfaction</asp:Label>
    <asp:TextBox runat="server" ID="Range" TextMode="Range"
        Width="200" Height="30"></asp:TextBox>

    <asp:TextBox runat="server" ID="RangeValue" Width="50"></asp:TextBox>
</li>
```

2. Next, add the code in bold to the script section:

```
<script type="text/javascript">
    function configureRange() {
        var range = document.getElementById("Range");
        range.min = 0;
        range.max = 200;
        range.step = 20;

        updateRangeValue();
    }
```

```
        function updateRangeValue() {
            document.getElementById("RangeValue").value
                = document.getElementById("Range").value;
        }
    </script>
```

3. The `updateRangeValue()` function takes the current value of the range control and stores it in the text box. Also, the `configureRange()` function that is called when the page is loaded, calls `updateRangeValue()` to set its initial value.

4. Now you'll need to call the `updateRangeValue()` function whenever the range control is updated. To do that, add the code in bold to the `Page_Load()` event handler in the `Feedback.aspx.cs` code-behind file:

```
public partial class Feedback : System.Web.UI.Page

{
    protected void Page_Load(object sender, EventArgs e)
    {
        Range.Attributes.Add("onChange", "updateRangeValue()");
    }
}
```

5. Save your changes and execute the page. As you move the slider, the selected value is displayed as shown in Figure 2-23. Notice that it is updated in increments of 20 (if the step attribute is still set at 20).

9. Overall satisfaction   [slider]   140

Figure 2-23. *Displaying the range value*

Summary

In this chapter you created a basic ASP.NET web form application using the template provided by Visual Studio. After briefly trying out the email control you then created a feedback page that demonstrated each of the other input types. Using some simple JavaScript, you configured the range control and provided a real-time display of its value.

Along the way I also provided some useful information regarding the development environment including:

*   Configuring browsers to test with

*   Using the Page Inspector

*   Accessing the default SQL Server database

*   Using the `HTML5Test.com` web site to research browser support

CHAPTER 3

■ ■ ■

MVC Web Applications

In this chapter you will use ASP.NET MVC to create a feedback form that will demonstrate several of the new input types. I will first provide a brief introduction of the Model-view-controller (MVC) framework included with the .NET platform and then show you how to build an HTML5-based web page using MVC. The end result will be something similar to what you did in Chapter 2 but the implementation will be quite different. As you will see, the solution will rely heavily on the ability to extend the MVC framework to incorporate the new HTML5 features.

Model-view-controller (MVC) is an architectural pattern that has been around since as early as the late 1970s. The primary benefit of this pattern is the separation of concerns, allowing independent development, testing, and maintenance of each. The model provides the data and business logic. If the application was presenting a product catalog, for example, the model would provide the product details. If changes are made, the model is responsible for persisting the data. The view provides the user experience; both formatting the presentation of data as well as enabling user interaction with input controls, buttons, and links. The controller handles the user requests, passing this to the model and invoking the appropriate view. This process is illustrated in Figure 3-1.

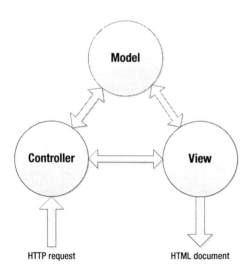

Figure 3-1. *The model-view-controller architectural pattern*

Introducing ASP.NET MVC4

ASP.NET MVC is a framework based on .NET that was first released in 2009 and implements the MVC pattern. The initial release used the same .aspx web forms syntax that was used in the traditional ASP.NET framework. In 2010, a new view engine called Razor was released, which is a more natural, HTML-like syntax. Also, instead of a code-behind file, the Razor engine allows the code to be included in the markup file. MVC version 4.0 is included with the Visual Studio 2012 release.

Like the traditional ASP.NET web forms I discussed in the previous chapter, MVC4 does not support many of the new HTML5 tags out-of-the-box. However, the MVC framework is much more extensible, making it relatively easy to add HTML5 support. In this chapter I will explain different techniques for extending the MVC framework to incorporate the new HTML5 features. There are also several open-source extensions that you can install and I will briefly demonstrate one of these as well.

Creating an ASP MVC Project

In this chapter you'll create an ASP.NET MVC project using the standard template in Visual Studio 2012. This will create a web application that looks very similar to the one you created in Chapter 2. Start Visual Studio 2012 (or the free version Visual Studio Express for Web). From the Web category, select the ASP.NET MVC 4 Web Application template, enter **Chapter 3** for the project name, and select an appropriate location as shown in Figure 3-2. Click the OK button to continue.

Figure 3-2. *Selecting the MVC 4 project*

You will be prompted to pick a template; select the Internet Application as shown in Figure 3-3. This will create a membership-based internet application just like the project in Chapter 2. Make sure the Razor view engine is selected.

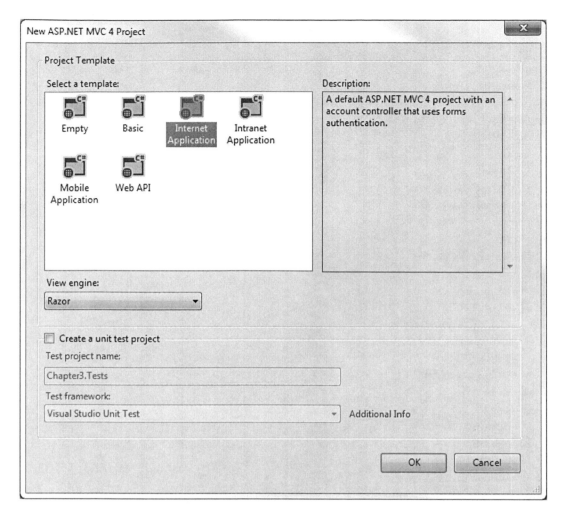

***Figure 3-3.** Selecting the Internet Application template*

After the project has been created, you'll see a number of folders in the Solution Explorer. Notice there are separate folders for controllers, models, and views as shown in Figure 3-4. The sample project includes several examples of each of these items.

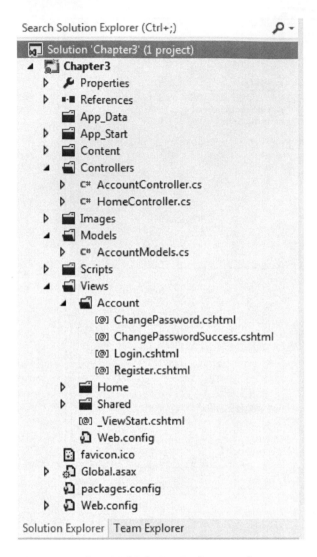

Figure 3-4. The initial Solution Explorer window

Exploring a Razor View

For a quick demonstration of the Razor view syntax you can look at the existing views provided by the project template. Open the `Register.cshtml` file, which you'll find in the Views\Account folder. This implements the view for the registration page. The `fieldset` section of the page is shown in Listing 3-1.

Listing 3-1. The initial Register.cshtml implementation

```
<fieldset>
    <legend>Registration Form</legend>
    <ol>
```

```
    <li>
        @Html.LabelFor(m => m.UserName)
        @Html.TextBoxFor(m => m.UserName)
    </li>
    <li>
        @Html.LabelFor(m => m.Email)
        @Html.TextBoxFor(m => m.Email)
    </li>
    <li>
        @Html.LabelFor(m => m.Password)
        @Html.PasswordFor(m => m.Password)
    </li>
    <li>
        @Html.LabelFor(m => m.ConfirmPassword)
        @Html.PasswordFor(m => m.ConfirmPassword)
        @Html.ValidationMessageFor(m => m.ConfirmPassword)
    </li>
  </ol>
  <input type="submit" value="Register" />
</fieldset>
```

In the Razor syntax an @ indicates the text that follows is code instead of literal markup. The code will generate HTML content at run time. You'll notice that much of the code uses the Html class. This is a helper class with methods that generate HTML markup. The LabelFor() method, for example, generates markup to insert a label control.

For each of the fields in the form, the code uses the LabelFor() and TextBoxFor() methods of the Html helper class. (The password fields use the PasswordFor() method.) Each of these methods takes a lambda expression, e.g. m =>m.UserName, that specifies a data element from the associated model. The model that is used for the view is defined by the following instruction at the top of the file:

```
@model Chapter3.Models.RegisterModel
```

If you look at the AccountModels.cs file, you'll find the definition of the RegisterModel class. This class has four public properties:

- UserName

- Email

- Password

- ConfirmPassword

Each of these properties has some metadata attributes such as Required and DataType that are used to generate the correct HTML. I will explain this further later in the chapter.

Using Editor Templates

The TextBoxFor() method will output a standard textbox control. To use the new HTML5 input types you'll need to modify this implementation. The MVC framework allows you to use the EditorFor() method instead of TextBoxFor(). By itself that doesn't change the markup that is generated since the default implementation of EditorFor() will still use the type = "text" attribute. I'll show you how to create an editor template to override this default behavior.

```
EXERCISE 3-1. ADDING AN EDITOR TEMPLATE
```

1. Open the `Register.cshtml` file, which you'll find in the Views\Account folder.

2. For the `Email` field, replace `TextBoxFor` with **EditorFor**. The code will look like this:

   ```
   @Html.LabelFor(m =>m.Email)
   @Html.EditorFor(m =>m.Email)
   ```

3. In the Solution Explorer, right-click on the Views\Shared folder and select the Add ➤ New Folder links. Enter **EditorTemplates** for the folder name.

■ **Caution**   Later in the chapter I will explain how the appropriate editor template is selected for each property. Editor templates must be in the EditorTemplates folder for the MVC framework to be able to use them. Because this folder was added to the Views\Shared folder, they are available to all views in your projects. You could create the EditorTemplates folder in the Views\Account folder. This would make them available to all views in the Account folder but not in other folders such as the Home folder. This also allows you to create a separate set of editor templates for each folder if you want the Home template to be different from the Account templates.

---

4. Right-click the Views\Shared\EditorTemplates folder and select the Add ➤ View links.

5. In the Add View dialog box, enter **EmailAddress** as the view name and make sure all the check boxes are unselected as shown in Figure 3-5.

Figure 3-5. *Adding the EmailAddress template*

6. This will generate a view page named `EmailAddress.cshtml`. Delete the entire content and replace it with the following code. This uses the TextBox() method but specifies some additional attribute including `type` and `placeholder`.

```
@Html.TextBox("", null, new { @class = "text-box single-line", type = "email",
    placeholder = "Enter an e-mail address" })
```

7. Save your changes and debug the application. Go to the Registration page and you should see the placeholder text displayed in the empty Email address field as shown in Figure 3-6.

Figure 3-6. *The blank Register form*

8. If you look at the page's source or the Page Inspector, the actual HTML will be similar to:

```
<input class="text-box single-line" data-val="true"
       data-val-required="The Email address field is required."
       id="Email" name="Email"
       placeholder="Enter an e-mail address" type="email" value=""/>
```

9. Close the browser and stop the debugger.

■ **Tip**   As with the previous chapter, I will be using the Opera browser for most of the exercises since it has the best support for the new input types.

ATTRIBUTE DRIVEN VALIDATION

Data validation in ASP.NET MVC starts with the model. If you look at the AccountModel.cs file you'll see metadata attributes such as Required attached to each property. For example, the Username property looks like this:

```
[Required]
[Display(Name = "User name")]
public string UserName { get; set; }
```

The `TextBoxFor()` helper function uses the metadata attributes to generate HTML like this:

```
<input name="UserName" id="UserName" type="text"
       data-val-required="The User name field is required."
       data-val="true" value=""></input>
```

Specifically, the `data-val` and `data-val-required` HTML attributes are generated. The view also includes these jQuery libraries:

```
<script src="~/Scripts/jquery.validate.min.js"></script>
<script src="~/Scripts/jquery.validate.unobtrusive.min.js"></script>
```

These JavaScript libraries use the HTML attributes such as data-val to perform client-side validation. For more information, see the article at: http://rachelappel.com/asp-net-mvc/how-data-annotations-for-asp-net-mvc-validation-work.

Adding a Feedback Page

You will now create a feedback form and use this to demonstrate how to implement the new HTML5 capabilities. You'll start by creating a model and then implement a strongly-typed view based on this model. You'll then add a controller action as well as a link to the new page.

■ **Tip**   Adding a page to the web application usually involves adding a model, adding a view, and creating or modifying a controller. The MVC pattern allows these to be developed separately and in a large project you will often have different people responsible for the views and models. You may be able to use an existing model. However, in a small project like this, where you are the sole developer, you will generally need to touch all three areas to add a page.

Creating the Feedback Model

A model defines the data elements that can be included on your page. By designing the model first, you can simplify the view implementation.

In the Solution Explorer, right-click the Models folder and select the Add ➤ Class links and enter **FeedbackModel** for the class name. Click the OK button to create the class. For the class implementation, enter the code shown in Listing 3-2.

■ **Note**   The view files use the new Razor syntax and have the `.cshtml` (or `.vbhtml`) extension. However, the model and controller files are standard C# (or VB) classes.

Listing 3-2. The FeedbackModel class

```
using System;
using System.Collections.Generic;
using System.Linq;
using System.Web;
using System.ComponentModel.DataAnnotations;
```

```
namespace Chapter3.Models
{
    public class FeedbackModel
    {
        [Display(Name = "Name", Prompt = "Enter your full name"),
         Required]
        public string Name { get; set; }

        [Display(Name = "Average Score", Prompt = "Your average score"),
         Range(1.0, 100.0),
         Required]
        public decimal Score { get; set; }

        [Display(Name = "Birthday"),
         DataType(DataType.Date)]
         public DateTime? Birthday { get; set; }

        [Display(Name = "Home page", Prompt = "Personal home page"),
         DataType(DataType.Url),
         Required]
        public string Homepage { get; set; }

        [Display(Name = "Email", Prompt = "Preferred e-mail address"),
         DataType(DataType.EmailAddress),
         Required]
        public string Email { get; set; }

        [Display(Name = "Phone number", Prompt = "Contact phone number"),
         DataType(DataType.PhoneNumber),
         Required]
        public string Phone { get; set; }

        [Display(Name = "Overall Satisfaction")]
        public string Satisfaction { get; set; }
    }
}
```

Press F6 to build the application. This will make the model available when defining the view.

Defining the Feedback View

Now you'll define a new view based on this model. Initially, this will be a simple form with a single field. Then you will add a link on the home page and a controller action to handle this. Later in the chapter you'll add more fields to the form.

EXERCISE 3-2. DESIGNING THE INITIAL FEEDBACK FORM

1. In the Solution Explorer, expand the Views folder. Right-click the Home folder and select the Add ➤ View links. Enter the name **Feedback**, select the "Create a strongly-typed view" check box, and select the FeedbackModel as shown in Figure 3-7. Again, make sure the Razor view engine is selected.

Figure 3-7. *Creating the Feedback view*

2. The new view is generated with a single empty div. Enter the code shown in bold from Listing 3-3. This code includes an input control for the Email property using the EditorFor() method.

Listing 3-3. Defining the initial form

```
@model Chapter3.Models.FeedbackModel
@{
    Layout = null;
}
```

```
<!DOCTYPE html>

<html>
<head>
    <meta name="viewport" content="width=device-width" />
    <title>Feedback</title>
</head>
<body>
    <div>
      @using (Html.BeginForm((string)ViewBag.FormAction, "Home"))
      {
        <fieldset>
        <legend>Feedback Form</legend>
        <div>
            @Html.EditorFor(m => m.Email)
        </div>
        <p>
            <input type="submit" value="Submit" />
        </p>
        </fieldset>
      }
    </div>
</body>
</html>
```

3. Views are invoked by a controller so you'll need to add a controller action that will load this page. Open the `HomeController.cs` class, which you'll find in the Controllers folder.

4. Add the following method:

```
public ActionResult Feedback()
{
    return View();
}
```

5. Finally, you'll need a link that triggers this controller action. Open the `_Layout.cshtml` in the View\Shared folder.

6. Add the line shown in bold:

```
<ul id="menu">
    <li>@Html.ActionLink("Home", "Index", "Home")</li>
    <li>@Html.ActionLink("About", "About", "Home")</li>
    <li>@Html.ActionLink("Contact", "Contact", "Home")</li>
    <li>@Html.ActionLink("Feedback", "Feedback", "Home")</li>
</ul>
```

7. Save your changes and press F5 to debug. You should now have a Feedback link on the home page as shown in Figure 3-8.

Figure 3-8. The Feedback link on the home page

8. Click this link to display the feedback form, which is shown in Figure 3-9.

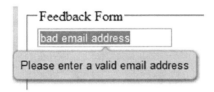

Figure 3-9. The initial feedback form

9. Enter an invalid email address and click the submit button. You should see the standard HTML5 validation error as shown in Figure 3-10.

Figure 3-10. The standard HTML5 validation error

10. View the source of the feedback form, which should be similar to this:

```
<form action="/Home/Feedback" method="post">
    <fieldset>
        <legend>Feedback Form</legend>
        <div>
            <input class="text-box single-line" data-val="true"
                   data-val-required="The Email field is required."
                   id="Email" name="Email"
                   placeholder="Enter an e-mail address"
                   type="email" value="" />
        </div>
        <p>
            <input type="submit" value="Submit" />
        </p>
    </fieldset>
</form>
```

Completing the Feedback Form

Now you'll add the remaining fields to the feedback form. You'll also need to provide editor templates for the additional data types. I'll also show you how the framework determines which template to use.

Adding the Other Fields

You'll start by adding the other fields that are defined in the FeedbackModel.cs class. For each one you'll include a label and use the EditorFor() method to generate the input field.

EXERCISE 3-3. COMPLETING THE FEEDBACK FORM

1. Open the Feedback.cshtml file and add the code shown in bold in Listing 3-4.

    Listing 3-4. The Feedback view implementation

    ```
    <div>
        @Html.EditorFor(m => m.Email)
    </div>

    <div class="editor-label">
        @Html.LabelFor(m => m.Name)
    </div>
    <div class="editor-field">
        @Html.EditorFor(m => m.Name)
    </div>
    <div class="editor-label">
        @Html.LabelFor(m => m.Birthday)
    </div>
    <div class="editor-field">
        @Html.EditorFor(m => m.Birthday)
    </div>
    <div class="editor-label">
        @Html.LabelFor(m => m.Homepage)
    </div>
    <div class="editor-field">
        @Html.EditorFor(m => m.Homepage)
    </div>
    <div class="editor-label">
        @Html.LabelFor(m => m.Phone)
    </div>
    <div class="editor-field">
        @Html.EditorFor(m => m.Phone)
    </div>
    <div class="editor-label">
        @Html.LabelFor(m => m.Score)
    </div>
    <div class="editor-field">
        @Html.EditorFor(m => m.Score)
    </div>
    ```

```
<div class="editor-label">
    @Html.LabelFor(m => m.Satisfaction)
</div>
<div class="editor-field">
    @Html.EditorFor(m => m.Satisfaction)
</div>

<p>
    <input type="submit" value="Submit" />
</p>
```

2. Save your changes and press F5 to view the modified form. Click the Feedback link to display the page, which will look similar to Figure 3-11.

Figure 3-11. *The feedback form*

3. Notice that all the new fields use the standard TextBox control and do not include a placeholder text. This is because there is no editor template defined for these data types.

Adding Editor Templates

You may have been asking yourself, how does the framework know which template to use? The framework tries to use the correct template based on the data type of the property. This is not very reliable as e-mail, urls, and phone numbers are all stored in a string variable. The preferred method is to define this using metadata.

If you include the System.ComponentModel.DataAnnotations namespace in your model class you can include metadata in your model. There are two metadata attributes that are used to determine the appropriate template:

*   DataType
*   UIHint

The DataType attribute is specified using the DataType enum. This includes a fairly large but fixed set of values, such as the contextual types EmailAddress, CreditCard, Currency, PostalCode, and Url. If you add a DataType attribute, the editor template with the matching name is used. You included the DataType attributes when you implemented the FeedbackModel.

The UIHint attribute is specified with a string and you can therefore use any value to want. If you want a property displayed in green font, you can specify the UIHint("GreenFont") attribute in the model and then provide a GreenFont.cshtml template. The UIHint takes precedence over the DataType attribute when determining the appropriate template to use.

■ **Tip** My GreenFont example was used to illustrate how the UIHint attribute works. You should not use it for setting style properties as this is the role of the style sheets. A more appropriate application of the UIHint attribute will be demonstrated later in this chapter when you implement a range control.

---

4. Right-click the Views\Shared\EditorTemplates folder and select the Add ➤ View links. In the Add View dialog box, enter the name **Date** and unselect all of the check boxes. Replace the view implementation with the following code:

```
@Html.TextBox("", null, new { @class = "text-box single-line",
    type = "date" })
```

5. In the same way, add another editor template named **Url** and use the following implementation:

```
@Html.TextBox("", null, new { @class = "text-box single-line", type =
    "url", placeholder = "Enter a web address" })
```

6. Create a **PhoneNumber** template using the following code:

```
@Html.TextBox("", null, new { @class = "text-box single-line", type =
    "tel", placeholder = "Enter a phone number" })
```

7. Create a **Number** template using the following code:

```
@Html.TextBox("", null, new { @class = "text-box single-line", type =
    "number", placeholder = "Enter a number" })
```

Save your changes and press F5 to debug your application. The feedback form should now use the HTML5 controls as shown in Figure 3-12.

Figure 3-12. The form using HTML5 controls

Generating Custom HTML

The editor templates that you have implemented are all based on the TextBox() method of the Html helper class. The templates simply add some additional attributes such as type and placeholder. However, you can implement templates that will output any HTML content you want. To demonstrate that, I'll show you how to build your own helper extension that generates the markup from scratch. You will use this to replace the EmailAddress template.

Adding a Custom Helper Class

You can create your own helper class and add it as a property of the existing Html helper class. You can then access your custom method as:

```
@Html.<CustomClass>.<CustomMethod>()
```

EXERCISE 3-4. CREATING A HELPER EXTENSION

1. In the Solution Explorer, right-click the Chapter 3 project and select the Add ➤ Class links. Enter the name **Html5** when prompted for the class name.

2. Enter the source shown in Listing 3-5.

    Listing 3-5. The initial HTML5 helper class

    ```
    using System;
    using System.Collections.Generic;
    using System.Linq;
    using System.Web;
    using System.Globalization;
    ```

```
namespace System.Web.Mvc
{
    public class Html5Helper
    {
        private readonly HtmlHelper htmlHelper;

        public Html5Helper(HtmlHelper htmlHelper)
        {
            this.htmlHelper = htmlHelper;
        }
        private static CultureInfo Culture
        {
            get
            {
                return CultureInfo.CurrentCulture;
            }
        }

        // Add custom methods here…

    }

    public static class HtmlHelperExtension
    {
        public static Html5Helper Html5(this HtmlHelper instance)
        {
            return new Html5Helper(instance);
        }
    }
}
```

There are a couple of things to point out here. First, note that the namespace is set as System.Web.Mvc and not your application's namespace, Chapter3. Your custom helper class is named Html5Helper and its constructor takes an HtmlHelper parameter. This is a reference to the standard helper class, which is stored as a private class member. Your custom methods will need this to access data from the framework such a view and model information. Finally, this code also declares a static HtmlHelperExtension class, which provides a static method that returns your custom class. Notice that the method name is Html5, so you will access your custom class from the view as:

```
@Html.Html5().<CustomMethod>()
```

The purpose of having your own custom helper class is to be able to implement custom helper methods. So let's add one now. The first method will generate an email input control. You will then use this in your EmailAddress.cshtml template.

3. Add the code shown in Listing 3-6 to your custom class where the // Add custom methods here placeholder is.

Listing 3-6. The EmailControl implementation

```
public IHtmlString EmailControl()
{
    string id;
    string name;
```

```
            string placeHolder;
            string value;
            string valueAttribute;
            ViewDataDictionary viewData = htmlHelper.ViewData;
            ModelMetadata metaData = viewData.ModelMetadata;

            // Build the HTML attributes
            id = viewData.TemplateInfo.GetFullHtmlFieldId(string.Empty);
            name = viewData.TemplateInfo.GetFullHtmlFieldName(string.Empty);

            if (string.IsNullOrWhiteSpace(metaData.Watermark))
                placeHolder = string.Empty;
            else
                placeHolder = "placeholder=\"" + metaData.Watermark + "\"";

            value = viewData.TemplateInfo.FormattedModelValue.ToString();
            if (string.IsNullOrWhiteSpace(value))
            valueAttribute = string.Empty;
            else
            valueAttribute = "value=\"" + value + "\"";

            // Determine the css class
            string css = "text-box single-line";

            ModelState state;
            if (viewData.ModelState.TryGetValue(name, out state)
                && (state.Errors.Count > 0))
                css += " " + HtmlHelper.ValidationInputCssClassName;

            // Format the final HTML
            string markup = string.Format(Culture,
                "<input type=\"email\" id=\"{0}\" name=\"{1}\" {2} {3} " +
                "class=\"{4}\"/>", id, name, placeHolder, valueAttribute, css);

            return MvcHtmlString.Create(markup);
        }
```

This method gathers the various HTML attributes such as id, name, class, and placeholder. This information is extracted from the model or the model metadata. At the end of this method, the markup string is built using the standard string.Format() method, which assembles the various attributes. This is then passed to the static MvcHtmlString.Create() method to provide this as the IHtmlString interface that the MVC framework requires.

The primary difference in this implementation of the EmailAddress template is that the placeholder attribute is set using the model metadata. The previous implementation used a hard-coded placeholder, "Enter an e-mail address". Unfortunately, the property names are completely inconsistent. In the model, this is specified using the Prompt attribute (Prompt = "Preferred e-mail address"). In the ModelMetadata class, this value is provided as the Watermark property. And, of course, this is included in the HTML document as a placeholder attribute.

Re-implementing the Custom Email Template

Now you'll replace the EmailAddress template with a much simpler one that uses the new helper extension that you've just implemented.

EXERCISE 3-5. RE-IMPLEMENTING THE EMAIL TEMPLATE

1. Save the changes and open the `EmailAddress.cshtml` template.

2. Replace the entire implementation with the following:

   `@Html.Html5().EmailControl()`

3. Save the changes and press F5 to debug. The placeholder text should now reflect the prompt specified in the model metadata as demonstrated in Figure 3-13.

   ┌─Feedback Form────────────────────────────────
   │ ┌─────────────────────────────┐
   │ │ Preferred e-mail address   │
   │ └─────────────────────────────┘

   Figure 3-13. The modified Email field

4. View the source of this page and the HTML markup for the Email field should look like:

   ```
   <input type="email" id="Email" name="Email" placeholder="Preferred e-mail address"
           class="text-box single-line"/>
   ```

Implementing a RangeControl

As you saw in the previous chapter, the range control supports some additional attributes that are not available in the standard TextBoxFor (or even EditorFor) implementations. To implement this using the MVC framework, you'll implement a custom helper method. You'll then provide an editor template that calls this custom method. Finally, you'll add a UIHint attribute in the model metadata that will tell the framework to use the new template.

Implementing a Custom Helper Method

The first step is to create a custom helper method that will generate the appropriate markup for a range control. This will be similar to the `EmailControl()` method that you just implemented except that is doesn't include the placeholder attribute. Also, the min, max, and step attributes are passed in to the method.

Add the code in Listing 3-7 to the `Html5.cs` file (inside the `Html5Helper` class).

Listing 3-7. The RangeControl implementation

```
public IHtmlString RangeControl(int min, int max, int step)
{
    string id;
    string name;
    string value;
    string valueAttribute;

    ViewDataDictionary viewData = htmlHelper.ViewData;

    // Build the HTML attributes
    id = viewData.TemplateInfo.GetFullHtmlFieldId(string.Empty);
    name = viewData.TemplateInfo.GetFullHtmlFieldName(string.Empty);
```

```
    value = viewData.TemplateInfo.FormattedModelValue.ToString();
    if (string.IsNullOrWhiteSpace(value))
        valueAttribute = string.Empty;
    else
        valueAttribute = "value=\"" + value + "\"";

    // Determine the css class
    string css = "range";

    ModelState state;
    if (viewData.ModelState.TryGetValue(name, out state)
        && (state.Errors.Count > 0))
        css += " " + HtmlHelper.ValidationInputCssClassName;

    // Format the final HTML
    string markup = string.Format(Culture,
        "<input type=\"range\" id=\"{0}\" name=\"{1}\" " +
        "min=\"{2}\" max=\"{3}\" step=\"{4}\" {5} class=\"{6}\"/>",
        id, name, min.ToString(), max.ToString(), step.ToString(),
        valueAttribute, css);

    return MvcHtmlString.Create(markup);
}
```

Adding the Range Template

Now you'll need to create an editor template for the range control that will use this new custom method.

EXERCISE 3-6. ADDING A RANGE TEMPLATE

1. Right-click the Views\Shared\EditorTemplates folder and select the Add ➤ View links.

2. In the Add View dialog box, enter the name **Range** and unselect all of the text boxes.

3. Replace the default implementation with the following:

   ```
   @Html.Html5().RangeControl(0, 200, 20)
   ```

4. Open the FeedbackModel.cs file and add the UIHint attribute to the Satisfaction property like this:

   ```
   [Display(Name = "Overall Satisfaction"), UIHint("Range")]
   public string Satisfaction { get; set; }
   ```

5. While you have the FeedbackModel.cs file open, add a UIHint attribute for the Score property as follows:

   ```
   [Display(Name = "Average Score", Prompt = "Your average score"),
    Range(1.0, 100.0), UIHint("Number"),
    Required]
   public decimal Score { get; set; }
   ```

6. Save your changes and press F5 to debug. Go to the Feedback page and the page should look like Figure 3-14.

Figure 3-14. *The updated raneg control*

Using Open Source Extensions

So far you have created two editor templates that are based on custom helper methods and four simple templates based on the TextBox() method. However, you will likely need quite a few other templates beside these. Before you spend all that time implementing them you might be wondering if someone else has already done this for you? Well, the answer is yes.

There are a lot of third-party libraries and tools that are available to you. Visual Studio provides a package manager called NuGet that makes it easy to find, download, install, and manage these third-party packages. I'll show you how to use NuGet to install a package of editor templates so you don't have to write them yourself. Of course, now that you know how to write your own, feel free to do so if any of these don't work quite like you want them to.

EXERCISE 3-7. INSTALLING EDITOR TEMPLATES

1. When the third-party package is installed, it will not overwrite any existing templates. So before you begin, you'll need to delete the existing editor templates. Delete all of the files in the EditorTemplates folder except for Range.cshtml (the third-party package does not include this template).

2. In Visual Studio, with the Chapter 3 project still open, select these links from the menu: Tools ➤ Library Package Manager ➤ Manage NuGet Packages for Solution.

3. This will display the Manage NuGet Packages dialog box. If you select the Installed packages link it will list the packages currently installed. You might be surprised to find that quite a few have already been installed by the project template.

4. Select the Online ➤ "NuGet official package source" links to view the packages that are available. At the time of this writing there are over 200 pages of packages to choose from so finding the right one might seem like a daunting task.

5. In the search field, enter **html5**, which should narrow the list down considerably (at the time of this writing it was only six pages).

6. Scroll down and select the package named "HTML5 Editor Templates for MVC 3" as shown in Figure 3-15. The right-hand pane displays details of this package including author, description, and links for more information.

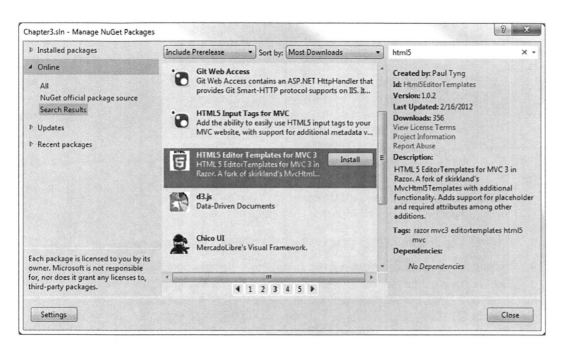

Figure 3-15. *Selecting the HTML5 Editor Templates for MVC 3 package*

7. Click the Install button. You will see the Select Projects dialog box shown in Figure 3-16. If there are multiple projects in your solution, you can use this dialog box to select which project(s) the package should be added to. Make sure the Chapter 3 project is selected and click the OK button.

Figure 3-16. *Selecting the project(s) to update*

8. Once the install has completed, close the Manage NuGet Packages dialog box.

9. You should now see quite a few templates in the EditorTemplates folder. Open the
   EmailAddress.cshtml file. The third-party implementation for this template is shown
   in Listing 3-8. While this is implemented differently from yours, it accomplishes
   basically the same thing, including getting the placeholder from the metadata.

Listing 3-8. *The open source Email template*

```
@{
    var attributes = new Dictionary<string, object>();

    attributes.Add("type", "email");

    attributes.Add("class", "text-box single-line");
    attributes.Add("placeholder", ViewData.ModelMetadata.Watermark);

    //since this is a constraint, IsRequired and other constraints
    //won't necessarily apply in the browser, but in case script
    //turns off readonly we want the constraints passed
    if (ViewData.ModelMetadata.IsReadOnly)
```

```
    {
        attributes.Add("readonly", "readonly");
    }

    if (ViewData.ModelMetadata.IsRequired)
    {
        attributes.Add("required", "required");
    }
}
@Html.TextBox("", ViewData.TemplateInfo.FormattedModelValue, attributes)
```

10. Press F5 to debug the application and navigate to the Feedback page, which should look like Figure 3-17.

Figure 3-17. *The feedback page using third-party templates*

Adding Literal HTML

Using the Html helper class, including the EditorFor() method is the recommended way to implement forms with ASP.NET MVC. This provides tight integration with the model including the model metadata and the separation of concerns (business rules and user experience). However, you can always embed the actual HTML markup in your view. An appropriate use of this would be to include static content or a control that is not connected to a model, such as a progress bar.

I'll now demonstrate three examples of inserting one of the new HTML5 control into the feedback form using direct HTML markup:

- Range

- Progress

- Meter

Adding a Range Control

You already included a range control using a custom editor template. Now you'll insert another one by simply adding the appropriate HTML markup. And just for fun, you'll make this a vertical slider by adjusting the width and height styles. To do this, add the code in bold from Listing 3-9 to the feedback form.

Listing 3-9. Adding a range control in HTML

```
<fieldset>
    . . .
    <div>
        @Html.LabelFor(m => m.Satisfaction)
    </div>
    <div>
        @Html.EditorFor(m => m.Satisfaction)
    </div>
    <div>
        Custom range
        <input type="range" id="CustomRange" name="CustomRange"
                class="range" style="width: 50px; height: 200px"
                min="0" max="200" step="20" />
    </div>
    <p>
        <input type="submit" value="Submit" />
    </p>
</fieldset>
```

Save your changes and press F5 to debug. The form should look like Figure 3-18.

■ **Note**   The value of this control is not part of the model and will not be saved with the form. This is appropriate if the control is used solely to aid the user experience and does not need to be persisted. For example, it could control the volume of a video or audio clip.

Figure 3-18. *Adding an vertical range control*

Adding a Progress Bar

Next, you'll add a progress bar by inserting a progress tag in the form. Add the following code in bold after the submit button:

```
<p>
    <input type="submit" value="Submit" />
</p>
<div>
    <progress id="FormProgress" value="60" max="100">
        <strong>Progress: 60%</strong>
    </progress>
</div>
</fieldset>
```

The progress tag does not support a `min` attribute but only a `max` attribute. The minimum value is assumed to be zero. The `value` attribute specifies the current progress. Press F5 to debug the application and navigate to the feedback form. The progress should appear as shown in Figure 3-19.

Figure 3-19. The progress control in Opera

The code within the `progress` tag is used for browsers that do not support the *progress* tag. For example, in IE9, the form would look like Figure 3-20.

Figure 3-20. The progress control in IE9

Updating the Progress Bar

However, a static progress bar is not very interesting; one might even find a progress bar that never changes to be very frustrating. Now you'll add some JavaScript code to update the progress bar as fields on the form have been entered.

First, you'll create a function called `calculateProgress()` that iterates through all the input fields to see which ones have a value. There are six fields so you'll give each one a value of 17 (6 x 17 = 102). This code uses the `document.getElementsByClassName()` selector that returns all elements with the specified class attribute. In this case, you want elements with the "text = box single-line" class. The function then updates the value of the progress bar using the computed value.

Then, you'll need to call this function whenever an input field is changed. To do that, you'll create a function named `bindEvents()` and use the same `getElementsByClassName()` selector. This time, you'll use the `addEventListener()` function to bind the `calculateProgress()` function to the `onChange` event. Finally, you'll call `bindEvents()` function in the `onLoad` event handler.

Enter the code in bold from Listing 3-10 to your feedback form.

Listing 3-10. Adding JavaScript to update the progress bar

```
<head>
    <meta name="viewport" content="width=device-width" />
    <title>Feedback</title>

    <script type="text/JavaScript">
        function calculateProgress() {
            var value = 0;
            var fieldList = document.getElementsByClassName("text-box single-line");
            for (var i = 0; i < fieldList.length; i++) {
                if (fieldList[i].value > "")
                    value += 17;
            }
```

```
            if (value > 100)
                value = 100;
            var progress = document.getElementById("FormProgress");
            progress.value = value;
        };
        function bindEvents() {
            var fieldList = document.getElementsByClassName("text-box single-line");
            for (var i = 0; i < fieldList.length; i++) {
                fieldList[i].addEventListener("change", calculateProgress, false);
            }
        }
    </script>
</head>

<body onload="bindEvents();">
```

■ **Note**   In calculating the progress this code ignores the range control used for the Satisfaction field. This was done because it always has a value and so you can't tell when a value was "entered".

Also, change the initial value property of the progress tag from 60 to 0 like this:

```
<progress id="FormProgress" value="0" max="100">
```

Press F5 to debug the application. As you enter values in the input fields, notice that the progress bar is automatically updated. To demonstrate how browser implementation varies, try this in Google Chrome. Notice that the progress bar is animated with a lighter section moving horizontally through the part of the control that is already filled in. Also, notice that it does not support vertical range controls as shown in Figure 3-21.

Figure 3-21. *The progress and range controls in Chrome*

Using the Meter Control

For the last example, you'll add a meter control, which is very similar to the progress bar. A meter allows you to define intervals within the range that will enable the color-coding of the status indicator. For example, consider an oil-pressure gauge on a car. A "normal" range is indicated on the gauge and low or high values are highlighted. I don't need to know what the oil-pressure is or even what it should be; I just want to know if it's in the normal range.

Like the range control, the meter control supports the min and max attributes as well as the current value. It also provides low, high, and optimum attributes that define the normal range. Enter the following code in bold:

```
<div>
    <progress id="FormProgress" value="0" max="100">
        <strong>Progress: 60%</strong>
    </progress>
</div>
<div>
    <meter id="Meter" value="50" min="20" max="120"
           low="50" high="100" optimum="75">
        <strong>Meter:</strong>
    </meter>
</div>

</fieldset>
```

To demonstrate how different values are displayed, you'll add some JavaScript code to update the control with a random value every second. To do that, add the following code in bold to the bindEvents() function:

```
function bindEvents() {
    var fieldList = document.getElementsByClassName("text-box single-line");
    for (var i = 0; i < fieldList.length; i++) {
        fieldList[i].addEventListener("change", calculateProgress, false);
    }

    setInterval(function () {
        var meter = document.getElementById("Meter");
        meter.value = meter.min + Math.random() * (meter.max - meter.min);
    }, 1000);
}
```

This code uses the setInterval() function so the anonymous function is called every 1000 milliseconds. Press F5 to start the application. Depending on the value the color will change from green to yellow as shown in Figure 3-22.

Figure 3-22. *The meter control*

In case, you've gotten lost in all the various updates, the complete implementation of the Feedback.cshtml view is shown in Listing 3-11.

Listing 3-11. The final Feedback.cshtml implementation

```
@model Chapter3.Models.FeedbackModel

@{
    Layout = null;
}

<!DOCTYPE html>

<html>
<head>
    <meta name="viewport" content="width=device-width" />
    <title>Feedback</title>
    <script type="text/JavaScript">
        function calculateProgress() {
            var value = 0;
            var fieldList = document.getElementsByClassName("text-box single-line");
            for (var i = 0; i < fieldList.length; i++) {
                if (fieldList[i].value > "")
                    value += 17;
            }
            if (value > 100)
                value = 100;
            var progress = document.getElementById("FormProgress");
            progress.value = value;
        };
        function bindEvents() {
            var fieldList = document.getElementsByClassName("text-box single-line");
            for (var i = 0; i < fieldList.length; i++) {
                fieldList[i].addEventListener("change", calculateProgress, false);
            }
            setInterval(function () {
                var meter = document.getElementById("Meter");
                meter.value = meter.min + Math.random() * (meter.max - meter.min);
            }, 1000);
        }
    </script>
</head>
<body onload="bindEvents();">
    <div>
      @using (Html.BeginForm((string)ViewBag.FormAction, "Home"))
      {
        <fieldset>
            <legend>Feedback Form</legend>
            <div>
                @Html.EditorFor(m => m.Email)
            </div>
            <div class="editor-label">
                @Html.LabelFor(m => m.Name)
            </div>
```

```
<div class="editor-field">
    @Html.EditorFor(m => m.Name)
</div>
<div class="editor-label">
    @Html.LabelFor(m => m.Birthday)
</div>
<div class="editor-field">
    @Html.EditorFor(m => m.Birthday)
</div>
<div class="editor-label">
    @Html.LabelFor(m => m.Homepage)
</div>
<div class="editor-field">
    @Html.EditorFor(m => m.Homepage)
</div>
<div class="editor-label">
    @Html.LabelFor(m => m.Phone)
</div>
<div class="editor-field">
    @Html.EditorFor(m => m.Phone)
</div>
<div class="editor-label">
    @Html.LabelFor(m => m.Score)
</div>
<div class="editor-field">
    @Html.EditorFor(m => m.Score)
</div>
<div class="editor-label">
    @Html.LabelFor(m => m.Satisfaction)
</div>
<div class="editor-field">
    @Html.EditorFor(m => m.Satisfaction)
</div>
<div>
    Custom range
    <input type="range" id="CustomRange" name="CustomRange"
           class="range" style="width: 50px; height: 200px"
           min="0" max="200" step="20" />
</div>
<p>
    <input type="submit" value="Submit" />
</p>
<div>
    <progress id="FormProgress" value="0" max="100">
        <strong>Progress: 60%</strong>
    </progress>
</div>
```

```
        <div>
            <meter id="Meter" value="50" min="20" max="120"
                    low="50" high="100" optimum="75">
                <strong>Meter:</strong>
            </meter>
        </div>
    </fieldset>
    }
    </div>
</body>
</html>
```

Summary

In this chapter you used some of the new HTML5 input types in an ASP.NET MVC project. As with the traditional web forms project, you have to do a little extra work to use them but it's fairly easy to incorporate the new HTML5 features. In particular, the MVC framework is designed to be extensible, which provides a clean platform for building HTML5 applications.

The MVC pattern provides models that define the data elements used on the forms. By including some metadata attributes in the model and then providing custom templates you can take advantage of the HTML5 semantic-specific controls. There are open-source extensions that you can download and install, making it easy to build HTML5 compliant applications. However, in this chapter I showed you how to build your own custom helper extension and build your own editor templates. If you find yourself in a unique situation where you need a specific implementation, you can always build your own.

With the MVC Razor view engine you can also include literal HTML markup so you have ultimate control of the user experience. I also introduced two new HTML controls, progress and meter and demonstrated how these work with some simple JavaScript to manipulate them.

CHAPTER 4

Cascading Style Sheets

In Chapters 2 and 3, I showed you the some of the new HTML elements and how to use them in ASP.NET applications. The second major area in the overall HTML5 umbrella includes the improvements in the style sheets. As I explained in Chapter 1, the CSS3 recommendations are broken down into more than 50 modules, most of which are still in draft (as of this writing). However, there is quite a bit of new functionality that is already available in most browsers.

In this chapter I will demonstrate many of the more useful features. I will start by explaining the basics of creating styles sheets. If you have some experience with CSS this may seem like review but some of this is new with CSS3, especially the selectors, which have been significantly improved with CSS3. You'll then create a single web page using some of the new structural elements like nav, aside, and footer. With the page content complete, I'll then explain some of the fun things you can do with CSS.

Reviewing Style Syntax

A style sheet is comprised of a set of rules. Each rule consists of a selector that indicates what elements the rule applies to and one or more declarations. Each declaration contains a property-value pair. A rule is specified with the following syntax:

```
<selector>{<property:value>; <property:value>;...}
```

For example, if you wanted all of the paragraph tags to use a green 12px font, the rule would look like this:

```
p {color:green; font-size:12px;}
```

As with HTML, white space is ignored in a style sheet so this rule could also be written as:

```
p
{
    color:green;
    font-size:12px;
}
```

I will use this format throughout the rest of this chapter as I think it's a little easier to read.

Using Selectors

There were a lot of different ways to select elements from the document and the CSS3 specifications nearly double this list. I'll provide an overview of the selectors that are available. Many of these will be demonstrated later in the chapter.

Element Selectors

The first one that I just showed you is an *element* selector. To use this, simply specify the element type such as p, h1, input, ol, div, and so on. HTML5 introduces a large number of new tags that were added primarily with CSS in mind. These context-specific elements like article, footer, and nav, communicate their purpose more clearly, and therefore make it more likely that consistent formatting will be applied to all pages. These new element types are:

- article – a stand-alone portion of content such blog entry.

- aside – content usually put to one side of the page; typically used for navigation or related information.

- details – used for expandable content that can be hidden or displayed based on user input.

- figcaption – used with figure to associate a caption with an image

- figure – used to wrap embedded content such as an image or graphic

- footer – the page or section footer

- header – the page or section header

- hgroup – used to group header elements like h1, h2, etc.

- nav – used to contain a group of links

- output – contains output such as the result of a user action

- section – used to organize content in to logical sections

- summary – usually used in conjunction with one or more details elements

Using Combinators

If you want to apply the same declarations to more than one element type, you can group them like this:

```
p, h1, h2
{
    color:green;
    font-size:12px;
}
```

The comma (",") character serves as a logical OR operation. For example, all elements of type p OR h1 OR h2. This is just a special case of a selector combinator. You can also combine selectors to specify certain element hierarchies. By combining elements with one of the following operators you can create a more complex selector:

- , - (e.g. p, h1) Selects all p elements as well as all h1 elements.

- space – (e.g. header p) Selects the second element when it is inside the first element. For example, if you want all p elements that are inside a header element, use header p. The header element does not have to be the immediate parent, just somewhere in node's parentage.

- * - (e.g. header*p) selects the second element when it is a grandchild or later descendant of the first element.

- > - (e.g. header > p) Selects the second element when the first element is the immediate parent. The header > p selector returns all p elements whose parent (immediate) is a header element.

- +-(e.g. header+p) Selects the second element when the first element is the preceding sibling.

- ~-(e.g. p~header) Selects the second element when it follows the first element (not necessarily immediately).

To illustrate the last two, if your document looks like this:

```
<h1>Some header</h1>
<h2>Some sub-header</h2>
<p>Some text</p>
```

The h1+p selector will not return any element but both h2+p and h1~p will both return the p element.

Class and ID Selectors

The class selector allows you to select elements with a specific class attribute. For this reason, the class attribute is often referred to as the css class. A class selector is created by prefixing the class name with ".." like this:

```
.featured
{
  background-color:yellow;
}
```

This will apply the background color for all elements that have class = "featured" attribute. The class selector looks for whole words that match the selector value. An element can have multiple words in the class attribute like class = "the featured article" and the .featured selector will return it.

■ **Caution**   In the HTML document, the class attribute is a string that can have any value you want to give it. However, to be able to use it in a class selector it must not have any white space or other characters that are not compatible with the CSS syntax. For example, you cannot select class = "featured content" in a class selector. Instead you'll need to use an attribute selector, which I will demonstrate later.

An ID selector works just like a class selector except that it uses the id attribute instead of class and you prefix it with a hash symbol ("#") like this:

```
#Submit
{
    color:blue;
}
```

An ID selector specifies a single element based on its unique id so, by definition, the style will not be reused. It is better to define styles based on elements or classes so similar elements can be styled the same way. ID selectors should be used sparingly and only for unique situations where the style does not need to be reused.

Using Attribute Selectors

Attribute selectors give you a great deal of flexibility, allowing you to select elements based on any of the element's attributes. These are specified as [attribute = value] like this:

```
[class="book"]
{
    background-color:yellow;
}
```

This is functionally equivalent to using the .book class selector; however, the attribute selector allows you to select using only portions of the attributes value. To do that, prefix the equal sign ("=") with one of the following:

- ~- (e.g. [class~="book"]) The attribute value must include the word indicated by the selector value (e.g. class = "some **book** titles"). This is exactly how the class selector works.

- |- (e.g. [class|="book"]) The attribute value must begin with a word that matches the selector value (e.g. class = "**book** titles")

- ^= (e.g. [class^="book"]) The attribute value must begin with the selector value (e.g. class="**book**s")

- $- (e.g. [class$="book"]) The attribute value must end with the selector value (e.g. class="check**book**")

- *- (e.g. [class*="book"]) The attribute value must contain the selector value (e.g. class="over**book**ed")

You can specify the attribute without a value, which will return all elements that have the attribute. A good example of this is the [href] selector, which will select all elements that have the href attribute, regardless of its value. You can also include an element selector before an attribute selector to further restrict the selected elements. For example, img[src^="https"] will return all img elements whose src attribute begins with https.

Pseudo-Class Selectors

There are quite a few selectors that are based on dynamic properties of an element. Consider a hyperlink, for example. If the page referenced by the link has been displayed, the link is usually displayed with a different color. This is achieved using a CSS rule that uses the visited property like this:

```
a:visited
{
    color: purple;
}
```

This will change the color of all a elements that have the visited flag set. Several of these selectors have been available for some time but CSS3 defines a fairly large set of new ones. Here is the complete list:

- :active – selects the active link

- :checked – selects elements that are checked (applies to check boxes)

- :disabled – selects elements that are currently disabled (typically used for input elements)

- :empty – selects elements that have no children (elements that include text are not selected)

- :enabled – selects elements that are enabled (typically used for input elements)

- :first-child – selects the elements that are the first child of its immediate parent

- <tag>:first-of-type – select the elements that is the first of the specified type within its parent

- :focus – select the element that currently has the focus

- :hover – select the element that the mouse is currently hovering over

- :lang(value) – selects the elements that have a lang attribute that start with the specified value

- :last-child – selects the elements that are the last child within its parent

- :link – selects all unvisited links

- <tag>:last-of-type – select the elements that are the last of the specified type within its parent

- :nth-child(n) – selects the elements that are the nth child within its parent

- :nth-last-child(n) – selects the elements that are the nth child within its parent, counting in reverse

- <tag>:nth-last-of-type(n) – selects the nth child of the specified type within its parent, counting in reverse

- <tag>:nth-of-type(n) – selects the nth child of the specified type within its parent

- :only-child – selects the elements that are the only child element of its parent

- <tag>:only-of-type – selects the elements that are the only sibling of the specified type within its parent

- :root – selects the root element of the document

- :target – selects the elements with a target attribute where the target is the active element

- :visited – select all visited links

The nth-child(n) selector counts all child elements of the parent, while the nth-of-type(n) only counts child elements of the specified type. The distinction here is subtle but important. The same is true with the only-child and only-of-type selectors.

▓ **Caution**   There are four pseudo classes that can be used with an anchor (<a>) element (:link, :visited, :hover, and :active). If you use more than one, they should appear in this order in the style rules. For example, :hover must come after :link and :visited if they are used. Likewise, :active must come after :hover.

These pseudo-elements can be used to return a portion of the selected elements:

- :first-letter – selects the first character of every selected element

- :first-line – select the first line of every selected element

- :selection – returns the portion of an element that is selected by the user

You can add the :before or :after qualifiers to a selector to insert content in the document before or after the selected elements. Use the content: keyword to specify the content and include any desired style commands (the style only applies to the inserted content). For example, to add "Important!" before each p tag that immediately follows a header tag, use the following rule:

```
header+p:before
{
    content:"Important! ";
    font-weight:bold;
    color:red;
}
```

You can also prefix a selector with :not to return all the elements not selected. For example, :not(header+p) selects all elements except p tags that immediately follow a header tag.

Understanding Unions

You can also combine complex selectors in a logical OR relationship by separating them with commas. For example, the p, h1, h2 selector I showed earlier in this chapter is an example of a union. It will return all elements that satisfy any of the included selectors. Each selector can be any of the more complex types. This is also a valid selector:

```
header+p, .book, a:visited
```

It will return all elements that are either a p element that immediately follows a header element, an element with the book class, or a visited a element.

■ **Tip** For a definitive list of available selectors see the article at http://www.w3schools.com/cssref/css_selectors.asp.

Using CSS Properties

All of these selectors are provided so you can specify the appropriate elements that you want to apply the desired style properties to. This is the real meat of CSS. There are literally hundreds of CSS properties available and I can't describe them all here. I will demonstrate many of the newer, more useful features in the rest of this chapter. A really good reference of all CSS properties can be found at http://www.w3schools.com/cssref/default.asp.

Using Vendor Prefixes

Oh the joys of living on the edge! As with other areas of HTML5, browser vendors will have varying support for the CSS specifications. In many cases, however, these vendors implement new properties before they become part of the official recommendation. In fact, much of what is being included in the CSS3 specification has already been available from one or more browsers.

When a browser vendor adds a new feature that is not part of the CSS3 recommendation, the property is given a vendor-specific prefix to indicate this is a non-standard feature. If this becomes part of the recommendation, the prefix is eventually dropped. To take advantage of some of the newer properties you may need to use the vendor-specific properties, and since you want your page to work on all vendors, you'll need to add all of them. For example, to specify the border-radius, in addition to the standard border-radius property, you may need to set all of the vendor-specific properties as well like this:

```
header
{
    -moz-border-radius: 25px;
    -webkit-border-radius: 25px;
    -o-border-radius: 25px;
    -ms-border-radius: 25px;
    border-radius: 25px;
}
```

The most common prefixes are listed in Table 4-1. There are others but this list will cover that vast majority of browsers.

Table 4-1. *Vendor prefixes*

Prefix	Browser vendor
-moz-	Firefox
-webkit-	Chrome, Safari
-o-	Opera
-ms-	Internet Explorer

You can't blindly assume that all vendor-prefixed properties have the same name as the standard property, with the prefix added, although that is true most of the time. Here is a good article that lists many of the vendor-specific properties: http://peter.sh/experiments/vendor-prefixed-css-property-overview

■ **Caution**   You should always list the standard property last so it will override the vendor-specific version. Some browsers will support both and, while most of the time the implementation is identical, sometimes the vendor-specific version behaves differently.

Understanding the Box Model

Each element in the document takes up a certain amount of space, which depends on the content of that element. In addition, factors such as padding and margin affect this as well. *Padding* is the space between the content and the element's border. The *margin* is the space between the border and adjacent elements. This is illustrated in Figure 4-1.

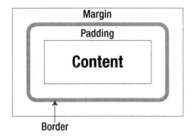

Figure 4-1. *The box model*

You can specify the margin with the margin declaration and specify the values either in pixels or as a % of the page size. You can specify the top, right, bottom, and left margin individually using the margin-top, margin-right, margin-bottom, and margin-left declarations or with the margin declaration specifying all four values (in that order – top, right, bottom, and left). You can also use the margin declaration with a single value, which will set all four margins to this value. You set the padding property the same way using the padding declaration.

When determining the space used, remember to include the border width as well. For example, if the padding is set to 10px, the margin set to 5px and the border-width set to 3px, the space used (in addition to the actual element content) will be $(2 * 10) + (2 * 5) + (2 * 3) = 36px$.

Applying Style Rules

Styles are specified from various sources and in several different ways and as the name suggests, they are cascaded, or inherited. It's important to understand how this works, especially when there are conflicting declarations.

Including Style Specifications

There are three sources of style sheets:

- Author – these are the style sheets created by the web developer and what we normally think of when referring to a style sheet.

- User – a user can also create a style to control how web pages are displayed for them specifically.

- User Agent – a user agent (web browser) will have a default style sheet. For example, if you create a document with no style rules, the browser will display the content using a default font family and size. These are actually defined in a style sheet that is specific to the browser.

For author styles, which are the only source you can control, there are three ways to include style rules in an HTML document:

- Inline – the style is set directly in the element using the `style` attribute like this `<p style="color:red">This is red text</p>`. Of course, with this method you don't use a selector since the style only applies to the current element (as well as all child elements).

- Internal – style rules can be included in the actual HTML document using the `style` element. This is normally placed in the head tag and applies to the entire document. Styles defined this way will require a selector to indicate on which element(s) the style should be used. This approach is sometimes referred to as *embedded* styles.

- External – the most common way to apply styles is to place all of the style rules in a separate file with a .css extension. The style rules are formatted just like the internal styles. The obvious benefit of using an external style sheet is that the same set of rules can be applied to multiple pages. Each page references this style sheet with a `link` element like this:

```
<link rel="stylesheet" type="text/css" href="MyStyleSheet.css" />
```

Cascading Rules

When rendering a page, the browser has to process styles from all of these sources to determine the appropriate style for each element. When there are conflicting rules, the author style sheet takes precedence over the user style sheet, which takes precedence over the user agent styles (browser defaults). The author styles can be specified using the three methods I explained earlier (inline, internal, and external). Within the author styles, inline declarations take precedence over internal declarations and external styles sheet are considered last. So if a page uses an internal `style` element and also uses the `link` element to include an external style sheet, the internal declarations will override conflicting rules in the external style sheet.

■ **Caution**   If an external style sheet is referenced after the `style` tag, it will take precedence over the internal styles. If you have both external style sheets and an internal `style` element, you should reference the external sheet first so the precedence rules work as expected.

In addition, consider that even within a single style sheet there may be conflicting declaration. For example, a style sheet may include the following:

```
p
{
    color: black;
}

header p
{
    color: red;
}
```

A p element within a header element is selected by both rules so which one is used. In this case the specificity rule applies which states that the more specific selector is used, which is the header p selector. With all the selectors that are available, determining which one is more *specific* is not as straightforward as you might think. ID selectors are considered more specific than class or attribute selectors, which are more specific than element selectors. If there are only element selectors, the rule with the most elements takes precedence so header p, which contains two elements, is more specific than just p.

Finally, what if the same exact selector is used twice in the same style sheet with different declarations? For example, if p { color:black; } appears in the style sheet and later p { color:green } appears. In this case, the rule that appears last takes precedence, so you'll have green text.

Using the Important Keyword

The one sort of "ace-in-the-hole" is the important keyword. If this is used in a style rule, this trumps all other rules. You can add the important keyword like this:

```
p
{
    color: red;
    !important;
}
```

If two conflicting rules both have the important keyword then the precedence is determined based on the rules I already mentioned. There is one significant difference, however. Normally rules in the author style sheet override rules in the user style sheet. If they have the important keyword this is reversed, the user style sheet will override the author rules. That may seem odd at first but this has a very important application. This allows the user to override the author styles for certain properties. For example, someone who is visually impaired may need to increase the font size. The important tag will ensure that this style does not get overridden.

■ **Caution**   You might be tempted to use the important keyword to make a quick fix and override a cascaded style rule. With all the precedence rules that I just described, you shouldn't need to do this. I recommend using this as a last resort. Overuse of the important keyword can make your style sheets difficult to maintain.

Creating a Web Page

For the rest of this chapter I will show you how to build a single web page that will demonstrate many of the new CSS features. To keep the project simple, I will be using the Web Matrix application instead of Visual Studio to create a single web page. The style rules will use the internal style element so everything can be placed in a single file. The small amount of JavaScript will also be included in the single file.

I will be using the Chrome browser for this project as it supports all of the CSS features that I will be demonstrating. At the time of this writing the other browsers do not support one or more of these features. By the time you read this other browsers may support these also.

■ **Note**   I explained how to install the Web Matrix application in Chapter 1. This is a free download provided by Microsoft. If you prefer, you can also implement the web site using Visual Studio with the MVC4 project template. After creating the project using the Basic template, add a **Home** folder under the View folder and create a view named **Index**. You'll also need to create a controller named **HomeController** using the Empty MVC controller template. Follow the instructions in the rest of this chapter using the `Index.cshtml` file (instead of `Default.cshtml`). You can also download the completed Visual Studio project that is included in the source code from `www.apress.com`.

Planning the Page Layout

Before creating a new web page, it's a good idea to sketch out the basic page structure. This will help you visualize the overall layout and see how the elements are nested together.

The page that you will develop in this chapter will use a `header` and `nav` element at the top and a `footer` element at the bottom. The main area in the middle will use a `div` element and have two side-by-side areas, each with a series of `article` tags. The larger area will be enclosed with another `div` element and provide the primary content, which is organized into articles. The smaller area, on the right, will use an `aside` element and will contain a `section` element. This will contain a series of `article` elements that will present related information. This is illustrated in Figure 4-2.

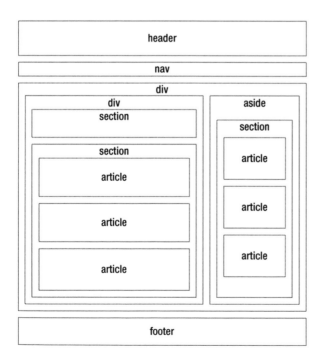

Figure 4-2. *Planning the page layout*

■ **Note** This diagram shows spaces between each of the elements to make it easier to understand. In the actual web page, in most cases this space is removed by setting the `margin` attribute to 0.

Creating the Web Project

With the content planned out you're ready to begin building the web page. You'll start by creating a project using WebMatrix and enter the basic page structure. Then you'll add content to each element. Later, I'll show how to implement the style rules.

Start the WebMatrix application and click the Templates button as shown in Figure 4-3.

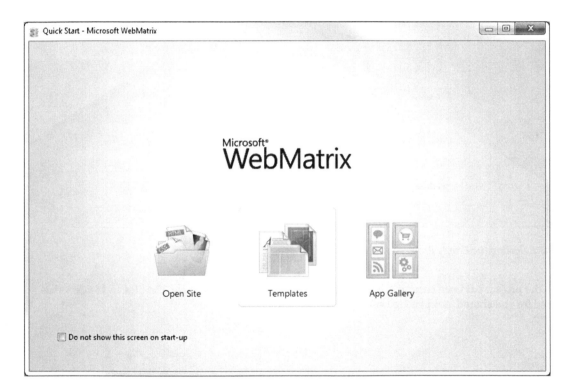

Figure 4-3. *Launching the WebMatrix application*

■ **Tip** For future reference, the App Gallery button will display a fairly large list of pre-built web applications that you can download and use to build your web project. This includes packages like WordPress, Joomla, and Drupal.

There are several templates to choose from. The Starter Site, for example, will create an ASP.NET MVC project. For this chapter you'll use Empty Site template. Select this and enter **Chapter4** for the site name as shown in Figure 4-4. Click the OK button to create the project.

Figure 4-4. *Selecting the Empty Project template*

When the project has been created, click the Files button in the navigation pane. The files and folders that were created for you should look like Figure 4-5.

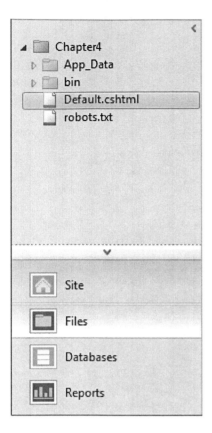

Figure 4-5. *The initial files and folders*

There should be a single web page named Default.cshtml. Double-click the file name in the navigation page to open it. The initial contents will look like this:

```
@{

}
<!DOCTYPE html>
<html lang="en">
    <head>
        <meta charset="utf-8" />
        <title></title>
    </head>
    <body>

    </body>
</html>
```

Defining the Page Structure

I find it helpful to start by entering the structural elements first before adding the contents. This will give you an opportunity to see the structure clearly, uncluttered by the actual content. Open the Default.cshtml file and enter the elements shown in Listing 4-1.

Listing 4-1. Entering the page structure

```html
<!DOCTYPE html>

<html lang="en">
    <head>
        <meta charset="utf-8"  />
        <title>Chapter 4 - CSS Demo</title>
    </head>
    <body>
        <header class="intro">
        </header>

        <nav>
        </nav>

        <div id="contentArea">

            <div id="mainContent">
                <section class="rounded">
                    <header>
                    </header>
                </section>

                <section>
                    <article class="featuredContent">
                        <a id="feature"></a>
                        <header>
                        </header>

                        <div>
                        </div>
                    </article>

                    <article class="otherContent">
                        <a id="other"></a>
                        <header>
                        </header>

                        <div>
                        </div>
                    </article>

                    <article class="otherContent">
                        <a id="another"></a>
                        <header>
                        </header>

                        <div>
                        </div>
                    </article>
                </section>
            </div>
```

```
            <aside id="sidebar">
                <section id="titles">
                    <article class="book">
                        <header>
                        </header>
                    </article>

                    <article class="book">
                        <header>
                        </header>
                    </article>

                    <article class="book">
                        <header>
                        </header>
                    </article>

                    <article class="book">
                        <header>
                        </header>
                    </article>

                    <article class="book">
                        <header>
                        </header>
                    </article>
                </section>
            </aside>
        </div>

        <footer>
        </footer>

    </body>
</html>
```

This is just basic HTML structure that you could have inferred from the diagram shown in Figure 4-2. The article elements have the class attribute assigned as you will use this for styling purposes. I assigned the id attribute to a few of the top-level elements. I also added an anchor element (<a id="feature"></a>) to each of the main content articles. You will setup navigation links to these in the nav element.

Adding the Content

There's nothing particularly special about the content. It's a lot of text (mostly Lorem ipsum), a few images, and some links.

In the Navigation pane, right-click the Chapter4 project and select the New Folder link. Enter **Images** for the folder name. An Images.zip file is included with the downloadable source code. Copy the images from this file to the new Images folder in your project.

I recommend downloading the content rather than entering it manually. There is a Default_content.cshtml file available in the source code. Replace your current implementation of this with the code in this file. It contains only the content of this page without any styles defined. If you want to enter the content manually, it is shown in Appendix A.

■ **Note** I wanted to point out one minor detail in the content. The footer element uses the new time element that was added with HTML5. As of this writing only the Opera browser supports it. The text between the begin and end tags (May 12th 2012) is displayed but the datetime attribute contains a machine-readable format that can be used by the browser, search engines, or JavaScript. Check out this article for more details: http://www.webmonkey.com/2012/02/the-html5-time-element-is-back-and-better-than-ever.

After the content has been added, click the Run button in the ribbon to see what the page looks like so far. It should be similar to Figure 4-6.

CSS Demo

Introducing the new HTML5 features

Use the new CSS3 features to build some of the most visually appealing web sites.

- Feature
- Article
- Archives
- Apress

Main content area

Lorem ipsum dolor sit amet, consectetur adipisicing elit, sed do eiusmod tempor incididunt ut labore et dolore magna aliqua. Ut enim ad minim veniam, quis nostrud exercitation ullamco laboris nisi ut.

Featured Article

This is really cool...

Lorem ipsum dolor sit amet, consectetur adipisicing elit, sed do eiusmod tempor incididunt ut labore et dolore magna aliqua. Ut enim ad minim veniam, quis nostrud exercitation ullamco laboris nisi ut.

Figure 4-6. *The initial page with only default styles*

Implementing the Style Rules

Now we get to the fun part, adding style. There is a huge number of style attributes that are available to you and I will demonstrate some of the more useful techniques that are new to CSS3. Many of these styles have been used for a while but prior to CSS3, their implementation was more complicated, often requiring JavaScript. After assigning some basic style rules I'll show you how to use more advance features including:

- Rounded corners
- Gradient backgrounds
- Tables
- Multiple columns
- Box shadows
- Zebra striping
- 3D transforms
- CSS Animation

Adding Basic Styles

Before you start adding the new styling features, you'll need to define the basic style formats. Add a style element inside the head element at the top of the Default.cshtml file. Then add the rules shown in Listing 4-2. Again, if you prefer, you can download the Default_styled.cshtml file and copy the code from there.

Listing 4-2. Adding the basic styles

```
<style>
    /* Basic tag settings */
    body
    {
        margin: 0 auto;
        width: 940px;
        font: 13px/22px Helvetica, Arial, sans-serif;
        background: #f0f0f0;
    }

    h2
    {
        font-size: 18px;
        line-height: 5px;
        padding: 2px 0;
    }

    h3
    {
        font-size: 12px;
        line-height: 5px;
        padding: 2px 0;
    }
```

```css
h1, h2, h3
{
    text-align: left;
}

p
{
    padding-bottom: 2px;
}

.book
{
    padding: 5px;
}

/* Content sections */
.featuredContent
{
    background-color: #ffffff;
    border: 2px solid #6699cc;
    padding: 15px 15px 15px 15px;
}

.otherContent
{
    background-color: #c0c0c0;
    border: 1px solid #999999;
    padding: 15px 15px 15px 15px;
}

aside
{
    background-color: #6699cc;
    padding: 5px 5px 5px 5px;
}

footer
{
    margin-top: 12px;
    text-align:center;
    background-color: #ddd;
}

footer p
{
    padding-top: 10px;
}

/* Navigation Section */
```

```css
nav
{
    left: 0;
    background-color: #003366;
}

nav ul
{
    margin: 0;
    list-style: none;
}

nav ul li
{
    float: left;
}

nav ul li a
{
    display: block;
    margin-right: 20px;
    width: 140px;
    font-size: 14px;
    line-height: 28px;
    text-align: center;
    padding-bottom: 2px;
    text-decoration: none;
    color: #cccccc;
}

nav ul li a:hover
{
    color: #fff;
}
</style>
```

I won't say much about this because it's all pretty standard CSS stuff. It uses mostly element selectors with an occasional class selector. If you preview your webpage now it should look like Figure 4-7.

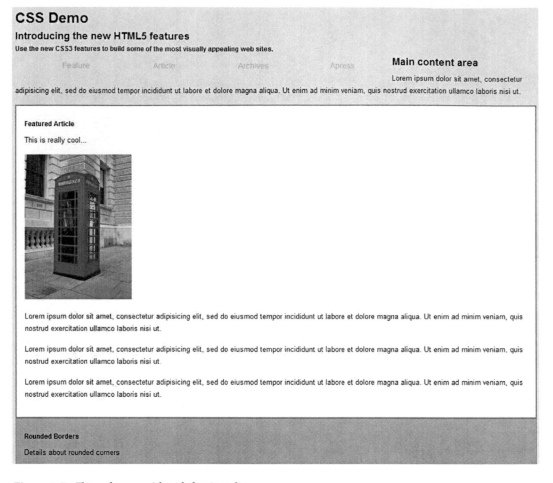

Figure 4-7. *The webpage with only basic styling*

■ **Note** To simplify the sample code, I will only use the Chrome vendor prefix, `-webkit-`, and only when the current version (19) doesn't support the standard attribute. I can get away with this because I am only expecting the page to work in the Chrome browser. Normally, you cannot make this assumption and will need to include all of the vendor prefixes.

Using Rounded Corners

Adding rounded corners is very easy to do with CSS3; just define the `border-radius` attribute. Your web page will use rounded corners for the `aside`, `nav`, and `footer` elements as well as elements with the `rounded` class.

■ **Note** In Chapter 7, I will show you how to implement rounded corners in older-browsers that do not support this feature. After reading that chapter you'll likely have a better appreciation for having features like this supported natively in the browser.

Add the rules shown in Listing 4-3 to the end of the style element.

Listing 4-3. Using rounded borders

```
/* Rounded borders */
.rounded
{
    border: 1px solid;
    border-color:#999999;
    border-radius:25px;
    padding: 24px;
}

aside
{
    border: 1px solid #999999;
    border-radius:12px;
}

/* Make the radius half of the height */
nav
{
    height: 30px;
    border-radius:15px;
}

footer
{
    height: 50px;
    border-radius:25px;
}
```

For the nav and footer elements, since they are fairly short sections, you'll set the radius to be half of the height. This will form a semi-circle on both ends. The top navigation section should look like Figure 4-8.

Figure 4-8. *Using rounded borders*

Working with Gradients

With CSS3 you can easily create a gradient by setting the `background-image` attribute using the `linear-gradient` function. With this function you can specify the beginning and ending color as well as the angle that the gradient should be applied. You'll use a gradient in the main heading, which has the `intro` class.

Add the following rule at the end of the `style` element:

```
/* Gradients */
.intro
{
    border: 1px solid #999999;
    text-align: left;
    padding-left: 15px;
    margin-top: 6px;
    border-radius: 25px;
    background-image: -webkit-linear-gradient(45deg, #ffffff, #6699cc);
    background-image: linear-gradient(45deg, #ffffff, #6699cc);
}
```

■ **Note** The IntelliSense in WebMatrix doesn't recognize the `linear-gradient` attribute and will show this as a CSS validation error. You can ignore this.

This will apply the gradient as a 45° angle. This also creates a rounded border. The page should now look like Figure 4-9.

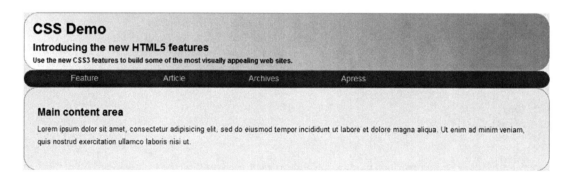

Figure 4-9. *Using a gradient background*

Creating Tables

It is generally considered bad practice to use tables in your markup for formatting purposes. This type of formatting is better done in the style sheet. You can then update the style if a different format is needed. You might have noticed that the current web page has the `aside` element following the main content instead of the two aligned side-by-side. You'll setup a table now using CSS to correct that.

Add the rules shown in Listing 4-4 at the end of the `style` element:

Listing 4-4. Creating a table

```
/* Setup a table for the content and sidebar */
#contentArea
{
    display: table;
}

#mainContent
{
    display: table-cell;
    padding-right: 2px;
}

aside
{
    display: table-cell;
    width: 280px;
}
```

These rules set the `display` attribute on the top-level elements. The `contentArea` element is set to `table` and the `mainContent` and `aside` elements are set to `table-cell`. These elements are then rendered as cells within the overall content element. To complete the alignment, the padding on the `mainContent` is set to 2px and the width of the `aside` element is set to 280px. The width of the mainContent is calculated automatically using the remaining space.

The page layout should now look like Figure 4-10.

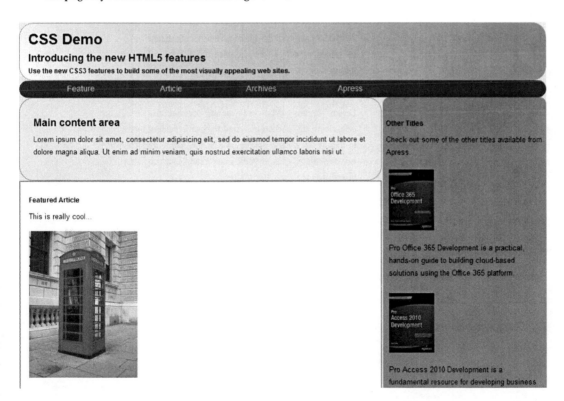

Figure 4-10. *The page layout with the sidebar on the right*

Adding Column Layout

Another neat feature that is new with CSS3 is the ability to format the content into columns like you would see in a newspaper or magazine. This is done using the `column-count` attribute. You should also specify the `column-gap` attribute that defines the vertical space between the columns. As of this writing these attributes were only available using the vendor-prefixed attributes.

Add the following rules at the end of the `style` element:

```
/* Setup multiple columns for the articles */
article div
{
    text-align:justify;
    padding:6px;

    -webkit-column-count: 2;
    column-count: 2;

    -webkit-column-gap: 20px;
    column-gap: 20px;
}
```

The articles should now be formatted with two columns as demonstrated in Figure 4-11.

Figure 4-11. *Using two columns*

Adding Box Shadows

Images can look a bit harsh and adding a shadow can soften the look and make the page more visually appealing. A shadow is easily added using the box-shadow attribute, which takes the following values:

- Horizontal position – the position of the horizontal shadow. If negative, the shadow is on the left side.

- Vertical position – the position of the vertical shadow. If negative, the shadow is at the top.

- Blur – the size of the blurred area just after the shadow.

- Spread – the width of the shadow.

- Color – the color of the shadow.

- Inset – makes the image appear lower than the surrounding area causing the shadow be on the image rather that outside the image.

The values are specified in a comma-separated list. It expects from two to four position/size values, an optional color property and the optional inset keyword. Only, the first two are required, which are the horizontal and vertical position. The blur and spread values will default to zero if not specified. Add the following rules to the end of the style element:

```css
/* Add the box shadow */
article img
{
    margin: 10px 0;
    box-shadow: 3px 3px 12px #222;
}

.book img
{
    margin: 10px 0;
    display: block;
    box-shadow: 2px 2px 5px #444;
    margin-left: auto;
    margin-right: auto;
}

aside
{
    box-shadow: 3px 3px 3px #aaaaaa;
}
```

The .book img rule also includes both the margin-left and margin-right attributes, which are both set to auto. This causes the images to be centered horizontally. Figures 4-12 and 4-13 show a close-up of the images in the featured content and the side bar items. Notice the first image has a larger blur area than the sidebar images.

Figure 4-12. *The shadow of the phone booth image in the featured content section*

Figure 4-13. *The shadow on the sidebar images*

Using Zebra Striping

One styling approach that has been used for a long time is to alternate the background when there is a list of items, which is sometimes referred to as *zebra-striping*. This goes back to the old blue-bar paper used to enter accounting journals. The alternating backgrounds make it easier to distinguish between each item. Prior to CSS3 this was accomplished with JavaScript that would programmatically change the background on every other element.

CSS3 introduces the nth-child selector which is perfect for this application because it returns every n^{th} element. Using this with n set to 2 will return every other element. Add the following code to the end of the style element:

```
/* Stripe the title list */
#titles article:nth-child(2n+1)
{
    background: #c0c0c0;
    border: 1px solid #6699cc;
    border-radius: 10px;
}

#titles article:nth-child(2n+0)
{
    background: #6699cc;
    border: 1px solid #c0c0c0;
    border-radius: 10px;
}
```

This rule uses a complex selector, #titles article:nth-child(2n+1), that first selects the #titles element. This is a section element that contains the book titles. Each book title is in a separate article element. The article:nth-child selector then return every nth article element inside the #titles element. The 2n+1 parameter may seem a bit odd, however. To get every other element, you specify 2n as the parameter, which would return the odd items (first, third, fifth, and so on). By using 2n+1, the list is offset by 1 so you will get the even items (second, fourth, sixth and so on). So the first rule formats the even items and the second rule, which uses 2n+0, will format the odd items. You could simply use 2n instead of 2n+0 as these are equivalent but I like using 2n+0 for consistency. The only difference between these two style rules is the background and border colors. The effect is shown in Figure 4-14.

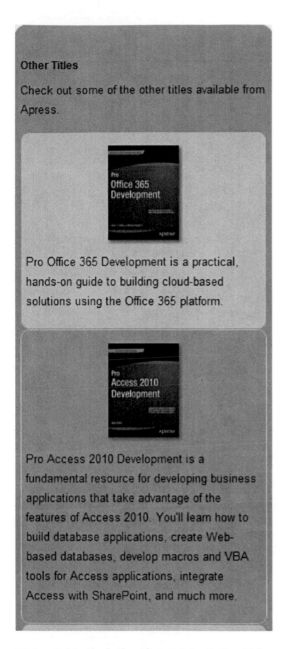

Figure 4-14. *Apply the zebra striping to the sidebar*

Using 3D Transforms

Adding a 3D transform can add some pizzazz to your web page. There's a lot that you can do with transforms but as the current support is rather limited, I won't spend too much time on it. I'll demonstrate a fairly simple application where you can flip the phone booth image in 3D.

■ **Note** As of this writing only Chrome and Safari support this feature.

You'll add a range control that you can use to change the rotation of the image. Insert the code shown in bold from Listing 4-5.

Listing 4-5. Adding a range control

```
<section>
    <article class="featuredContent">
        <a id="feature"></a>
        <header>
            <h3>Featured Article</h3>
        </header>

        <div class="rotateContainer">
            <p>This is really cool...</p>
            <img class="rotate" id="phone"
                src="images/phonebooth.jpg"
                alt="phonebooth" />
    <input type="range" min="-180" max="180" step="18"
        value="0" onchange="rotateImage(this.value)" />
    <br />
            <p>
                Lorem ipsum dolor sit amet, consectetur adipisicing
                elit, sed do eiusmod tempor incididunt ut labore et
                dolore magna aliqua. Ut enim ad minim veniam, quis
                nostrud exercitation ullamco laboris nisi ut.
            </p>
```

To format the 3D transformation, you'll specify a couple of attributes. First, you'll set the perspective property on the div that contains the image. This establishes the vanishing point that is used to determine how the 3D effect is rendered. Then, you'll set the preserve-3d attribute, which tells the browser to maintain the 3D perspective when rotating the image. To do this, add the following to the end of the style section:

```
.rotateContainer
{
    -webkit-perspective: 600px;
}

.rotate
{
  -webkit-transform-style: preserve-3d;
}
```

Now you'll add a JavaScript function that will change the rotation of the image as the range control is adjusted. Enter the code in bold in the head element:

```
<html lang="en">
    <head>
        <meta charset="utf-8" />
        <title>Chapter 4 - CSS Demo</title>
```

```
<script type="text/javascript">
  function rotateImage(value){
    document.getElementById("phone").style.webkitTransform
      ="rotateY(" + value + "deg)";
  }
</script>
```

```
</head>
```

The range control was created with a minimum value of –180 and a maximum of 180. The `rotateImage()` function is called whenever this value changes and simply calls the `rotateY()` function passing in the selected value. As you slide the range control you should see the image rotate as demonstrated in Figure 4-15.

Figure 4-15. *The rotated phonebooth – in 3D!*

Adding Animation

For the last effect, I'll show you how to create an animation effect without using any JavaScript. You can't modify the image with CSS because that is considered content, not format. However, you can change the background image and you'll take advantage of that to achieve the animation effect.

The `aside` element has a div defined as:

```
<div id="moon"></div>
```

Because there is no content or size defined, it has no effect on the page layout, currently. Now you'll use the animation feature in CSS3 to iterate through various images that illustrate the phases of the moon.

In CSS, animation is achieved by defining a set of keyframes. Each frame defines one or more CSS attributes. In this application you'll specify the appropriate background image but you could just as easily change the color or size or any other CSS attribute. For each frame you also specify the % of the animation duration when this frame should appear. You should always have a 0% and 100% frame, which specify the beginning and ending properties. You can include any number of steps in between. In this example, there are eight images so the frames will transition at 0%, 12%, 25%, 37%, 50%, 62%, 75%, 87%, and 100%.

Once you have defined the keyframes, you then then set the animation attributes on the element that you want to animate. You'll specify the name of the keyframes by setting the animation-name attribute. You can also set the duration (in seconds) that the animation will take using the animation-duration attribute. Add the code shown in Listing 4-6 to the end of the style section.

Listing 4-6. Defining the animation effect

```
/* Animate the moon phases */
@@-webkit-keyframes moonPhases
{
0%   {background-image:url("images/moon1.png");}
12%  {background-image:url("images/moon2.png");}
25%  {background-image:url("images/moon3.png");}
37%  {background-image:url("images/moon4.png");}
50%  {background-image:url("images/moon5.png");}
62%  {background-image:url("images/moon6.png");}
75%  {background-image:url("images/moon7.png");}
87%  {background-image:url("images/moon8.png");}
100%  {background-image:url("images/moon1.png");}
}

@@keyframes moonPhases
{
0%   {background-image:url("images/moon1.png");}
12%  {background-image:url("images/moon2.png");}
25%  {background-image:url("images/moon3.png");}
37%  {background-image:url("images/moon4.png");}
50%  {background-image:url("images/moon5.png");}
62%  {background-image:url("images/moon6.png");}
75%  {background-image:url("images/moon7.png");}
87%  {background-image:url("images/moon8.png");}
100%  {background-image:url("images/moon1.png");}
}

#moon
{
    width:115px;
    height:115px;
    background-image: url("images/moon1.png");
    background-repeat: no-repeat;
    -webkit-animation-name:moonPhases;
    -webkit-animation-duration:4s;
    -webkit-animation-delay:3s;
    -webkit-animation-iteration-count:10;
```

```
    animation-name:moonPhases;
    animation-duration:4s;
    animation-delay:3s;
    animation-iteration-count:10;
}
```

This code sets the total duration at 4 seconds so the image should transition every ½ second. It also specifies to wait 3 seconds before starting and to repeat the animation 10 times. When you refresh the web page, after about 3 seconds it should cycle through the phases of the moon as shown in Figure 4-16.

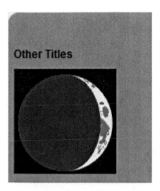

Figure 4-16. *Animating the moon's phases*

There are two other animation properties that were not applicable here, `timing-function` and `direction`. If you're using a simple animation and only define the begin and end values, the `timing-function` defines the speed of the transition. For example, if you're moving an element to a different position, setting this to linear will move the object at a constant rate. However, using the default value, ease, the transition will start out slow and then speed up and then slow down near the end. There are other options, like ease-in which will start out slow and then speed up for the remainder of the transition. The `direction` property, if set to alternate, will reverse the transition on alternating iterations. The default value, normal, will replay the exact same transition each time.

The complete style element is shown in Appendix B.

Summary

In this chapter I covered a lot of information about CSS, especially the new features in CSS3. The selectors are quite powerful giving a great deal of flexibility in applying styles. Prior to CSS3 much of this had to be done with a lot of JavaScript functions. I also showed you how to plan and structure a sample web page using a lot of the new structural HTML5 elements.

Using the WebMatrix application you created a simple web page, defined the basic structure and then populated the content. Using some if the new CSS3 features you then added some significant style features including:

- Rounded borders
- Gradients
- Tables
- Multiple columns

- Shadows
- Zebra striping
- 3D transforms
- Animation

In the next chapter I'll introduce some of the new features of HTML5 related to scripting.

CHAPTER 5

■ ■ ■

Scripting Enhancements

In this chapter I will demonstrate a few miscellaneous improvements that affect the scripting aspect of web development. So far, I have introduced the markup changes and the CSS enhancements. Scripting is the third leg of the overall HTML5 umbrella and a significant amount of attention was given to this area. This chapter will explain some improvements that have broad application, specifically:

- Query selectors
- Web workers
- Bundling and minification

Bundling and minification is not actually part of HTML5 but is a new feature of Visual Studio 2012. It is really easy to use and can make your page load much faster.

Using Query Selectors

In Chapter 4, I explained the CSS selectors that you can use to create powerful style rules. CSS3 introduced a significant improvement in this area. With the robust attribute selectors and quite a few new pseudo-classes such as nth-child that you used in Chapter 4, there is considerable functionality for selecting DOM elements. But it gets even better; all of this ability is available from JavaScript as well.

The HTML5 specification includes two new functions, querySelector() and querySelectorAll(). The querySelector() function returns a single element; the first one that matches the specified selector. The querySelectorAll() function returns an array of matching elements. For both functions you pass in the CSS selector, formatted just like you would in a style sheet. So once you've learned how to use CSS selectors, you can apply that same experience to JavaScript.

To try out these functions, you will use the same web page that you created in Chapter 4. The final version of the Chapter 4 project is available in the source code download if you want to use that.

Using querySelector

The querySelector() function can be used to replace the getElementByID() function. Of course it is much more useful than that, because you can pass in any type of CSS selector.

Open the Default.cshtml file and modify the rotateImage() function, replacing the getElementByID() function like this:

```
function rotateImage(value){
    document.querySelector("#phone").style.webkitTransform
        ="rotateY(" + value + "deg)";
}
```

■ **Caution**   Don't forget to prefix the ID with "#". Because the `querySelector()` function can be used with any type of selector, you'll need the hash symbol to indicate this is an ID selector.

Run the web page using Chrome (or Safari) and verify the range control still works.

Using querySelectorAll

That was a fairly trivial example so now I'll demonstrate a more complex selector. You'll add a JavaScript function that will change the color on all of the internal links in the nav element. Arguably you could just do this in the style sheet but there are times when you need to do it in code as well. For example, you might need to change the style programmatically based on user input.

Add the following function to the script element in the `Default.cshtml` page:

```
function adjustInternalLinks(){
    var links = document.querySelectorAll("nav ul li a[href ^='#']");
    for (var i=0; i < links.length; i++){
        links[i].style.color = "green";
    }
}
```

The CSS selector is nav `ul li a[href ^='#']`, which returns all a elements with an href attribute that begins with the # character. This is further filtered to only elements that have the nav, ul, and li parentage. This will exclude links that may appear in other sections.

The `querySelectorAll()` function returns an array so this code iterates through the array making each element green. Now you'll need to call this function. Add the code shown in bold to the body element:

```
<body onload="adjustInternalLinks()">
```

This will call the function when the page is loaded but you could just as easily call this based on some appropriate user input to make the style dynamic. Save the changes and reload the page. You should now have green links. Note that the link to `www.apress.com` is not green because it is an external link and doesn't start with "#".

Creating the Visual Studio Project

For the rest of the exercises in this chapter you'll use a Visual Studio project. You'll create an empty web site now and then add features to it later. Start Visual Studio 2012 and select the New Project link. Select the MVC4 project template and enter **Chapter5** for the name as shown in Figure 5-1.

Figure 5-1. *Creating the Chapter5 project*

In the second dialog select the Basic Project template and make sure the Razor view engine is selected.

Employing Web Workers

With more and more work being done on the client, making the client application multi-threaded becomes more important. Fortunately, the use of web workers is a convenient way to accomplish that. Functions that are CPU intensive or may take some time to complete can be executed on a background thread leaving the main UI thread available to respond to user actions.

Web workers use a fairly simple concept. You create a worker and pass it a JavaScript file that defines its execution. The web page can then communicate with the worker through messages. The worker implements the onmessage event handler to respond to an incoming message from the page and uses the postMessage() function to send data back to the caller. The caller must also handle the onmessage event to receive the messages from the worker. This is illustrated in Figure 5-2.

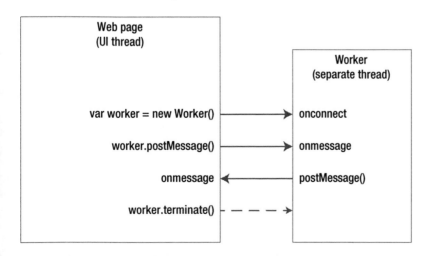

Figure 5-2. *Communicating with a dedicated web worker*

■ **Tip** For the demo application that you'll create in this chapter, the messages between the caller and the worker will be simple text messages. However they can be any format you want, including JSON encoded data.

One of the most significant limitations of web workers is that they cannot access the DOM, so you can't use them to update the page content or style. Also, they cannot access the window object, which means, among other things, that you can't use timers. With these limitations in mind you might be wondering when you would use a web worker.

Web workers are great for performing tasks such as retrieving data. For example, if you need to lookup information from an external source (such as a database, local file system, or web) you can pass the lookup parameters to the worker and when the lookup finishes the data can be passed back as a JSON message. This allows the web page to respond to user actions while the data is being retrieved.

Web workers come in two varieties: dedicated and shared. A single shared worker can be used by multiple web pages. Both dedicated and shared workers function the same basic way but the communication is a little different. You'll start by implementing a dedicated web worker.

Using a Dedicated Worker

A dedicated web worker, as its name implies, is dedicated to the web page that created it. The web page creates it, uses it as needed and closes it when it no longer needs it. A web page can create as many workers as it needs.

To demonstrate a dedicated web worker, you'll build a simple web page that will allow you to create a worker and send messages to it. It will also display the response so you can see the two-way communication. The worker implementation is trivial; simply echoing back the message that was sent to it.

EXERCISE 5-1. USING A DEDICATED WEB WORKER

1. In the Chapter5 project that you created earlier, right-click the Controller folder in the Solution Explorer and select the Add ➤ Controller links. Enter the name **HomeController** and select the Empty MVC controller template. Click the Add button to create the controller.

2. Right-click the View folder and select the Add ➤ New Folder links. Enter the name **Home**.

3. Right-click the new Home folder and select the Add ➤ View links. In the Add View dialog box, enter the name **Index**, make sure the Razor view engine is selected, and unselect all the check boxes as shown in Figure 5-3.

Figure 5-3. *Adding the Index view*

4. Replace the default implementation of the Index.cshtml view using the code shown in Listing 5-1. This will create a simple form with a text area for displaying messages and three buttons for communicating with the worker.

Listing 5-1. The Index view implementation

```
<!DOCTYPE html>

<html lang="en">
    <head>
        <meta charset="utf-8" />
        <title>Chapter 5 - Web Workers</title>
        <link rel="stylesheet" type="text/css" href="Content/Sample.css" />
        <script src="Scripts/controlWorker.js"></script>
```

```
        </head>
        <body>
            <header>

                <h1>Web Workers Demo</h1>
            </header>

            <div>

                <textarea id="output"></textarea>
            </div>

            <form id="control" method="post" action="">
                <input id="create" type="button" class="button" value="Create Worker"
                    onclick="createWorker()"><br>
                <input id="send" type="button" class="button" value="Send Message"
                    onclick="sendWorkerMessage()">
                <input id="message" type="text" class="text" value="Hello, World!"><br>
                <input id="kill" type="button" class="button" value="Close Worker"
                    onclick="closeWorker()">

            </form>

        </body>
    </html>
```

5. From the Solution Explorer, right-click the Content folder and select the Add ➤ New Item links. Select the Web category and then select the Style Sheet item and enter **Sample.css** for the file name as shown in Figure 5-4. Click the Add button to create the file.

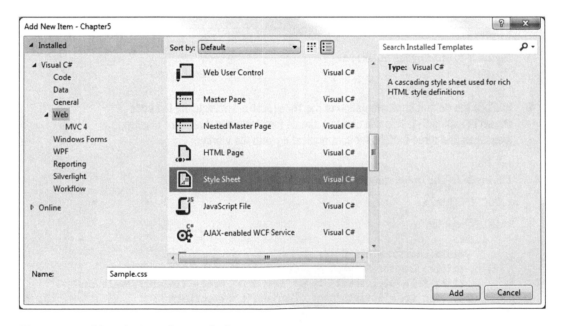

Figure 5-4. *Adding the Sample.css style sheet*

6. Replace the default implementation with the code shown in Listing 5-2.

    Listing 5-2. The Sample.css style sheet

    ```
    h1
    {
        font-size:22px;
        color:purple;
    }

    #output
    {
        width: 500px;
        height: 250px;
        background-color:#dfcaca;
    }

    .button
    {
        width:125px;
        height:25px;
        color:green;
    }

    .text
    {
        width:260px;
    }
    ```

7. Press F5 to debug the application and the form should look similar to Figure 5-5.

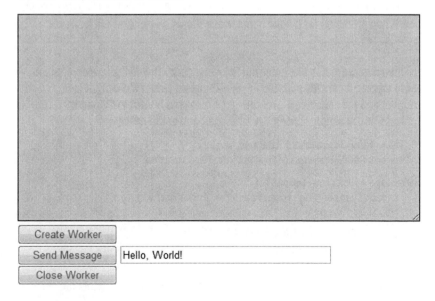

Figure 5-5. *The initial form design*

113

8. Close the browser and stop the debugger.

9. In the Solution Explorer, right-click the Scripts folder and select the Add ➤ New Item links. In the Add New Item dialog box, select the Web category and then select the JavaScript File item. Enter **worker.js** for the filename as shown in Figure 5-6.

Figure 5-6. *Adding the worker.js file*

■ **Tip** You can also right-click the Scripts folder and select the Add ➤ JavaScript File links, which will skip the Add New Item dialog box. When prompted for the file name, leave the `.js` extension off, however.

---

10. For the contents of this file, enter the following code. This is the implementation of the worker. It handles both the onconnect event (when the worker is first created) and the onmessage event (when a message is sent to the worker). The implementation simply echoes the message back to the caller.

```
/* This file implements the web worker */
onconnect = sendResponse("The worker has started");

onmessage = function (event) {
    sendResponse("Msg received: " + event.data);
}

function sendResponse(message) {
    postMessage(message);
}
```

11. Using the same instructions, add a **controlWorker.js** file in the Scripts folder.

12. Enter the code shown in Listing 5-3 for its implementation. I will explain this in more detail later in the chapter.

Listing 5-3. The controlWorker.js implementation

```
/* This file contains functions used to
   communicate with the web worker */

var myWorker;

function createWorker() {
    if (typeof(Worker) !== "undefined") {
        var log = document.querySelector("#output");
        log.value += "Starting worker process... ";

        myWorker = new Worker("Scripts/worker.js");

        log.value += "Adding listener... ";
        myWorker.onmessage = function(event){
            log.value += event.data + "\n";
        }

        log.value += "Done!\n";
    }
    else {
        alert("Your browser does not support web workers");
    }
}

function sendWorkerMessage(){
    if (myWorker !== null) {
        var log = document.querySelector("#output");
        log.value += "Sending message... ";

        var message = document.querySelector("#message");
        myWorker.postMessage(message.value);

        log.value += "Done!\n";
    }
}

function closeWorker(){
    if (myWorker !== null) {
        var log = document.querySelector("#output");
        log.value += "Closing worker... ";

        myWorker.terminate;
        myWorker = null;

        log.value += "Done!\n";
    }
}
```

13. Press F5 to debug the application. Click the Create Worker button and then click the Send button. Modify the message and try clicking the Send Message button again. Finally, click the Close Worker button. The text area should look like Figure 5-7.

```
Starting worker process... Adding listener... Done!
The worker has started
Sending message... Done!
Msg received: Hello, World!
Sending message... Done!
Msg received: Hello again
Closing worker... Done!
```

Figure 5-7. *The message log*

The `controlWorker.js` file contains three functions that provide the implementation for the three buttons on the form. It first declares a `myWorker` variable, which holds a reference to the dedicated web worker.

- `createWorker()` – This function first checks to see if the browser supports web workers by seeing if the `Worker` class is defined. If not, an alert is raised. It then creates an instance of the `Worker` class saving its reference in the `myWorker` variable. The worker implementation is passed to its constructor by referencing the `worker.js` script file. It then creates the `onmessage` event handler that adds the incoming message to the `output` field.

- `sendWorkerMessage()` – This simply calls the worker's `postMessage()` method passing in the text specified in the `message` field. Notice it is using the `querySelector()` method that I explained earlier in this chapter.

- `closeWorker()` – This calls the worker's `terminate()` method and sets the `myWorker` variable to null. The worker is closed immediately without any ability to perform any clean-up operations.

■ **Tip** In the same way that you added an `onmessage` event handler you can also create an `onerror` event handler to respond to errors from the worker.

With this simple implementation you can see how easy it is to create a worker and use messages to communicate with it.

Creating a Shared Worker

A shared web worker allows you to create a worker and then reuse it from other pages. There are a couple of advantages to using shared workers. The most obvious one is that multiple pages can share the same thread instead of having to create a new worker thread for every page. The other, which I'll explain later, is to share state information across pages.

Now you'll create a shared worker, which is implemented in a JavaScript file. The concept is essentially the same but the communication is done a little differently. You'll add a few more buttons to the web page and implement a new set of JavaScript functions to communicate with the shared worker.

EXERCISE 5-2. CREATING A SHARED WORKER

1. Open the `Index.cshtml` file and add the following script reference in the `head` element after the previous reference:

```
<script src="Scripts/controlSharedWorker.js"></script>
```

2. Add the code shown in bold in Listing 5-4 to the form element. This will add another set of buttons to control the shared worker.

Listing 5-4. The additional buttons in Index.cshtml

```
<form id="control" method="post" action="">
    <input id="create" type="button" class="button" value="Create Worker"
            onclick="createWorker()"><br>
    <input id="send" type="button" class="button" value="Send Message"
            onclick="sendWorkerMessage()">
    <input id="message" type="text" class="text" value="Hello, World!"><br>
    <input id="kill" type="button" class="button" value="Close Worker"
            onclick="closeWorker()">

    <br><br>
    <input id="createS" type="button" class="button" value="Create Shared"
            onclick="createSharedWorker()"><br>
    <input id="sendS" type="button" class="button" value="Send Shared Msg"
            onclick="sendSharedWorkerMessage()">
    <input id="messageS" type="text" class="text" value="Hello, World!"><br>
    <input id="killS" type="button" class="button" value="Close Shared"
            onclick="closeSharedWorker()">

</form>
```

3. From the Solution Explorer, add another file to the Scripts folder named **sharedWorker.js** and enter the code shown in Listing 5-5. This is the implementation of the shared worker.

Listing 5-5. The sharedWorker.js implementation

```
/* This file implements the shared web worker */
var clients=0;

onconnect=function(event) {
    var port=event.ports[0];
    clients++;

    /* Attach the event listener */
    port.addEventListener("message", function(event){
        sendResponse(event.target, "Msg received: " + event.data);
    }, false);

    port.start();

    sendResponse(port, "You are client # " + clients + "\n");
}
```

```
function sendResponse(senderPort, message) {
    senderPort.postMessage( message);
}
```

4. Add another file in the Scripts folder named **controlSharedWorker.js** and enter the implementation shown in Listing 5-6. I will explain this code later.

Listing 5-6. The controlSharedWorker.js implementation

```
/* This file contains functions used to
   communicate with the web worker */

var mySharedWorker;

function createSharedWorker() {
    if (typeof(Worker) !== "undefined") {
        var log = document.querySelector("#output");
        log.value += "Starting shared worker process... ";

        mySharedWorker = new SharedWorker("Scripts/sharedWorker.js");

        log.value += "Adding listener... ";
        mySharedWorker.port.addEventListener("message", function(event){
            log.value += event.data + "\n";
        }, false);

        mySharedWorker.port.start();

        log.value += "Done!\n";
    }
    else {
        alert("Your browser does not support web workers");
    }
}

function sendSharedWorkerMessage(){
    if (mySharedWorker !== null) {
        var log = document.querySelector("#output");
        log.value += "Sending message... ";

        var message = document.querySelector("#messageS");
        mySharedWorker.port.postMessage(message.value);

        log.value += "Done!\n";
    }
}

function closeSharedWorker(){
    if (mySharedWorker !== null) {
        var log = document.querySelector("#output");
        log.value += "Closing worker... ";

        mySharedWorker.port.terminate;
        mySharedWorker = null;

        log.value += "Done!\n";
    }
}
```

5. Press F5 to debug the application. Create a shared worker and send a message to it. It should work just like the previous exercise.

6. Leaving the browser tab running, create a new tab and enter the same URL as the first tab. This will open the same site in a second tab. Create a shared worker from the second tab. Then click the Send Shared Message button to test the connection. Notice the message says that you are the second client as demonstrated in Figure 5-8.

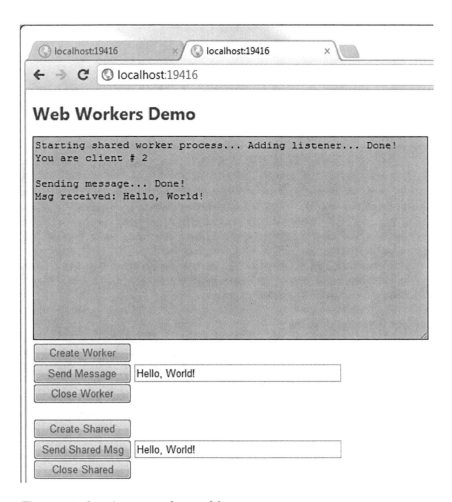

Figure 5-8. *Opening a second copy of the page*

7. The Chrome browser has a small wrench icon at the top-right corner. Click this and then select the Tools ➤ Task Manager links to open the task manager, which should look similar to Figure 5-9. Notice that there are two copies of your page but only one copy of the web worker.

Figure 5-9. Displaying the Task Manager

Now let's look at how the shared worker was implemented. Just like the dedicated worker, it must handle the onconnect and onmessage events. However you can't attach the ommessage handler directly to the worker; instead you must access a port and attach to that. The onconnect event receives an event parameter and you access the port by event.ports[0]. Once you have the port you can attach the event handler to it. You use the port's addEventHandler() method. This takes two parameters. The first is the name of the event, message in this case. The second parameter is the function that will be called when the event is raised.

When sending a message back you must also use the port object. This port object is provided in the event.target property of the incoming message. Both this event handler and the onconnect event handler use the sendResponse() function passing in the port object.

The functions in the controlSharedWorker.js file are almost identical to their dedicated counterparts. However, they must also use the port object.

Notice in the sharedWorker.js file that the clients variable is declared and then incremented in the onconnect event handler. This is used to keep track of how many clients have connected to the shared worker. I added this just to demonstrate how this variable is global to all the clients attached to the worker. In fact, there is no per-port instance data; all data is global.

Also, when a message comes in, the event parameter includes the port that the response should be sent to. The worker doesn't "remember" the port for each client. It just does what it's instructed to do and returns a response on the specified port.

Using Visual Studio Bundling and Minification

When a browser loads a page, all of the referenced files such as style sheets and JavaScripts must be loaded as well. Each file is retrieved from the server with an HTTP request, so a separate round-trip is required for each file. Also, while we like white space and comments to make our code more manageable, this is extra data that must be downloaded but ignored by the browser. If you're concerned about your page loading faster, there are two techniques that can make a big difference.

- Bundling – *Bundling* is the process of taking all the individual files and concatenating them into a single file. This will reduce the amount of server round-trips it will take to load your page.

- Minification – The *minification* process trips out all white space and comments making the referenced files as small as possible.

Prior to Visual Studio 2012, both of these were a manual process that you would need to do with each build. Now, as I will show you, much of this work is done for you. First, let's see how the current page works without bundling.

Run your application. You can verify the files that were downloaded by using the Developer Tools in the Chrome browser. Click the wrench icon at the top of the browser window and select the Tools ➤ Developer tools links to display the tools pane. You could also use the Ctrl+Shift+I shortcut. Select the Network link to see the server requests. Refresh the page to see the network traffic, which should look like Figure 5-10.

Name / Path	Method	Status / Text	Type	Initiator	Size / Content	Time / Latency	Timeline
:19416/	GET	200 OK	text/html	Other	1.30KB 3.26KB	631ms 627ms	
jquery.ui.resizable.css /Content/themes/base	GET	200 OK	text/css	:19416/ 8 Parser	(from c...	11ms 10ms	
jquery.ui.selectable.css /Content/themes/base	GET	200 OK	text/css	:19416/ 9 Parser	(from c...	11ms 11ms	
jquery.ui.accordion.css /Content/themes/base	GET	200 OK	text/css	:19416/ 10 Parser	(from c...	14ms 12ms	
jquery.ui.autocomplete.cs /Content/themes/base	GET	200 OK	text/css	:19416/ 11 Parser	(from c...	16ms 15ms	
jquery.ui.button.css /Content/themes/base	GET	200 OK	text/css	:19416/ 12 Parser	(from c...	18ms 17ms	
jquery.ui.core.css /Content/themes/base	GET	200 OK	text/css	:19416/ 7 Parser	(from c...	10ms 10ms	
jquery.ui.dialog.css /Content/themes/base	GET	200 OK	text/css	:19416/ 13 Parser	(from c...	18ms 16ms	
jquery.ui.slider.css /Content/themes/base	GET	200 OK	text/css	:19416/ 14 Parser	(from c...	18ms 16ms	
jquery.ui.tabs.css /Content/themes/base	GET	200 OK	text/css	:19416/ 15 Parser	(from c...	20ms 18ms	
jquery.ui.datepicker.css /Content/themes/base	GET	200 OK	text/css	:19416/ 16 Parser	(from c...	20ms 19ms	
jquery.ui.progressbar.css /Content/themes/base	GET	200 OK	text/css	:19416/ 17 Parser	(from c...	20ms 19ms	
jquery.ui.theme.css /Content/themes/base	GET	200 OK	text/css	:19416/ 18 Parser	(from c...	21ms 19ms	
site.css /Content	GET	200 OK	text/css	:19416/ 19 Parser	(from c...	21ms 18ms	
modernizr-2.0.6-develop /Scripts	GET	200 OK	applica...	:19416/ 21 Parser	(from c...	23ms 22ms	
Sample.css /Content	GET	200 OK	text/css	:19416/ 21 Parser	(from c...	22ms 18ms	
controlWorker.js /Scripts	GET	200 OK	applica...	:19416/ 21 Parser	(from c...	22ms 22ms	
controlSharedWorker.js /Scripts	GET	200 OK	applica...	:19416/ 21 Parser	(from c...	24ms 22ms	
jquery-1.6.2.js /Scripts	GET	200 OK	applica...	:19416/ 21 Parser	(from c...	28ms 22ms	

Figure 5-10. *Viewing the network traffic*

This graph lists the files that are downloaded from the web server. As you can see, it's a pretty long list. The first file listed is the html document. The rest are JavaScript or CSS files referenced by your page (or the master layout page). Your three files, Sample.css, controlWorker.js, and controlSharedWorker.js are shown near the end of the list.

To simplify this demonstration, edit the _Layout.cshtml view to remove the standard references. You don't need them for this application. Comment out the referenced files by adding the code shown in bold:

```
<!DOCTYPE html>
<html>
<head>
    <meta charset="utf-8" />
    <meta name="viewport" content="width=device-width" />
    <title>@ViewBag.Title</title>
    <!-- @Styles.Render("~/Content/themes/base/css", "~/Content/css")
    @Scripts.Render("~/bundles/modernizr") -->
</head>
<body>
    @RenderBody()

    <!-- @Scripts.Render("~/bundles/jquery") -->
    @RenderSection("scripts", required: false)
</body>
</html>
```

Now run the application and the network traffic should look like Figure 5-11.

Figure 5-11. *Network traffic with the standard files removed*

A bundle is a set of files that the server concatenates for you. You reference the bundle name in your web page, and all the individual files are returned in one HTTP request. Visual Studio builds default bundles for you for all the standard files. However, you might want to create your own custom bundles. You can build a custom bundle to include just the files you need.

EXERCISE 5-3. CREATING A CUSTOM BUNDLE

1. Visual Studio will only generate bundles when not in Debug mode. This is controlled by the compilation setting in the web.config file. To enable bundling you'll need to set this flag manually. Open the web.config file in the root folder and edit the code shown in bold:

    ```
    <system.web>
      <compilation debug="false" targetFramework="4.5" />
      <authentication mode="Forms">
    ```

2. Open the Global.asax.cs file and change the code to comment out the RegisterBundles() method line like this:

    ```
    //BundleConfig.RegisterBundles(BundleTable.Bundles);
    ```

3. Add the following code to the `Application_Start()` method to create two custom bundles:

```
BundleTable.Bundles.Add(new ScriptBundle("~/Scripts/myJs").Include(
    "~/Scripts/controlWorker.js",
    "~/Scripts/controlSharedWorker.js"));

BundleTable.Bundles.Add(new StyleBundle("~/Content/myCss").Include(
    "~/Content/Sample.css"));
```

This code first creates a `Bundle` object, specifying the logical name that it will be referenced by. It then uses the `Include()` method to list the appropriate files that should be included in the bundle. Finally, the new bundle is added to the `BundleTable` object so it will be available to the web page.

4. Change the script reference in the `Index.cshtml` file to use the `myJs` and `myCss` bundles using the `Scripts.Render()` and `Styles.Render()` helper functions. Also, comment out the existing script and css references. Your file references should look like this:

```
<head>
    <meta charset="utf-8" />
    <title>Chapter 5 - Web Workers</title>

    @Scripts.Render("~/Scripts/myJs")
    @Styles.Render("~/Content/myCss")

    <!--<link rel="stylesheet" type="text/css" href="Content/Sample.css" />
    <script src="Scripts/controlWorker.js"></script>
    <script src="Scripts/controlSharedWorker.js"></script>-->
</head>
```

■ **Note** The `Scripts.Render()` and `Styles.Render()` helper functions will generate the appropriate references to access the specified bundles. However, in debug mode when bundles are disabled, it will generate references to the individual files.

---

5. Because you changed the debug setting to false, you won't be able to debug the application. Instead, Press Ctrl-F5 to run the application. Check the network traffic, which should look like Figure 5-12.

Name Path	Method	Status Text	Type	Initiator	Size Content	Time Latency	Timeline	43ms	65ms	87ms	108ms	130ms
:19416/	GET	200 OK	text/html	Other	1.29KB 2.33KB	26ms 21ms						
myJs /Scripts	GET	200 OK	text/ja...	:19416/:20 Parser	(from c...	6ms 6ms						
myCss /Content	GET	200 OK	text/css	:19416/:20 Parser	(from c...	4ms 4ms						

Figure 5-12. The final network activity

123

The minification process strips out white space and comments making the file more compact and therefore faster to download. The bundling process automatically minifies the bundle. It uses a different minification function for `.css` and `.js` files. The appropriate one is used by specifying either the `StyleBundle` or `ScriptBundle` class. You can create your own minification function as well.

Summary

In this chapter you tried out a few very useful techniques that you may likely use in many of your web projects. The features you used are:

- Query selectors – take advantage of the same powerful CSS selectors in your JavaScript code.

- Web workers – execute CPU intensive or slow operations on a separate thread to improve overall responsiveness.

- Bundling – create custom bundles to download just the files you need in a single server round-trip.

- Minification – compress the referenced files for faster download.

In Chapter 6, I'll show you how the HTML5 improvements can be used in create mobile-friendly web applications.

CHAPTER 6

■ ■ ■

Mobile Web Applications

So far, we have only looked at desktop browsers, however, one of the really great aspects of HTML5 is how well it is supported on a wide variety of devices including mobile phone, tablets, and TVs. In fact, the number of HTML5 devices is expected to exceed 1 Billion by 2013 (see the article at http://www.strategyanalytics.com/default.aspx?mod=pressreleaseviewer&a0=5145). As of this writing, the Opera Mobile and Firefox Mobile platforms lead the pack with 369 and 325 points, respectively, as reported by Html5Test.com. When Blackberry 10 releases, it is expected to receive a whopping 447 points out of a possible 500.

On a mobile device you will use native applications as well as web applications. Native apps are developed for a specific mobile platform and installed on the device, or downloaded through the phone service. Native apps can often provide the best user experience because they can make maximum use of the device's specific hardware and OS features. However, Web apps, due in part to the popularity of HTML5, are increasingly in demand as well. And they can be developed almost as easily as those used by desktop browsers.

In this chapter I will introduce some of the emulators that are available to help you test your site on various mobile devices. The biggest challenge that you'll face is supporting a variety of form factors. I will show you some techniques that will allow your web page to dynamically adjust to different screen resolutions. This will enable you to take advantage of a larger screen when it's available and still support even very small devices from the same code.

Using Emulators

To see how your web site works on a mobile device you can use a number of phone emulator applications. While these may not function exactly as the actual hardware they provide a reasonable approximation. I'll show you how to install and use several of the more common utilities.

Installing the Windows Phone Developer Tools

I'll start with the Windows Phone Emulator, which is part of the Windows Phone SDK 7.1. You can download and install the SDK from this site: http://www.microsoft.com/en-us/download/details.aspx?id=27570. The SDK is only supported on Visual Studio 2010 and includes VS 2010 Express for Windows Phone. However, you will only be using the emulator application which is not specific to any version of Visual Studio.

After installing this, start the emulator, which you'll find in the Windows Phone SDK 7.1 start menu. After the application has loaded, click the Internet Explorer application and then enter the URL of your web site from Chapter 4. Make sure to include the **http://** prefix in front of localhost. You'll need to click the keyboard buttons on the phone emulator to enter the address. The site will look like Figure 6-1.

Figure 6-1. *The Windows Phone emulator*

The browser on the Windows Phone 7.1 is essentially IE9 so it doesn't support much of the HTML5 features. In the next chapter I will show you how to use polyfills to retrofit some of the new features in older browsers. For now however, you will use other phone emulators as they provide better HTML5 support.

Using the Opera Mobile Emulator

Opera provides a free mobile emulator application, which you can download from this site:
http://www.opera.com/developer/tools/mobile. One thing that is particularly nice about this utility is
that you can choose, from a pretty long list, which device you want to emulate. After you have installed this
application, start it and you should see the Launch window shown in Figure 6-2.

Figure 6-2. *The Opera Emulator launch window*

When you select a device, the window displays the hardware details such as screen resolution. Select the LG
Optimus One device and click the Launch button. With this emulator you can either use the device keypad or
your desktop keyboard. Enter the URL of your site from Chapter 4, which should look like Figure 6-3.

Figure 6-3. *Emulating the LG Optimus One device*

Notice that page is scaled to fit in the screen, which makes it mostly unreadable. You will deal with that later in the chapter. You can try some other devices such as the Nokia N800, which is shown in Figure 6-4. As you might expect, the larger form factors handle the page better.

Figure 6-4. *Emulating the Nokia N800*

Installing Chrome Ripple

Emulating a mobile device on Chrome and Firefox requires a different approach by using add-ons to the desktop browser. When using the emulators you are essentially using the desktop browser with some add-on functionality to simulate the device's form factor.

Start the Chrome desktop browser and go to this site: `http://ripple.tinyhippos.com/download`. This will display the Ripple page. Click the "Add to Chrome" button and follow the instructions to install this.

Figure 6-5. *The Ripple emulator download page*

Once you have installed the add-on, use the Chrome browser and enter the URL of the Chapter4 web site. On the right-hand corner, there is a button that is used to start the emulator. Click this button and then click the Enable button as shown in Figure 6-6.

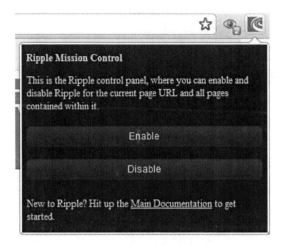

Figure 6-6. Enabling the Ripple emulator

This will display the current page using the emulator mode. The first time you start Ripple for a specific URL, you'll see the prompt shown in Figure 6-7. Click the "BlackBerry 10 WebWorks" button to choose this platform to emulate.

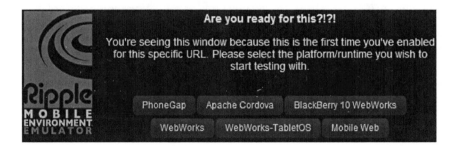

Figure 6-7. Selecting the desired platform

Your web page on the BlackBerry 10 device should look like Figure 6-8.

Figure 6-8. *The web page on the BlackBerry 10 device*

There are two small buttons at the top-left and top-right corners of the browser window with arrows on them. Use these to show/hide the option windows. For example, the one on the left, shown in Figure 6-9, allows you to change the device orientation or to choose a different platform to emulate. It also provides some technical details of the current device such as the screen resolution. The button on the right includes the Settings tab where you can switch between dark and light themes.

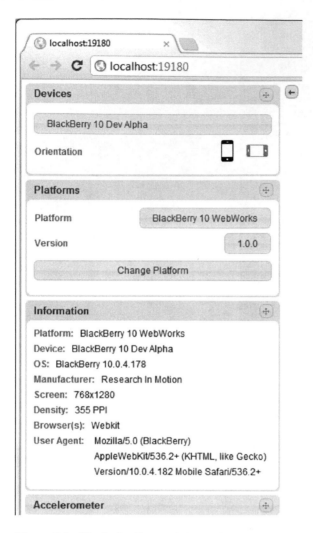

Figure 6-9. Displaying the emulator options

Emulating the Other Devices

To simulate your web site on an iPhone, using Chrome, go to this site: `http://iphone-emulator.org`. When the emulator is displayed, enter the URL of the Chapter4 site into the search box on the device. The site will look like Figure 6-10.

Figure 6-10. *Emulating the web page on an iPhone*

Notice the buttons at the top of the page that enable you to also emulate other devices such as the iPad and Android.

Handling Form Factors

The biggest challenge when creating web applications that work well on mobile devices is handling the various form factors. On the larger devices you'll want to take advantage of the extra space while still making a reasonable appearance on the smaller ones. In the samples that I've shown you so far, the device either scaled the page to fit or cropped it. Neither approach is optimal.

There are three techniques that will help you improve how your site looks across all form factors:

- Media queries – This allows you to apply different styles based on attributes of the existing viewport. I will spend most the rest of this chapter demonstrating this.

- Flexible images and videos – This simply instructs the browser to stretch or shrink the image to fit the available space.

- Use a CSS grid template layout – This is similar to designing forms with Windows Presentation Foundation (WPF) that allows the browser to resize or move elements dynamically based on the window size. Unfortunately, this is not something that is currently available and the specification is still in draft, but watch for this in future browser updates.

■ **Tip**   One of the things that the various emulators do is limit the window size based on the device characteristics. You can accomplish the same thing by simply resizing your browser window. For your initial testing you can shrink the window and see how the layout responds. Then use the emulators for the final testing.

Understanding Media Queries

CSS 2.1 introduced the media keyword, allowing you to define a printer-friendly style sheet. For example you can use something like this:

```
<link rel="stylesheet" type="text/css" href="screen.css" media="screen" />
<link rel="stylesheet" type="text/css" href="print.css" media="print" />
```

You can then define a different style sheet for the print version of your webpage. Alternatively, you could embed media-specific style rules within a single style sheet. For example this will change the font size when printed:

```
@media print
{
    h1, h2, h3
    {
        font-size: 14px;
    }
}
```

■ **Tip**   There are other media types that are supported including aural, braille, handheld, projection, tty, and tv. As you can see, the media type was initially used to represent the type of device that is rendering the page. Also, the all type is supported but is also implied if no media type is specified. Styles with the all type are applied for every device.

With CSS3, this has been enhanced significantly to allow you to query various attributes to determine the appropriate styles. For example, you can apply a style when the width of the windows is 600px or smaller like this:

```
@media (max-width:600px)
{
    h1
    {
        font-size: 12px;
    }
}
```

The features that can be selected in a media query are:

- `width`
- `height`
- `device-width`
- `device-height`
- `orientation`
- `aspect-ratio`
- `device-aspect-ratio`
- `color`
- `color-index`
- `monochrome`
- `resolution`
- `scan`
- `grid`

Most of these support a `min-` and `max-` prefix, which avoids having to use a greater than or lesser than operator. For example, if you wanted a style for windows between 500px and 700px, inclusive, you would specify this as

```
@media screen and (min-width: 500px) and (max-width: 700px)
```

Notice in this example I also included the `screen` media type. In this case, this style is ignored for all other types such as `print`.

■ **Tip**   For a complete definition on each of these features, see the W3 specification at
`http://www.w3.org/TR/css3-mediaqueries/#media1`.

Using Media Queries

There is a lot that you can do with media queries to dynamically style your web page. For example, you could use the `color` and `monochrome` features to apply more appropriate styles when displayed on a monochrome device. The `color` feature returns the number of colors supported so (`min-color: 2`) will select all color devices. You can also use (`orientation: portrait`) and (`orientation: landscape`) to arrange the elements based on the devices orientation.

For this demonstration you will focus on the width of the window but the same basic concept applies to the other features as well. As the width of the window shrinks, the styles will gradually adjust to accommodate the size while retaining as much of the original layout as possible.

A typical approach is to plan for three different styles: large, medium, and small. The large style is probably how the site is initially designed, as is the case with your Chapter4 site. There are side bars and multiple columns of content. The medium style will keep the same basic layout but start to shrink areas as needed. A useful technique is to use relative sizing so as the window shrinks, each element gradually shrinks as well. The small style will be used for handheld devices and you'll generally keep the layout to a single column. Since the page will tend to be longer now, links to bookmarks on the page become more important.

Modifying the Chapter4 Site

To demonstrate these techniques, you'll add some additional style rules to the site that you built in Chapter 4. You'll use media queries to selectively apply these styles based on the width of the window.

▓ **Tip** The Chapter4 site was created using the Web Matrix application. However, the source code download provides this as both a Web Matrix project as well as a Visual Studio project. You'll find these in the Chapter4 folder. You can use whichever you prefer. The instructions will tell you how to modify the `Default.cshtml` file. If you're using Visual Studio this will be the `Index.cshtml` file, the changes are identical in both files.

Open the Chapter4 project and run the application. Use the Chrome browser as it supports all of the styling features that were demonstrated in Chapter 4. Try shrinking the width of the browser window. Notice that the page does not scale at all; the browser simply clips whatever does not fit in the window. That's your first clue that you have some work to do. Web pages should be fluid and adjust to the window size.

Configuring the Medium Layout

The current layout of your web page is based on a relatively large window such as a desktop browser. When designing a web page, you should also consider the appropriate layout for smaller devices. I suggest creating a separate design for very small resolution devices such as a typical mobile device. In this chapter you'll use media queries to implement small, medium, and large configurations. However, the medium layout is often a compromise between small and large. Starting with a large layout and then designing the small layout usually works best.

Scrolling horizontally is not intuitive and should be avoided if at all possible. So if you have a narrow resolution you should stack elements vertically. The aside element, for example, will need to go to the bottom of the page. You might consider eliminating the images or changing the font sizes.

Once you have a small layout in mind, you can gradually introduce these changes as the width shrinks. The approach I like to take is to gradually start shrinking the width of the browser window and see what breaks. Then make the corrections to deal with that and try shrinking it some more. With the small layout already designed, you'll know where you're going as you make adjustments in this iterative process.

Now you'll define the style for the medium and small layouts, starting with medium. On medium-sized devices, you'll use the same basic layout but just shrink some of the elements. For this site, medium will be defined as widths between 600px and 940px. The size of the web page is 940px so if the window is wider than that, no adjustment is necessary. The 600px minimum size is somewhat arbitrary. I'll explain how I arrived at that figure later.

The medium layout needs little adjustment. You'll use a simple trick of defining the elements with relative sizes. This allows them to automatically shrink or stretch as the window is resized. Open the `Default.cshtml` file and add the rules shown in Listing 6-1 to the existing `style` element. Add this after all the existing rules.

Listing 6-1. Defining the medium layout

```
@@media screen and (max-width: 940px)
{
    body
    {
        width: 100%;
    }
```

```
aside
{
    width: 30%;
}
nav ul li a
{
    width: 100px;
}
}
```

▨ **Note**   In the Razor syntax, an ampersand (@) is used to indicate that what follows it is code; not content. To include an ampersand in the context such as a media query, you'll need to use a double ampersand.

By setting the body width to 100% it will automatically shrink to fit the window. It won't stretch past 940px, however, because this style is only applied when the width is smaller than that. The aside element is set to 30%. The current ratio (280px/940px) is approximately 30%. As you continue shrinking the window, the links in the nav element will eventually be clipped, so this style also reduces their width, moving them closer together.

Run the application and try shrinking the window. You should notice a nice fluid layout that adjusts to the window size as shown in Figure 6-11.

Figure 6-11. Displaying the medium layout

Configuring the Small Layout

Eventually, however, the layout doesn't work very well, as illustrated in Figure 6-12.

Figure 6-12. *The medium layout when shrunk too much*

There are several issues here that you'll address:

- The header text is wrapping to another line and overlapping.

- The navigation links are wrapping to the next line (and now outside the nav element).

- The picture overlaps the adjacent text.

- The text columns are too narrow; this size cannot adequately support three content columns.

The primary change that you'll make that will adjust the layout, is to move the aside element to the bottom of the page rather than alongside the other content. As you resize the window, the other changes were gradual but this change will cause a jump. The main content will go from 70% of the window size to 100%. You'll need to determine the appropriate width that should trigger the change. I choose 600px but you can experiment with other values and see how the page works.

Enter the code in Listing 6-2 to the end of the existing style element.

Listing 6-2. Defining the small layout

```
@@media screen and (max-width: 600px)
{
    /* Move the aside to the bottom of the page */
    #contentArea, #MainContent, aside
    {
        display: block;
    }

    aside
    {
        width: 98%;
    }

    /* Use a single column for the article content */
    article div
    {
        -webkit-column-count: 1;
        column-count: 1;
    }

    /* Move the links closer together */
    nav ul li a
    {
        margin-right: 15px;
        width: auto;
    }

    /* Fix the line spacing of the header */
    h2, h3
    {
        line-height:normal;
    }

    /* Force the intro element to stretch to fit the content */
    .intro
    {
        height: min-content;
    }

    /* Move the book images to the left */
    .book img
    {
        float: left;
```

```
        margin-right: 10px;
        margin-bottom: 5px;
    }

    /* Make the book elements tall enough to fit the image */
    .book
    {
        min-height: 120px;
    }
}
```

■ **Note**   The previous style that you added for the medium size also applies to the small style since both apply to widths less than 940px. The small style will define additional rules but keep in mind the previous styles apply as well.

The small layout rules make the following adjustments:

- The aside element is moved to the bottom. This is done by undoing the table and cell attributes that you entered in Chapter 4 and then changing the width to be 98%. Previously, the #contentArea element had the display attribute set to table and the #mainContent and aside elements were set to table-cell. By setting all three of these to block, the virtual table is removed.

- The content is displayed in two columns and this will be reduced to a single column.

- To keep the links from wrapping, a 15px margin is defined and then the width is sized automatically based on the content. This will remove most of the blank space between them.

- Since the header text can now use more than one line, change the line height so the lines do not overlap.

- Force the intro section to stretch vertically to ensure all the content fits.

- Move the book images to the left and the corresponding text to the right.

- Ensure the book elements are large enough to fit the image.

Display the web page with these changes and resize the window. With even very narrow pages, the site still looks good, as shown in Figure 6-13.

CSS Demo

Introducing the new HTML5 features

Use the new CSS3 features to build some of the most visually appealing web sites.

Feature   Article   Archives   Apress

Main content area

Lorem ipsum dolor sit amet, consectetur adipisicing elit, sed do eiusmod tempor incididunt ut labore et dolore magna aliqua. Ut enim ad minim veniam, quis nostrud exercitation ullamco laboris nisi ut.

Featured Article

This is really cool...

Lorem ipsum dolor sit amet, consectetur adipisicing elit,

Figure 6-13. *The web page with a very narrow window*

Scroll down and see how the `aside` section is formatted, which should look like Figure 6-14.

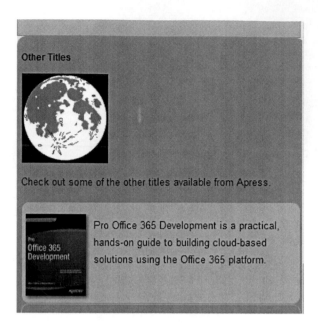

Figure 6-14. *The layout of the aside section*

Using Flexible Images

If you continue to shrink the web page, the phone booth window will eventually be clipped. To prevent that, set the `max-width` property to 100%. This will cause the images to be re-sized to fit the width of the container. This is not done inside a media query and this format will be applied at all resolutions. Enter the following code to the end of the `style` element:

```
#phone
{
    max-width: 100%;
    height: auto;
}
```

Setting the height to auto will change the height to maintain the existing aspect ratio. Refresh the web page and continue shrinking the window. Notice that the image will start shrinking as well. You can still rotate it as shown in Figure 6-15.

Figure 6-15. *The shrinking window*

You can do the same thing with video elements using the following style rule:

```
.video embed, .video object, .video iframe
{
    width: 100%;
    height: auto;
}
```

Viewing the Page on a Mobile Device

For a final test, display the site using Chrome and enable the Ripple emulator as I showed you earlier. Select the PhoneGap platform. Your page should look like Figure 6-16.

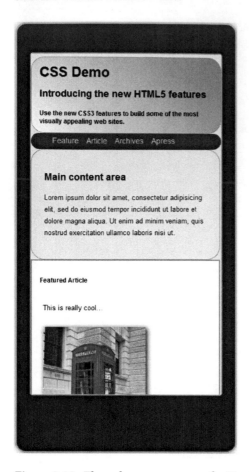

Figure 6-16. *The web page as seen on the Ripple emulator*

Summary

In this chapter I showed you how to install and use several mobile device emulators including:

- Windows Phone Emulator
- Opera Mobile Emulator
- Chrome Ripple add-on
- iPhone emulator

To handle the various form factors, media queries were used to selectively apply styles based on the window width. We implemented large, medium, and small layouts that scale cleanly as the window is resized. Also, by setting the width to 100% we can auto-size images and video.

PART 3

■ ■ ■

Developing with HTML5

While browser support for HTML5 is rapidly growing, you will likely need to deal with older browsers that do not support most of the HTML5 features. In Chapter 7 I will show you how to use several open-source solutions for polyfilling the new features on an older browsers. You really shouldn't need to spend too much time with this. These techniques will come close to the native browser support with little work on your part.

Having explored the basic HTML5 features, it's time to try out some of the really cool new features. Chapter 8 demonstrates the new audio and video elements that enable you to easily embed this into your application. I'll explain the codecs supported by each browser and how to make your site support multiple browsers. You will also build your own controls to manipulate the audio and video files.

Chapters 9 and 10 demonstrate both graphic platforms, Scalable Vector Graphics (SVG) and Canvas, respectively. These tools use very different approaches but both provide some impressive capabilities for creating graphical applications.

■ ■ ■

CHAPTER 7

Supporting Older Browsers

So now you've got this great looking, HTML5 compliant web page that you created in Chapter 4. You want to show it off so you send a link to a colleague who just happens to still use IE 8 and they see something like Figure 7-1.

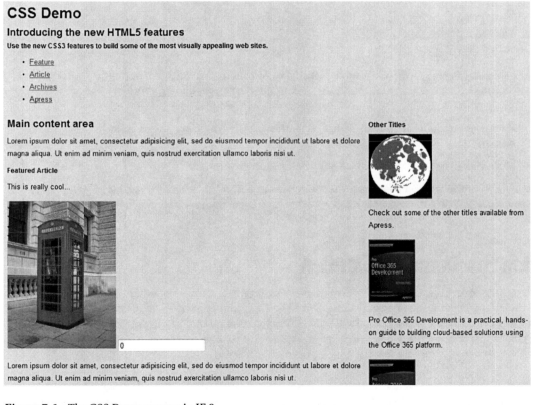

Figure 7-1. *The CSS Demo as seen in IE 8*

The page looks awful and nothing like what you were expecting. You're certainly not going to win any prizes for it. Not to be deterred you send the link to your boss and things get worse. They are using IE 7 and they see something like Figure 7-2.

CSS Demo

Introducing the new HTML5 features

Use the new CSS3 features to build some of the most visually appealing web sites.

- Feature
- Article
- Archives
- Apress

Main content area

Lorem ipsum dolor sit amet, consectetur adipisicing elit, sed do eiusmod tempor incididunt ut labore et dolore magna aliqua. Ut enim ad minim veniam, quis nostrud exercitation ullamco laboris nisi ut.

Featured Article

This is really cool...

Figure 7-2. *The CSS Demo as seen in IE 7*

Now the sidebar is no longer on the side but tacked on at the bottom of the page. Your boss begins wondering what you've been doing in all your spare time. You've just learned two important lessons – the hard way:

1. Always control your demo environment; in this case, let them see the page on your browser.

2. More importantly, test your web site on several different browsers.

In this chapter, I will show you some fairly simple techniques to get your page looking its best even with older browsers. You don't have to write much code because there is a lot of open source code that you can easily add to your site.

Creating the Demo Application

To work the exercises in this chapter, you'll use the same web page that you developed in Chapter 4. In this case, however, you'll implement it using Visual Studio. I'll first show you how to create the project and copy the web page from the previous WebMatrix project. In the rest of the chapter, I'll demonstrate the techniques you'll use to make this page look great, even in IE 7.

■ **Tip**　The source code download that is available at `www.apress.com` contains the initial Visual Studio project for this chapter. If you want to skip exercise 7-1, you can use the project from the Chapter07\Initial folder instead.

EXERCISE 7-1. CREATING THE DEMO SITE

1. Start Visual Studio 2012 and from the Start Page click the New Project link.

2. Select the "ASP.NET MVC 4 Web Application" template and enter **Chapter7** for the project name as shown in Figure 7-3. Click OK to continue.

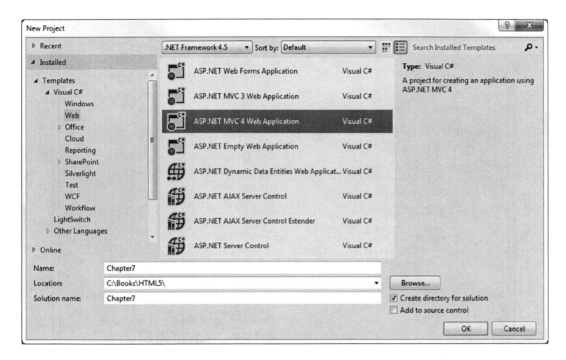

Figure 7-3. *Creating a new MVC4 project*

3. In the next dialog box select the Basic template and make sure the Razor view engine is selected. Click OK to create the project.

4. When the project has been created, from the Solution Explorer, right-click the Views folder and select the Add ➤ New Folder links. Enter the name **Home**.

5. Right-click the Views\Home folder and select the Add ➤ View links.

6. In the Add View dialog box, enter the name **Index** and unselect all of the check boxes as shown in Figure 7-4. Click the Add button to create the view.

Figure 7-4. Adding the Index view

7. Open your WebMatrix project from Chapter 4, copy the entire contents of
    Default.cshtml, and paste it into the new Index.cshtml file, replacing the default
    implementation.

8. From the Solution Explorer, right-click the Controllers folder and select the
    Add ➤ Controller link.

9. In the Add Controller dialog box, enter the name **HomeController** and make sure the
    "Empty MVC controller" template is selected as shown in Figure 7-5.

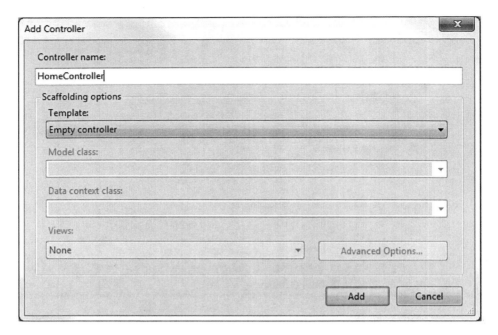

Figure 7-5. *Adding the Home controller*

10. From the Solution Explorer, right-click the Chapter7 project and select the Add ➤ New Folder links. Enter the name **Images**.

11. Using Windows Explorer, copy the images from the Chapter4 project to the Chapter7\Images folder. (There should be 14 images in this folder.)

12. From the Solution Explorer, right-click the Images folder and select the Add ➤ Existing Item links. In the Add Existing Item dialog box, navigate to the Chapter7\Images folder, select all the images, and click the Add button.

13. Open the Global.asax.cs file and find the Application_Start() method. Remove the following line from this method. This will prevent the MVC framework from including the default script and content files.

    BundleConfig.RegisterBundles(BundleTable.Bundles);

14. Save your changes and select Internet Explorer as the default browser. Press F5 to debug the application. Depending on what version of Internet Explorer you will have varying results.

■ **Caution**   I'm using IE 9; if you have a different version you might need to adjust some of the following instructions.

---

15. In Internet Explorer, from the tools menu, select the Developer Tools link. This provides several features for analyzing the current web page.

16. At the top of the tools pane, you can select the browser mode as shown in Figure 7-6.

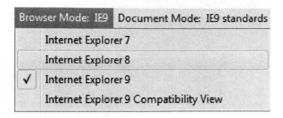

Figure 7-6. Selecting the browser mode

17. Select Internet Explorer 7 for the browser mode and the page should look like Figure 7-2. You can use the browser mode to see how your page will look in some of the older versions of Internet Explorer.

Making Some Simple Changes

There are a couple of really easy changes that will make the web page look much better. You'll start with those and then later I'll show you some of the more involved solutions.

Using Modernizr

When supporting older browsers, the first thing you should do is employ the Modernizr open source JavaScript library. This library performs two essential functions:

- Detect the current browser's available features and provide this information as queryable properties. For example, in your JavaScript, you can place conditional logic like this:

```
if (!Modernizr.cssanimations) {
    alert("Your browser does not support CSS animation");
}
```

- Provide shims to implement missing functionality. This includes the html5shim library that allows you to style your content using the new elements such as header, footer, nav, and aside.

■ **Tip** For more information, check out the Modernizr web site at http://modernizr.com.

So let's add the Modernizr library to your page and see what happens! The version of Modernizr that is added to your MVC4 project is modernizr-2.0.6-devlopment-only.js. There are newer versions available from the modernizr site but this will do fine for this exercise.

At the top of your Index.cshtml file, just after the DOCTYPE tag, add the following code:

```
<script src="~/Scripts/modernizr-2.0.6-development-only.js"></script>
```

Press F5 to debug the application. In Internet Explorer, go to the developer's tools and change the browser mode to IE7 as I explained earlier. Your page should look like Figure 7-7.

Figure 7-7. *The demo page with modernizr as viewed in IE 7*

Resetting the Styles

Wow! You thought Modernizr was supposed to make the page look better, right. Well, it's really not that bad; a simple change will straighten things up.

It is generally a good idea to explicitly define default styles for basic things like margin, padding, and font size rather than rely on the browser's defaults. Remember from Chapter 4, any style attribute not explicitly defined in your style sheet will revert to the browsers native style sheet. Since you can't control the browser's default styles, it's best to set these yourself. Typically these basic rules are placed in a separate style sheet that is often referred to as a reset style sheet.

■ **Tip**   Here's a good article on reset style sheets, with some links to publicly available styles
`http://sixrevisions.com/css/css-tips/css-tip-1-resetting-your-styles-with-css-reset`.

This is particularly important with HTML5 since it introduced a set of new elements types like nav and
aside. Older browsers do not know what these elements are and do not have any reasonable default styles for
them. The biggest problem is that the display attribute defaults to inline (placed side-by side) but the style
should be blocked (stacked vertically).

Add the following rule to the top of your style element:

```
/* Reset */
article, aside, footer, header, nav, section
{
    display:block;
}
```

Now press F5 to debug your application and switch to IE7 mode. Your page should now look like Figure 7-8.

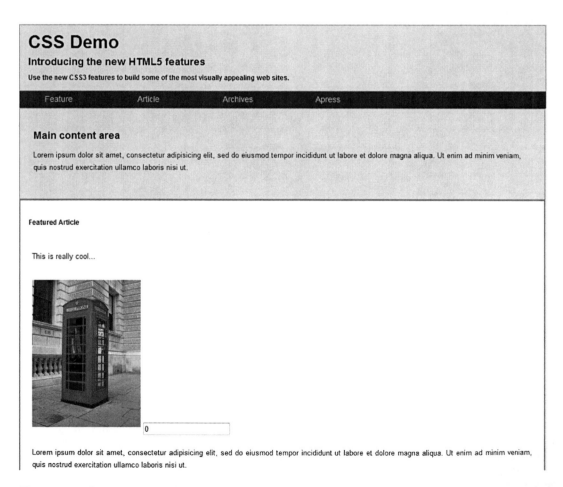

Figure 7-8. *The Demo page after resetting the styles*

> ■ **Note** A shim is a thin object, often made of wood that is used to fill a gap between two objects. In this context the term refers to a relatively small piece of code that fills in the gap between a browser's current functionality and the full HTML5 specification. The term "shim" has been used in software development circles for a long time. The term polyfill was introduced for referring to a browser-related shim. So, in this context, the two terms are synonymous.

Adding More Polyfills

Now you're probably starting to feel a little better. With just two pretty easy changes (adding Modernizr and resetting the styles), the page looks decent. However, upon closer inspection, there is a fairly long list of features that are not working, including

- Tables
- Rounded corners
- Gradient background fills
- Striped articles
- Animation
- 3D Transforms
- Multiple-columns

Given a sufficient amount of patience and persistence (and of course time) you could probably implement all of these features so that your page looks the same in both IE 7 and the latest version of Chrome. However, I don't recommend that you do that. Essentially, you should make sure your page works great on the latest HTML5 compliant browsers and works acceptably on older browsers. It doesn't have to work great on every browser. Consider the following:

- Most users are not going to compare your site on a host of browsers and compare the experience of each. Your page does not need to look identical in every browser.
- If someone is using IE6, they are used to bad looking web sites. Implementing just a few of these polyfills will probably make your page stand out as one of the better sites they've visited.
- HTML5 is supposed to make your job as web developer easier. However, if you try to make every page work like native HTML5 on older browsers, you'll be spending far more time, not less.

For each feature that your page uses that is not natively supported by commonly used browsers, you have the following options:

- Fail – Simply display an error stating this browser does not support the necessary features and offer some suggested browsers to use. For example, the primary purpose of the sample site you created in Chapter 5 was to demonstrate how web workers are used. If the page is viewed by a browser that doesn't support web workers, there's no point trying to make the page work. Just fail!

- Polyfill – Implement an alternate solution to provide the needed feature. This can range from very simple solutions to rather complex. For example, if a gradient fill is not supported you could just use a solid color fill, or you could provide a shim and implement a gradient using JavaScript.

- Ignore – Just leave the feature unimplemented. For example, you could ignore rounded corners; in older browsers they'll be square corners.

There are no hard and fast rules here; you'll need to decide on a case-by-case basis which features are important to you and how much time you're willing to spend making them work on older browsers. In the rest of this chapter I will demonstrate some techniques to backfill some of these features using mostly-open source shims that are publicly available. I don't want to leave you with the impression, however, that you have to backfill every feature. In fact, several of these features for this demo, including multi-column support, 3D transforms, and animation will be ignored as they are just not that important.

■ **Tip**　There are a plethora of shims and polyfills available. This article provides a good reference if you're looking for something specific: `https://github.com/Modernizr/Modernizr/wiki/HTML5-Cross-Browser-Polyfills`. Keep in mind that these may not always work properly so test them and keep what works. Also, combining various shims can create some interesting results, as the side effects from one can break another one.

Displaying Tables

As you test your page in several browsers, note the features that are not working correctly and then prioritize them. In this case, the `aside` element should be alongside the main content, not at the end of the page. In my opinion, this is the most critical issue and should therefore be addressed first.

■ **Tip**　Tables were first supported in IE8. If you change the browser mode to IE8, you'll see the sidebar is alongside the main content. So table support is only an issue for IE7 and older. You might consider simply ignoring the issue and explain that your site works best with IE8 and newer. To see how many users that would affect, check out the latest browsers' stats at `http://www.w3schools.com/browsers/browsers_stats.asp`. According to these statistics, that's only about 2% of the total number of browsers in use. These statistics represent an overall usage; you may have a specific target audience that can have different characteristics.

To support tables in IE6 and IE7, you'll use a behavioral CSS extension, which allows you to embed a JavaScript in a style sheet. An extension is invoked by adding a rule like this:

```
header
{
    behavior: url(customBehavior.htc);
}
```

The implementation is provided in an HTML component (HTC) file with the `.htc` extension. There are a few things about using `.htc` files that you should be aware of.

- In general, you can open an html file in a browser without using IIS. For example, you could rename the Index.cshtml file in your Visual Studio project to Index.html and simply open the file with Internet Explorer (or any browser) and the page would work fine. However, .htc files are ignored if the page is not actually served up by a web server such as IIS or Apache.

- You may need to define the HTC content type on your web server. IIS and IIS Express both support this by default but you may need to add this with Apache or other web servers.

- Even though the .htc file is typically referenced in a CSS file, the URL specified in the behavior attribute must be relative to the location of the html document that invoked the style sheet. If you put the .htc file in the Content folder (with all the other style sheets), you'll need to reference it with a relative path ~/Content/customBehavior.htc.

To display tables you will use an open-source HTC that can be downloaded from this site: http://tanalin.com/en/projects/display-table-htc.

EXERCISE 7-2. SUPPORTING TABLES

1. Download the latest .zip file from this site: http://tanalin.com/en/projects/display-table-htc. (The latest file as of this writing is display-table.htc_2011-11-25.zip.) This file contains an uncompressed and a minimized version. Copy the display-table.htc to the Content folder.

2. Right-click the Content folder and select the Add ➤ Existing Item links. Browse to the Content folder and select the display-table.htc file. Click the Add button to load the file.

3. Open the Index.cshtml and find the portion where the table is defined. Add the code shown in bold from Listing 7-1 to the existing style rules. This specifies a vendor-prefixed version of the display attribute and invokes the display-table.htc component.

Listing 7-1. Defining a new table

```
/* Setup a table for the content and sidebar */
#contentArea
{
    display: table;

    -dt-display: table;
    behavior: url(Content/display-table.htc);
}

#mainContent
{
    display: table-cell;

    -dt-display: table-cell;

    padding-right: 2px;

    behavior: url(Content/display-table.htc);
}
```

```
aside
{
    display: table-cell;

    -dt-display: table-cell;

    width: 280px;

    behavior: url(Content/display-table.htc);
}
```

4. Save your changes and press F5 to debug the application. Change the browser mode to IE7 and you should now see a table setup as shown in Figure 7-9.

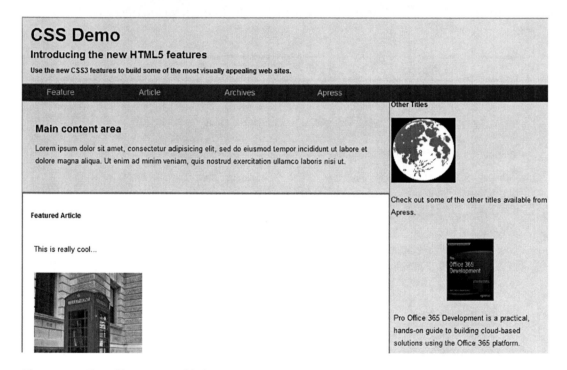

Figure 7-9. *The table support added in IE7*

■ **Note** The `display-table.htc` file uses its own vendor-specific prefix. So you needed to add the −dt-display attribute.

---

5. Now there's one more thing that needs to be fixed. You'll notice that the aside element is missing some styles such as background-color and padding. This is a side-effect of the CSS extension. To create the table in your page, this code created real table elements for you such as <tr> and <td>. So once the JavaScript runs, the aside element is removed and replaced with rows and cells. Since there is no aside element anymore you can't use an element selector to style it. However, there is only one aside element in your source document and it has the sidebar id attribute.

6. Close the browser, which will stop the debugger.

7. Replace all aside selectors with #sidebar., including the one you just added. There are several places in the Index.cshtml file that you'll need to change.

8. Press F5 to run the application and change the browser mode to IE7. The sidebar should now have a background color and there is also padding around the text.

Adding Rounded Corners

If the browser does not support rounded corners, you can easily add them thanks to a nifty jQuery plug-in written by Dave Methvin. In addition to rounded corners, this plugin can also create a number of other patterns, which are displayed on their web site (http://jquery.malsup.com/corner). This is provided through an open-source license so you can freely download and use it in your application.

You'll use this plugin to implement rounded corners for the nav and footer elements. However, this should only be done if rounded corners are not supported natively. So the first question is how do you know if the browser supports rounded corners? The answer again is: Modernizer. Adding a statement like this will conditionally call the custom method:

```
if (!Modernizr.borderradius)
```

■ **Tip**   I will show you another technique for rounding corners later in this chapter.

```
┌─────────────────────────────────────────────────────────────┐
│            EXERCISE 7-3. ADDING ROUNDED CORNERS              │
└─────────────────────────────────────────────────────────────┘
```

1. Go to the web site referenced above (http://jquery.malsup.com/corner). Click the jquery.corner.js link near the top of the page. This will download the latest version. Save the file in your Scripts folder.

2. From the Solution Explorer, right-click the Scripts folder and select the Add ➤ Existing Item links. Navigate to the Chapter7\Scripts folder and select the jquery.corner.js file.

3. This function is based on jQuery so you'll also need to reference that in your page. The jQuery script is already included in the Script folder.

4. Open the Index.cshtml file and add these references near the top of the page, just after the modernizr script:

    ```
    <script src="~/Scripts/jquery-1.6.2.js"></script>
    <script src="~/Scripts/jquery.corner.js"></script>
    ```

5. Now invoke this by adding this `script` element at the end of the `Index.cshtml` file, after the footer element and just before the body closing tag.

```
<script>
if (!Modernizr.borderradius) {
$("nav").corner("15px");
$("footer").corner("25px");
}
</script>
```

6. This code uses the jQuery selector to find the `nav` and `footer` elements and calls the `corner()` method specifying the radius.

7. Save your changes and press F5 to debug your application. Switch the browser mode to IE7 and your page should look like Figure 7-10.

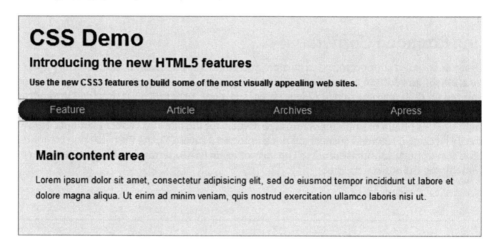

Figure 7-10. *The Demo page with rounded corners*

Adding Gradients

Next, you'll add a gradient background to the intro section using another open source solution from PIE (progressive internet explorer). This is implemented as an HTC file just like the table support that you added earlier. Once you have downloaded the component, you simply invoke it using the behavior property of your style sheet rule.

EXERCISE 7-4. ADDING BACKGROUND GRADIENTS

1. Go to the `http://css3pie.com` site and click the Download button. This will download a `PIE-1.0.0.zip` file (you may see a different version number; just download the latest version).

2. There are several files inside this `.zip` file. Copy the `PIE.htc` file to your Chapter7\ Content folder.

3. From the Solution Explorer, right-click the Content folder and select the Add ➤ Existing Item links. Navigate to the Content folder and select the `PIE.htc` file.

4. Open the `Index.cshtml` file and find where the rules for the `.intro` class are defined. Add the following lines shown in bold. This code will add another vendor-prefixed attribute (`-pie-`) and then invoke the PIE component using the `behavior` property.

```
/* Gradients */
.intro
{
    border: 1px solid #999999;
    text-align:left;
    margin-top: 6px;
    padding-left: 15px;
    border-radius:25px;
    background-image: -o-linear-gradient(45deg, #ffffff, #6699cc);
    background-image: -webkit-linear-gradient(45deg, #ffffff, #6699cc);
    background-image: linear-gradient(45deg, #ffffff, #6699cc);

    -pie-background: linear-gradient(45deg, #ffffff, #6699cc);
    behavior: url(Content/PIE.htc);
}
```

5. Save your changes, press F5 to debug the application, and switch the browser mode to IE7. You should now have a linear gradient that looks just like the native gradient. You might have also noticed that the corners are rounded as well. The `PIE.htc` shim also supports rounded corners and took care of that for you. However, you probably noticed that the padding on top of the `h1` text is missing. The height was not calculated correctly. That's an easy thing to fix.

■ **Note**   PIE is designed to backfill several CSS3 features, which are listed in this article: http://css3pie.com/documentation/supported-css3-features. It will attempt to address any of these features that are included in the element that references the `PIE.htc` shim. However, it does not do anything with features that are supported natively.

---

6. Close the browser, which will stop the debugger.

7. Open the `Index.cshtml` file and add the following rule to the style element:

```
h1
{
    padding: 20px 0;
}
```

8. Save your changes, press F5, and then select the IE7 browser mode. The page should now look like Figure 7-11.

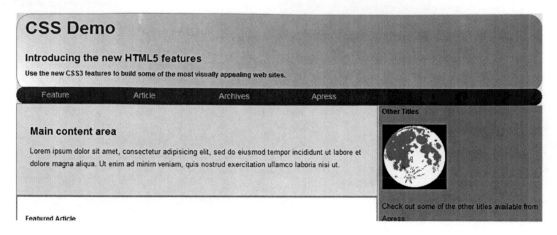

Figure 7-11. *The Demo page with a gradient background*

Striping the Book List

Recall from Chapter 4 that the list of books was styled using an :nth-child selector so alternating elements would have a different background. In older browsers that do not support this, you can accomplish this the old-fashioned way, by iterating the list in JavaScript and changing the style on alternating elements.

The trick, however, is determining if the :nth-child selector, is available as Modernizr does not provide this.

■ **Note** The solution provided here is based on a post by Lea Verou. I had to adjust this to work with IE, however. For more details, check out the article at

http://lea.verou.me/2011/07/detecting-css-selectors-support-my-jsconf-eu-talk/.

```
          EXERCISE 7-5. STRIPING THE BOOK LIST
```

1. Open the Index.cshtml file and add the following code to the script element at
    the bottom of the file after the existing function:

    ```
    function supportsSelector(selector) {
        var el = document.createElement('div');
        el.innerHTML = ['&shy;', '<style>', selector, '{}', '</style>'].join('');
        try
        {
            el = document.body.appendChild(el);
            var style = el.getElementsByTagName('style')[0],
                ret = !!(style.sheet.rules || style.sheet.cssRules)[0];
        }
    ```

```
            catch(e){
                ret = false;
            }
            document.body.removeChild(el);
            return ret;
        }
```

2. This code creates a new `style` element and adds the selector in question. It then checks to see if it is actually there. If not, the selector is not supported. This is done in a `try`/`catch` block in case older browsers do not support either the `style.sheet.rules` or `style.sheet.cssRules` properties.

3. Now with our handy `supportsSelector()` function, you can implement the manual striping technique. Add the following code to the same `script` element:

```
if (!supportsSelector(":nth-child(2n+0)")) {
    var titles = document.getElementById("titles");
    var articles = titles.getElementsByTagName("article");
    for (var i = 0; i < articles.length; i++) {
        var title = articles[i];
        if (i % 2) {
            title.style.background = "#6699cc";
            title.style.border = "1px solid #c0c0c0";
        }
        else {
            title.style.background = "#c0c0c0";
            title.style.border = "1px solid #6699cc";
        }
    }
}
```

4. If the `:nth-child` selector is not supported, this code gets the `#titles` element using the `getElementById()` function. This is the `section` element that contains a series of `article` elements; one for each book. It then gets an array of child `article` elements using the `getElementsByTagName()` function. Note that this method is invoked on the `titles` object and not the `document` object. Once it has the array of elements, the code simply iterates the array, modifying the `background` and `border` properties.

5. Save your changes and press F5 to debug the application. Change the browser mode to IE7 and the page should look like Figure 7-12.

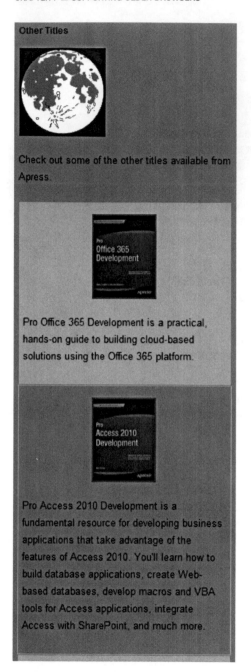

Figure 7-12. *The aside element with manual striping*

Hiding Unsupported Elements

As stated earlier in the chapter, for each nonsupported feature you need to decide if this is a deal-breaker and the page just needs to fail, if you want to polyfill that feature, or simply ignore it on older browsers. From the initial list of unsupported changes, there are three left that you have not implemented yet:

- CSS Animation

- 3D Transforms

- Multiple columns

You can fairly easily implement animation by using JavaScript to change the background image as a timer expires. That's the way it was normally done before we had CSS animation. Implementing a 3D transform in an older browser, however, just isn't going to work. I would categorize both of these as nice to have but not really worth the trouble so we'll leave these features out if the browser doesn't support them.

The one feature that would be nice to emulate is the multiple column support. There are shims available for this such as the one described in this article: http://www.csscripting.com/css-multi-column. And I guess they must work in some simple scenarios but they failed miserably with this page. Perhaps with enough time and patience I could get something to work but this is one of those hard decisions. Is it worth the effort? In some unique circumstances it might be but, in general, you probably shouldn't spend 80% of your time on a nice-to-have feature that will only affect a few percent of the expected audience.

One thing you should consider, though, is hiding elements that aren't functional. The range control, for instance, doesn't do anything and it's not even supported so it just looks like a textbox. You should hide that. Also, the now static picture of the moon isn't very interesting either. So you'll hide these elements. The range control is hidden by setting its visibility attribute to hidden. The div that contains the moon image needs to be shrunk down to 0px so it doesn't take up space. (You could also set the display property to None – either method accomplishes the same thing.)

EXERCISE 7-6. HIDING ELEMENTS

1. First, you'll need to assign an id attribute to the range control so it can be more easily selected in JavaScript. Add the code shown in bold to the input element:

```
<div class="rotateContainer">
    <p>This is really cool...</p>
    <img class="rotate" id="phone"
        src="images/phonebooth.jpg"
        alt="phonebooth" />
    <input type="range" min="-180" max="180" step="18"
        value="0" onchange="rotateImage(this.value)"
        id="rotateDegrees" />
    <br />
```

2. Then add the following code to the script element at the bottom of the Index.cshtml file:

```
if (!Modernizr.csstransforms3d) {
    document.getElementById("rotateDegrees").style.visibility = "hidden";
}

if (!Modernizr.cssanimations) {
    document.getElementById("moon").style.width = "0px";
    document.getElementById("moon").style.height = "0px";
}
```

3. This code simply hides the range control if 3D transforms are not supported and shrinks the moon `div` if CSS animations are not supported. Press F5 to debug the application and switch the browser mode to IE7. The final web page should look like Figure 7-13.

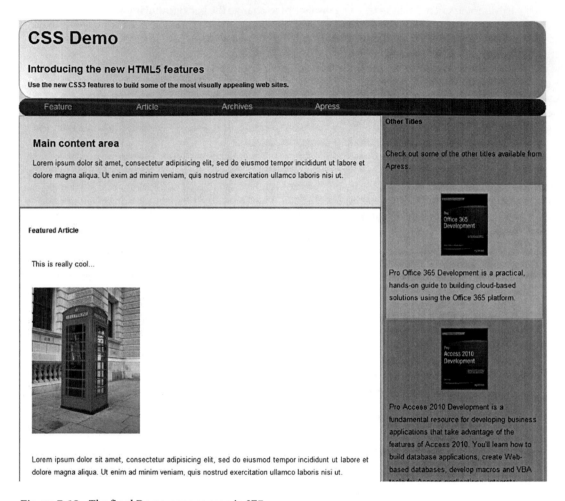

Figure 7-13. *The final Demo page as seen in IE7*

4. Finally, after all this work, you should try the page in a browser that supports all these features to make sure it still looks great there. The final version in Chrome should look like Figure 7-14.

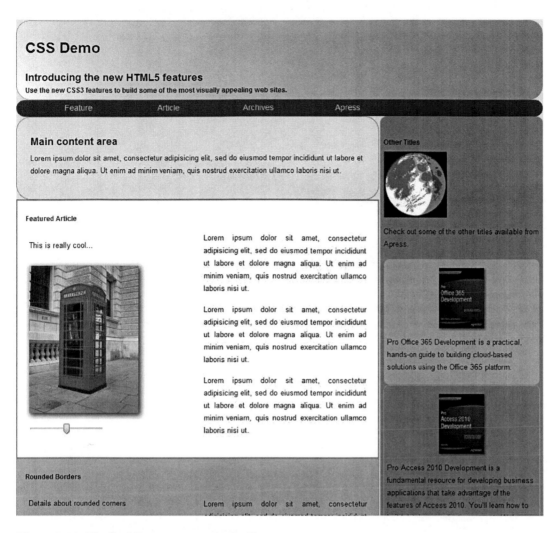

Figure 7-14. The final Demo page as seen in Chrome

■ **Tip**   The source code download contains the complete Index.cshtml file. Refer to this if there are any questions about exactly how or where a change should be made.

Summary

In this chapter, I showed you some techniques for making your web page look great even with older browsers that do not support the new HTML5 features. These techniques include:

- Using Modernizr for feature detection and basic element support
- Resetting the styles for elements not supported by the browser

- Displaying tables

- Adding rounded corners

- Supporting gradient background images

- Manually striping a list

- Hiding unsupported elements

For every unsupported feature you'll need to decide if:

- The feature is critical to the page (and if so the page should fail)

- The feature can be easily polyfilled

- The feature can be ignored

This is a bit of a balancing act because you want the page to look good in all browsers but you don't want to spend an excessive amount of time supporting every possible browser.

The final implementation of the demo page struck a good compromise. The site looks great and functions properly. While a few of the new HTML5 features are omitted, overall it's still a great site considering the browser support and the additional work was minimal.

In the next chapter, I'll show you how to use the new Audio and Video elements that were introduced in HTML5.

CHAPTER 8

■ ■ ■

Audio and Video

In this chapter, I will demonstrate the new audio and video elements introduced with HTML5. The two elements are identical in terms of their attributes and the methods and events that they support. I will spend most of the chapter discussing and demonstrating the audio element but just keep this in the back of your mind that everything I'm showing you applies to video as well. There are some exercises at the end of the chapter that will apply these same techniques to the video element so you can see this for yourself.

I will demonstrate how to add audio and video elements using the native controls provided by the browser. This approach makes embedding audio and video in your web site a trivial matter of adding some simple markup. If you want to write your own controls, however, this chapter will also demonstrate how to do that and to wire up all the events with JavaScript.

Because each browser supports different media formats, to make your site cross-browser compatible, you'll need to encode multiple versions of your media files. The audio and video elements can support multiple sources so each browser can chose the appropriate version to use. I'll also show you how you can use a couple of free utilities that will convert your audio and video files to the necessary formats.

■ **Note**   The video element supports three additional attributes (width, height, and poster) that the audio element doesn't. I will explain these later in the chapter.

Using the Audio Element

I'll start with a pretty simple exercise of adding an audio element to a web page. Then you'll support multiple formats and try your site on various bowsers.

Creating the Sample Project

In this chapter, you'll create a web site project that you'll use to try out the audio and video HTML5 elements. You'll create an empty web site now, and then progressively add features to it throughout the chapter.

EXERCISE 8-1. CREATING AN EMPTY PROJECT

---

1.   Start Visual Studio 2012 and select the New Project link. Select the MVC4 project template and enter **Chapter8** for the name, as shown in Figure 8-1.

Figure 8-1. *Creating the Chapter8 project*

2. In the second dialog select the Basic project template and make sure the Razor view engine is selected.

3. Right-click the Controller folder in the Solution Explorer and select the Add ➤ Controller links. Enter the name **HomeController** and select the Empty MVC Controller template. Click the Add button to create the controller.

4. Right-click the Views folder and select the Add ➤ New Folder links. Enter the name **Home**.

5. Right-click the new Home folder and select the Add ➤ View links. In the Add View dialog box, enter the name **Index**, make sure the Razor view engine is selected, and unselect all the check boxes as shown in Figure 8-2.

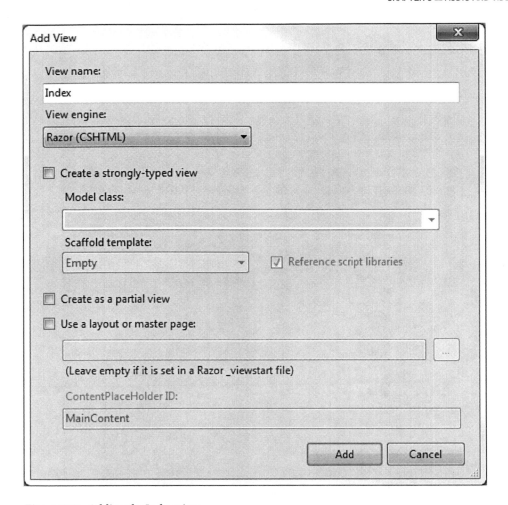

Figure 8-2. *Adding the Index view*

6. In the Solution Explorer, right-click the Chapter8 project, and select the Add ➤ New Folder links. Enter the name **Media**.

7. You'll need an MP3 file to use as a sample audio clip. The file I'm using is copyrighted so I can't include it with the source code. You should be able to find one on your computer or download one off the internet. You can also rip a CD through Windows Media Player and select MP3 as the format.

8. Drag the MP3 file from Windows Explorer to the Chapter8\Media folder in Visual Studio. Make sure you drop it onto the Solution Explorer in Visual Studio so it will also be added to the project.

9. Open the Index.cshtml file. In the empty div that was created by the project template, enter **< audio src** = and you should see a link that you can use to select the source from a file in your project, as shown in Figure 8-3.

171

```
<body>
    <div>
        <audio src=""
    </div>
</body>
</html>
```

Figure 8-3. *Using a the link to select the source*

10. Double-click the Pick URL link. In the Select Project Item dialog box, browse to the Media folder and select the audio clip as shown in Figure 8-4. Click OK to continue.

Figure 8-4. *Selecting the audio clip*

11. Enter the `autoplay` attribute and close the `audio` element. Add text inside the `audio` element like this:

```
<body>
    <div>
        <audio src = "~/Media/Linus and Lucy.mp3" autoplay>
            <p>HTML5 audio is not supported on your browser</p>
        </audio>
    </div>
</body>
```

12. Save your changes and make sure Internet Explorer is chosen as your default browser for debugging. Press F5 to debug your application.

13. Once the page has loaded, your audio clip should start playing. The page, however, will be blank.

14. Press F12 to open the developer tools pane, if not already opened. Change the browser mode to IE8. The music will stop and you'll see the "HTML5 audio is not supported on your browser" text displayed.

This first exercise demonstrated the basic use of the audio element. You simply enter the src attribute, which specifies the URL of the audio file. The content inside the audio element is used when the browser does not support the audio element. Since IE8 does not support the audio element, the text included in the p tag is displayed instead. You can take advantage of this to simply display a message as you did here. However, you could use this to provide a link to download the file or use a plugin to implement a fallback solution.

Using the Native Controls

In terms of the UI, there are basically three options:

- No controls – the audio plays but there are no controls available to the user. The clip can be started automatically when the page is loaded using the autoplay attribute. You can also start, pause, and stop the audio clip using JavaScript.

- Native controls – the browser provides controls for the user to play, pause, and stop the audio clip and control the volume.

- Custom controls – The page provides custom controls that interact with the audio element through JavaScript.

To enable the native control simply add the controls attribute like this:

```
<audio src="~/Media/Linus and Lucy.mp3" autoplay controls>
```

Press F5 to debug the application and the native controls should appear similar to Figure 8-5.

Figure 8-5. *Displaying the native audio controls in Internet Explorer*

In Opera, the controls look like Figure 8-6.

Figure 8-6. *The audio controls in Opera*

In Chrome the controls look like Figure 8-7.

Figure 8-7. *The audio controls in Chrome*

In Firefox, the controls look like Figure 8-8.

Figure 8-8. *The audio controls in Firefox*

In Safari, the audio controls look like Figure 8-9.

Figure 8-9. *The audio control in Safari*

As you can see, the controls are styled very differently in each browser. With native controls you have very little control over how the audio controls are displayed. You can change the width by setting the `style` attribute, which will stretch the progress bar. Changing the height will only add white space on top of the control as shown in Figure 8-10.

Figure 8-10. *Extending the size of the native controls*

▓ **Caution**   In IE9, if you set the height attribute less than 45px, the entire control will be hidden.

Reviewing Browser Support

If you tried to open your web page in one of the other browsers, you probably found that they didn't work. While all major browsers support the `audio` element, they don't all support the same audio formats. Fortunately all major vendors support one of two audio codecs, MP3 or Vorbis. Table 8-1 indicates the codecs that are supported by each browser.

Table 8-1. *Audio codec support*

Browser	MP3	Vorbis
IE 9	Yes	No
Firefox 4	No	Yes
Chrome 6	Yes	Yes
Safari 5	Yes	No
Opera 10.6	No	Yes

As you can see from this table, no single format is supported by all browsers. However, if you support both MP3 and Vorbis, your page will work in almost all browsers (IE8 and below do not support the audio element). To do this you'll need to first encode your audio clip in both formats. Fortunately, there are several free utilities that you can use to convert from one format to another.

The audio element allows you to specify multiple sources and the browser will iterate through the sources until it finds one that it supports. Instead of using a src attribute, you'll provide one or more source elements within the audio element, like this:

```
<audio autoplay controls>
    <source src="~/Media/Linus and Lucy.ogg" />
    <source src="~/Media/Linus and Lucy.mp3" />
    <p>HTML5 audio is not supported on your browser</p>
</audio>
```

The browser will use the first source that is supports so if it matters to you, the preferred file should be listed first. For example, Chrome supports both formats. If you prefer that the MP3 file be used, you should list it before the .ogg file.

While just listing the sources like this will work, the browser must download the file and open it to see if it is able to play it. That's not very efficient to download a fairly large file only to find out it can't be used. You should also include the type attribute, which specifies the type of resource this is. The browser can then determine if the file is supported by looking at the markup. The type attribute specifies the MIME format like this:

```
<source src="~/Media/Linus and Lucy.ogg" type="audio/ogg" />
<source src="~/Media/Linus and Lucy.mp3" type="audio/mp3" />
```

You can also specify the codec in the type attribute like this:

```
<source src="~/Media/Linus and Lucy.ogg" type='audio/ogg; codecs="vorbis"' />
```

Notice that the codecs value(s) are included within double-quotes so you'll need to use single-quotes around the type attribute value. Now you'll modify your web page so it will work on other browsers as well.

■ **Caution**   In Safari, the audio and video support is implemented by the QuickTime plugin. If you don't have this installed, you'll see the "HTML5 audio is not supported on your browser" text displayed. You can install QuickTime from this site: http://www.apple.com/quicktime. The instructions did not say so, but I've found that I needed to reboot my machine before this worked properly. I also found a few quirks when testing on Safari.

EXERCISE 8-2. ADDING MULTIPLE SOURCES

1. Create a vorbis encoded audio file of your sample audio clip that has the `.ogg` extension and copy this to the Chapter8\Media folder.

■ **Tip** I used a utility called XMedia Recode that you can download at `http://www.xmedia-recode.de/download.html`. You can use this utility to format both audio and video files. After you have installed this application, run it, click the Open File button in the ribbon, and select the mp3 file. In the Format tab, select the OGG format. Notice the File Extension is automatically set to .ogg and the Codec is set to Vorbis. Click the Add Job button in the ribbon. Select the Jobs tab to see the job that has been defined to convert this file. At the bottom of the window you can specify the location that the new file should be saved in. Click the Browse button and navigate to the Chapter8\Media folder. Finally, click the Encode button to start the job. A dialog will be displayed to show the progress of the job.

---

2. In the Solution Explorer, right-click the Media folder and select the Add ➤ Existing Item links. Navigate to the Chapter8\Media folder and select the `.ogg` file that you just encoded.

3. IIS Express already recognizes the `.mp3` extension but you'll need to add the `.ogg` extension to the `web.config` file. Open the `web.config` file in the root folder (not the one in the Views sub-folder). Add the `staticContent` section to the `system.webServer` section as shown below. This will enable the `.ogg` files as well as the video formats that you will be using later in the chapter.

```
<system.webServer>
. . .

    <staticContent>
       <mimeMap fileExtension=".ogv" mimeType="video/ogg" />
       <mimeMap fileExtension=".ogg" mimeType="audio/ogg" />
       <mimeMap fileExtension=".mp4" mimeType="video/mp4" />
       <mimeMap fileExtension=".webm" mimeType="video/webm" />
    </staticContent>

</system.webServer>
```

4. In the `Index.cshtml` file, replace the `audio` element with the following code:

```
<audio autoplay controls >
    <source src="~/Media/Linus and Lucy.ogg" type="audio/ogg" />
    <source src="~/Media/Linus and Lucy.mp3" type="audio/mp3" />
    <p>HTML5 audio is not supported on your browser</p>
</audio>
```

5. Save your changes and press F5 to debug the application. Open up the page using several browsers and verify that the controls are displayed and the audio starts playing when the page is loaded.

Building Your Own Controls

All of the DOM elements and events are available in JavaScript so it's a fairly straightforward process to create your own controls to work with the audio element. However, there are several facets that you'll need to control so it's not a trivial exercise. There are three areas that you'll need to address:

- Play/Pause
- Displaying progress and fast-forwarding/rewinding
- Adjust volume/mute

You will need to respond to events from both the custom controls as well as the audio element. In this exercise, you'll start by adding all the necessary controls to the page. Then I'll show you how to implement the event handlers that are needed for each area. The input elements that you'll use to control the audio element are:

- Play/Pause button – the label will toggle between "Play" and "Pause" depending on the state of the audio elements.
- Seek – this is a range control (introduced in Chapters 2 and 3) that will serve both to show the progress and allow the user to seek a specific location.
- Duration – this is a span element that displays both the current location and the total duration of the audio file.
- Mute button – the label will toggle between "Mute" and "Unmute".
- Volume – this is another range control that is used to specify the volume level.

The audio events that you'll provide handlers for include:

- onplay – raised when the audio is started
- onpause – raised when the audio is paused
- onended – raised when the audio has completed
- ontimeupdate – raised periodically as the audio clip is played
- ondurationchanged – raised when the duration changes, which occurs when the file is loaded
- onvolumnechanged – raised when the volume level changes or the mute property has changed

Adding the Custom Controls

You'll start by adding the custom controls and defining the event handlers that you'll need. Then I'll explain the JavaScript that you'll use to implement them.

EXERCISE 8-3. ADDING CUSTOM CONTROLS

1. Open the Index.cshtml file and remove the controls attribute. This will cause the audio element to be hidden.

2. Add the following div after the audio element. This will include all the input elements that you'll need to control the audio.

```
<div id="audioControls">
    <input type="button" value="Play" id="play" onclick="togglePlay()" />
    <input type="range" id="audioSeek" onchange="seekAudio()" />
    <span id="duration"></span>
    <input type="button" id="mute" value="Mute" onclick="toggleMute()" />
    <input type="range" id="volume" min="0" max="1" step="any"
        onchange="setVolume()" />
</div>
```

3. Modify the audio element to add the necessary event handlers by adding the code shown in bold. This also defines the id attributes that you'll use to access the audio and source elements.

```
<audio id="audio" autoplay
    onplay="updatePlayPause()"
    onpause="updatePlayPause()"
    onended="endAudio()"
    ontimeupdate="updateSeek()"
    ondurationchange="setupSeek()"
    onvolumechange="updateMute()" >

    <source src="~/Media/Linus and Lucy.ogg" type="audio/ogg" id="oggSource" />
    <source src="~/Media/Linus and Lucy.mp3" type="audio/mp3" id="mp3Source" />
    <p>HTML5 audio is not supported on your browser</p>
</audio>
```

4. In Visual Studio, change the debug browser to use Opera, as this supports the range controls that you are using. (You could also use Chrome if you prefer.) Save your changes and press F5 to debug the application. The page should look like Figure 8-11.

Figure 8-11. *The custom audio controls*

5. Close the browser and stop the debugger.

Implementing the Event Handlers

Now you're ready to implement the event handlers. I'll group these around the three main areas (play, seek, and volume) and explain one section at a time.

Supporting Play and Pause

Add the code shown in Listing 8-1 after the outer div, just before the end of the body element.

Listing 8-1. The initial script element

```
<script type="text/javascript">

var audio = document.getElementById("audio");

function setupSeek() {
    var seek = document.getElementById("audioSeek");
    seek.min = 0;
    seek.max = audio.duration;
    seek.value = 0;
    var duration = document.getElementById("duration");
    duration.innerHTML = "0/" + Math.round(audio.duration);
}

function togglePlay() {
    if (audio.paused || audio.ended) {
        audio.play();
    }
    else {
        audio.pause();
    }
}

function updatePlayPause() {
    var play=document.getElementById("play");
    if (audio.paused || audio.ended) {
        play.value="Play";
    }
    else {
        play.value="Pause";
    }
}

function endAudio() {
    document.getElementById("play").value = "Play";
    document.getElementById("audioSeek").value = 0;
    document.getElementById("duration").innerHTML = "0/" + Math.round(audio.duration);
}

</script>
```

This code first declares the audio variable that references the audio element. Since this is used by most of the functions, it's more efficient to get it once and store it in a variable that all functions can access.

The first method, setupSeek() is called in response to the ondurationchange event. When the page is first loaded, it doesn't know how long the audio clip is until the file is opened and the metadata is loaded. As soon as the metadata has been loaded, the duration can be determined and the event is raised. The setupSeek() function uses the duration property to set the max attribute of the audioSeek range control. It is also used to set the initial value of the span element. The duration property is expressed in seconds. Notice that the Math.round() function is called to round this value to the nearest integer.

The togglePlay() method is called when the user clicks on the Play button. If the current state of the audio element is paused or ended, it calls the play() function. Otherwise it calls the pause() method. The updatePlayPause() method sets the label of the play button. If the audio is currently playing, the text is changed to "Pause" since that will be the result if the button is clicked. Otherwise, the text is set to "Play".

■ **Tip** The `togglePlay()` function responds to the play button being clicked and the `updatePlayPause()` function responds to the `audio` element being started or paused. When the button is clicked, the `togglePlay()` method will change the state of the `audio` element. This state change will raise either an `onplay` or `onpause` event, which are both handled by the `updatePlayPause()` function. This is done this way because it is possible that the audio can be played or paused through means other than clicking the play button. For example, if you left the `controls` attribute, you would have both the native controls as well as the custom controls. Responding to the `onplay` and `onpause` events ensure the button label is always correct regardless of how the `audio` element is manipulated.

Finally, the `endAudio()` function is called when the audio has finished playing. This performs some synchronization including setting the button label, and initializing the range and span controls.

Supporting Progress and Seek

Next, add the functions shown in Listing 8-2 to the same `script` element.

Listing 8-2. Functions to support the range control

```
function seekAudio() {
    var seek = document.getElementById("audioSeek");
    audio.currentTime = seek.value;
}

function updateSeek() {
    var seek = document.getElementById("audioSeek");
    seek.value = audio.currentTime;
    var duration = document.getElementById("duration");
    duration.innerHTML = Math.round(audio.currentTime) + "/" + Math.round(audio.duration);
}
```

Just like with the play button, there is one event handler, `seekAudio()`, that responds to the input element and a separate event handler, `updateSeek()`, that responds to the `audio` element. The `seekAudio()` function is called when the user moves the slider on the range control. It simply sets the `currentTime` property using the value selected by the range control.

The `updateSeek()` function is called when the `ontimeupdate` event is raised by the `audio` element. This updates the range control to reflect the current position within the file. It also updates the span control to show the actual position (in seconds). Again, the `currentTime` property is rounded to the nearest integer.

Controlling the Volume

The last set of functions is used to support both the volume control and the mute button. Add the code shown in Listing 8-3 to the same `script` element that you have been using.

Listing 8-3. Controlling the volume

```
function toggleMute() {
    audio.muted = !audio.muted;
}
```

```
function updateMute() {
    var mute = document.getElementById("mute");
    if (audio.muted) {
        mute.value = "Unmute";
    }
    else {
        mute.value = "Mute";
    }
}
function setVolume() {
    var volume = document.getElementById("volume");
    audio.volume = volume.value;
}
```

As its name suggests, the toggleMute() function toggles the muted property of the audio element. When this is changed, the onvolumechange event is raised by the audio element. The updateMute() function responds to that event and sets the button label according to the current value of the muted property. Again, doing it this way ensures the button label is correct.

Finally, the setVolume() function is called when the user moves the slider on the second range control. It sets the volume property of the audio element to whatever was selected on the range control.

■ **Note** The volume property has a value between 0 and 1. You could think of this as 0% and 100%. When you defined the range control, the min attribute was set to 0 and max was set to 1, so the scale is correct. You can simply set the volume property using the range value. If you wanted to display the actual value of the volume property, just convert it to a percentage.

Now you're ready to try out your custom controls. Save your changes and press F5 to debug the application. The page should look similar to Figure 8-12.

Figure 8-12. *The completed custom controls*

You did not provide any style rules so the controls are displayed using default styles. But now you have access to the individual controls so you can arrange and style them anyway you want (refer to Chapter 4 for using CSS styles).

Changing the Audio Source

In this example, the audio source was defined in the markup. However, you can easily control this using JavaScript. If you're using a single src attribute as you did initially, you just need to change this attribute to reference a different file. However, if you're using multiple source elements you'll need to update all of these and then call the load() method.

To demonstrate this, when the clip has finished you'll change the source to a second audio clip and play that one as well.

EXERCISE 8-4. CHANGING THE AUDIO SOURCE

1. Close the browser and stop the debugger.

2. Create another audio file in both .mp3 and .ogg formats and copy these to the Chapter8\Media folder.

3. In the Solution Explorer, right-click the Media folder and select the Add ➤ Existing Item links. Navigate to the Chapter8\Media folder and select both the .mp3 and .ogg files that you just encoded.

4. Open the Index.cshtml file. At the top of the existing script element, declare the following variable. This will be used to keep track of how many songs were played.

   ```
   var songCount = 0;
   ```

5. Add the following code shown in bold to the endAudio() function. If the audio clip that just finished is the first one, the code will change the src attribute to reference the second file. The file is then loaded and played. (Note, you'll need to change these filenames to use the actual files that you included in your project.)

   ```
   function endAudio() {
       document.getElementById("play").value = "Play";
       document.getElementById("audioSeek").value = 0;
       document.getElementById("duration").innerHTML = "0/" + Math.
       round(audio.duration);

       if (++songCount < 2) {
           document.getElementById("oggSource").src = "/Media/Sample.ogg";
           document.getElementById("mp3Source").src = "/Media/Sample.mp3";
           audio.load();
           audio.play();
       }
   }
   ```

6. Save your changes and press F5 to debug the application. The initial song should start playing.

7. To save some time, fast-forward the clip to almost the end of the file and then wait for it to finish. The second file should automatically start playing. You should notice the span control was updated to show the duration of the second file.

Detecting Audio Support

You can programmatically determine if a source is supported by the browser by calling the canPlayType() method on the audio element, passing in the type attribute. To demonstrate this, add the following code to the beginning of the script block, after the audio variable declaration:

```
var sources = audio.getElementsByTagName("source");
for (var i = 0; i < sources.length; i++) {
    alert("[" + sources[i].type + "] - " + audio.canPlayType(sources[i].type));
}
```

This code iterates through all of the source elements and displays a pop-up indicating if the type is supported. Save your changes and try running this in Opera. You should see the results shown in Figures 8-13 and 8-14.

Figure 8-13. *The canPlayType() results for audio/ogg*

Figure 8-14. *The canPlayType() results for audio/mp3*

How do you like that? You ask a yes or no question and get back a "maybe" and no response. Well, as it turns out, the canPlayType() function does not return either "no" or "yes". Instead it returns either "maybe", "probably", or a blank string. The blank string can be interpreted as a "no". Let's talk about "maybe" and "probably".

The source file is a container that provides metadata about the media in addition to the actual data. Specifying a Mime type like audio/ogg merely indicates the type of container but doesn't explicitly state how the data is encoded (what codec is used). If the browser supports that container type, canPlayType() returns "maybe". There's no evidence to indicate it is not supported but can't tell for certain that it is. If the container type is not supported, like audio/mp3, a blank string is returned (meaning it is not supported).

▓ **Note**   A blank string is used to indicate not supported because in JavaScript, a blank string is a *falsy* value whereas "no" is a *truthy* value. So you can code if (canPlayType(type)) and only "maybe" and "probably" results will be selected.

If you also specify the codec value and the codec is supported then you'll get a "probably" returned. Change the type attribute on the first source element to this. (Again, watch the single- and double-quotes as you did earlier.)

```
type='audio/ogg; codecs="vorbis"'
```

Try running the application using Opera and the alert should look like Figure 8-15.

Figure 8-15. *The canPlayType() results for audio/ogg; codecs' "vorbis"*

"Probably" is as good as you'll get, with the `canPlayType()` method anyway; you don't ever get a "yes". The possible responses are illustrated in Table 8-2.

Table 8-2. *canPlayType() method responses*

Codec	Container Supported	Container Not Supported
Undefined	"maybe"	Blank
Supported	"probably"	Blank
Not Supported	Blank	Blank

Understanding Video Formats

As I said at the beginning of the chapter, the video element works just like the audio element so everything you have learned so far also applies to video.

Reviewing Browser Support

A video file usually contains both audio and video so all of the audio types and codecs that I covered earlier still apply. In addition, the video portion can be encoded in various ways. Fortunately, the industry seems to be narrowing down to three primary formats:

- MP4 – (*.mp4) using H.264 video encoding and MP3 audio encoding
- WebM – (*.webm) using VP8 video encoding and Vorbis audio encoding
- Ogg – (*.ogv) using Theora video encoding and Vorbis audio encoding

Table 8-3 lists the formats that are supported by the major browsers

Table 8-3. *Video/Audio codec support*

Browser	MP4	WebM	Ogg
IE 9	Yes	No	No
Firefox 4	No	Yes	Yes
Chrome 6	Yes	Yes	Yes
Safari 5	Yes	No	No
Opera 10.6	No	Yes	Yes

As with audio, you can encode a video file in multiple formats and provide several sources so the browser can select one that it supports. You can see from Table 8-2 that if you support MP4 plus either Ogg or WebM your page will be compatible with most browsers.

Converting Video Formats

The first thing you'll need is a sample video that is encoded in multiple formats. Windows provides a sample video clip named `Wildlife.wmv` that I'll use for the initial demo. To create an Ogg or WebM file, I recommend using the Firefogg plugin for Firefox. It's easy to install and use and I've found it to work well. If you prefer, there are other utilities that will convert to these formats including the XMedia Recode application that I mentioned earlier.

Using Firefogg

To install Firefogg, start Firefox and then navigate to the Firefogg site (`http://firefogg.org`). If the plugin is not installed the page provides a link to install it for you. Once this is installed, the Firefogg page should indicate that as shown in Figure 8-16.

Figure 8-16. *The main Firefogg page*

Click the "Make web video" link. In the next page, click the Select File button and then select the `Wildlife.wmv` file as the input source. The page will load the file and display the details. In the format dropdown you can choose either the WebM or Ogg format. Select the WebM format. In the Preset dropdown you can choose the size of the video. The original file is 1280 x 720 and you can use that or choose a smaller size.

Click the Encode button and then browse to the Chapter8\Media folder. Click the Save button to create the new file.

Creating an MP4 File

Firefogg will not create an MP4 file, which makes sense because Firefox doesn't support that format. The XMedia Recode utility is a nice utility that supports lots of formats including MP4. However, I've found that these files cannot be played by IE9. This is probably an IE bug because they work fine in Media Player and display properly using the Safari browser.

The only utility I have found that works with IE9 is the Any Video Converter application. You can download a free version at: http://www.any-video-converter.com/products/for_video_free. After you have installed it, start the application and click the Add Video Files button and then browse to the Wildlife.wmv file. In the Output profile dropdown, select the HTML5 Embed Video. Then select the HTML5 MP4 Movie option. The main window should look like Figure 8-17.

Figure 8-17. *The Any Video Converter application*

Now here's the critical part… click the Options button at the bottom-left corner. In the Options dialog box, select the Video tab and then select the "Flatten and add faststart to mp4 files" check box as shown in Figure 8-18. This is the option that will make the output file compatible with IE9. Click the OK button to save the options.

Figure 8-18. *Selecting the faststart option*

Finally, click the Encode Now button. This will create an HTML5 subfolder and create a file named `Wildlife_x264.mp4`. Rename this to `Wildlife.mp4` and move the file to the Chapter8\Media folder.

Downloading Sample Videos

If you don't want to convert your own video files, you can download the Big Buck Bunny trailer from Microsoft using this site: `http://ie.microsoft.com/testdrive/graphics/videoformatsupport/default.html`. This site provides several versions of this video clip so you can see how various browsers display them.

Open this site using Internet Explorer. Right-click the H.264 baseline profile video and select the Save Video As link. Browse to the Chapter8\Media folder and save the file as `BigBuckBunny.mp4`. Open the same site using Chrome or Opera and right-click the WebM version. Select the Save Video As link and browse to the Chapter8\Media folder. Save this as `BigBuckBunny.webm`.

Using the Video Element

Now that you have some video files to work with, you'll add a `video` element to your application. You'll add both sources to support all the major browsers. In the first exercise, you'll use the native controls and test it in several browsers. Then, you'll add custom controls that are implemented just like the audio controls.

Adding Video to the Demo Page

Adding video is a simple matter of adding the media files to your project and then adding some simple markup to the page to play it.

EXERCISE 8-5. ADDING A VIDEO ELEMENT

1. In the Solution Explorer, right-click the Media folder and select the Add ➤ Existing Item links. Select both versions of either the Wildlife or BigBuckBunny video files. I will be using the Wildlife files for this demo.

2. In the Index.cshtml file, remove the autoplay attribute from the audio element. You will autoplay the video and removing this will keep them from both playing at the same time.

3. Add the following markup, just after the div that contains the audio controls:

```
<video id="video" autoplay controls loop>
    <source src="~/Media/Wildlife.webm" type="video/webm" />
    <source src="~/Media/Wildlife.mp4" type="video/mp4" />
    <p>HTML5 video is not supported on your browser</p>
</video>
```

■ **Note** You already added the Mime types for webm, mp4, and ogg to the web.config file earlier in this chapter.

---

4. Save your changes and press F5 to debug the application.

5. Try it out in several browsers to make sure the video can be played in each.

For the video element you included the autoplay, controls, and loop attributes. You already used the autoplay and controls attributes when working with the audio element. The loop attribute will cause the video to start over at the beginning when it finishes. This is also supported by the audio element.

■ **Tip** The canPlayType() method that you used earlier on audio sources can also be used on video files. It works the same way, either returning a blank string indicating the file is not supported, or a "maybe" or "probably" result.

Adding Custom Video Controls

Now you'll add custom controls for the video element just like you did for the audio element. For this exercise I will be using the Big Buck Bunny video files.

EXERCISE 8-6. ADDING CUSTOM VIDEO CONTROLS

1. Modify the markup in the Index.cshtml file by replacing the video element with this:

```
<video id="video"
    onplay="updatePlayPauseVideo()"
    onpause="updatePlayPauseVideo()"
    onended="endVideo()"
    ontimeupdate="updateSeekVideo()"
```

```
        ondurationchange = "setupSeekVideo()"
        onvolumechange = "updateMuteVideo()">
        <source src = "~/Media/BigBuckBunny.webm" type = "video/webm" />
        <source src = "~/Media/BigBuckBunny.mp4" type = "video/mp4" />
        <p>HTML5 video is not supported on your browser</p>
    </video>
```

2. Add a new div after the video element and enter the following markup for it:

```
<div id = "videoControls">
    <input type = "button" value = "Play" id = "playVideo" onclick = "togglePlayVideo()" />
    <input type = "range" id = "videoSeek" onchange = "seekVideo()" />
    <span id = "durationVideo"></span>
    <input type = "button" id = "muteVideo" value = "Mute" onclick = "toggleMuteVideo()" />
    <input type = "range" id = "volumeVideo" min = "0" max = "1" step = "any"
        onchange = "setVolumeVideo()" />
</div>
```

3. Add a new script element using the code shown in Listing 8-4. This code is
    identical to the script used for the audio element except it uses the video element
    and the video controls.

Listing 8-4. The JavaScript functions for the video controls

```
<script type = "text/javascript">
var video = document.getElementById("video");

function setupSeekVideo() {
    var seek = document.getElementById("videoSeek");
    seek.min = 0;
    seek.max = video.duration;
    seek.value = 0;
    var duration = document.getElementById("durationVideo");
    duration.innerHTML = "0/" + Math.round(video.duration);
}

function togglePlayVideo() {
    if (video.paused || video.ended) {
        video.play();
    }
    else {
        video.pause();
    }
}

function updatePlayPauseVideo() {
    var play = document.getElementById("playVideo");
    if (video.paused || video.ended) {
        play.value = "Play";
    }
    else {
        play.value = "Pause";
    }
}
function endVideo() {
```

```
        document.getElementById("playVideo").value = "Play";
        document.getElementById("videoSeek").value = 0;
        document.getElementById("durationVideo").innerHTML = "0/"
            + Math.round(video.duration);
    }

    function seekVideo() {
        var seek = document.getElementById("videoSeek");
        video.currentTime = seek.value;
    }

    function updateSeekVideo() {
        var seek = document.getElementById("videoSeek");
        seek.value = video.currentTime;
        var duration = document.getElementById("durationVideo");
        duration.innerHTML = Math.round(video.currentTime) + "/"
            + Math.round(video.duration);
    }

    function toggleMuteVideo() {
        video.muted = !video.muted;
    }

    function updateMuteVideo() {
        var mute = document.getElementById("muteVideo");
        if (video.muted) {
            mute.value = "Unmute";
        }
        else {
            mute.value = "Mute";
        }
    }

    function setVolumeVideo() {
        var volume = document.getElementById("volumeVideo");
        video.volume = volume.value;
    }

</script>
```

4. Save your changes and select Opera as the debug browser. Press F5 to debug the application. Try out the video controls which should look like Figure 8-19.

Figure 8-19. *The video element and controls*

Adding a Poster

The poster attribute is supported by the video element (but not the audio element). Before the video is started you can use the poster attribute to specify the image that is displayed. If this is not specified, the browser will usually open the video and display the first frame. To add a poster, just include the image in your project and reference it in the poster attribute.

There's one thing to be careful about however. If you define a poster, the initial size of the video element will be the size of the poster image. If this is not the same as the video, the size will change when the video starts playing. You should either ensure the image is the same size or explicitly size the video element, which will stretch (or shrink) the poster image to fit.

EXERCISE 8-7. ADDING A POSTER IMAGE

1. Download an image file to use as the poster image. You can find images from this site: http://wiki.creativecommons.org/Case_Studies/ Blender_Foundation. Save the picture in the Chapter8\Media folder and name it **BBB_Poster.png**.

2. In the Solution Explorer, right-click the Media folder and select the Add ➤ Existing Item link. Browse to the Chapter8\Media folder and select the BBB_Poster.png image.

3. Modify the markup of the video element by adding the poster, width, and height attributes shown in bold:

```
<video id="video" poster="~/Media/BBB_Poster.png" width="852" height="480"
```

4. Save your changes and press F5 to start the application. You should now see the poster image until the video is started as shown in Figure 8-20.

Figure 8-20. The video element showing the poster image

Summary

In this chapter you created a simple web page that demonstrates the features of the audio and video elements. Cross-browser support is achieved by supplying the media files in multiple formats so each browser can use the one that it supports. This is pretty easy to do and fairly efficient since the browser can usually determine from the markup which file to download.

I showed you how to create your own controls for playing, pausing, and seeking within your audio and video files. By wiring up some simple JavaScript event handlers, making a custom media player becomes a straightforward exercise.

In the next chapter I'll demonstrate how to take advantage of scalable vector graphics (SVG) in HTML5.

CHAPTER 9

■ ■ ■

Scalable Vector Graphics

In this chapter I'll show you how to use scalable vector graphics (SVG) in an HTML5 web application using Visual Studio, ASP.NET MVC, and SQL Server. There are a lot of really cool things that you can do with SVG. I've picked out a fun demonstration that can be easily applied to many business applications. But first, let me give you an introduction to what SVG is.

Most people think of a graphic element as some form of bitmap; an array of rows and columns of pixels, and each pixel is assigned a specific color. In contrast, however, vector graphics express an image as a collection of formulas. For example, draw a circle with a center at point x,y and a radius r. More complex images are defined as a collection of graphic elements including circles, lines, and paths. While the rendering engine will ultimately determine the specific pixels that need to be set, the image definition is based on a formula. This fundamental difference provides two significant advantages to using vector graphics.

First, as its name suggests, vector graphics are scalable. If you want to expand the size of the image, the rendering engine simply recalculates the formula based on the new size and there is no loss of clarity. If you zoom in on a bitmap image you'll quickly start to see graininess and the image becomes blurry.

Secondly, each element in the image can be manipulated independently. If there are several circles in the image, for example, you can highlight one by simply changing the color of that image. Since vector graphics are formula based, you can easily adjust the formula to modify the image. What makes this particularly useful is that these elements can be styled using CSS, employing the powerful selectors and formatting capabilities that I showed you in Chapter 4.

Introducing SVG

You'll begin by creating a page that uses simple geometric shapes to draw a picture. Then you'll apply styles to these shapes using CSS. I'll show you how to save these markup elements in an .svg image file. This image file can be used just like other image files such as .jpg or .png files.

Creating the Sample Project

You'll first need to create a Visual Studio project that is similar to ones you created previously. This will use the Basic MVC4 project template.

EXERCISE 9-1. CREATING THE VISUAL STUDIO PROJECT

---

1. Start Visual Studio 2012. In the Start Page, click the New Project link.

2. In the New project dialog box, select the "ASP.NET MVC4 Web Application" template. Enter the project name **Chapter9** and select a location for this project as shown in Figure 9-1.

Figure 9-1. *Creating the Chapter9 project*

3. In the next dialog box, select the Basic template and make sure the Razor view engine is selected. Click the OK button and the project will be created (this may take a few seconds).

4. Right-click the Controller folder in the Solution Explorer and select the Add ➤ Controller links. Enter the name **HomeController** and select the Empty MVC Controller template. Click the Add button to create the controller.

5. Right-click the View folder and select the Add ➤ New Folder links. Enter the name **Home**.

6. Right-click the new Home folder and select the Add ➤ View links. In the Add View dialog box, enter the name **Index**, make sure the Razor view engine is selected, unselect all the check boxes, and click the Add button.

Adding Some Simple Shapes

To demonstrate how an svg element works you'll add some simple shapes like circles, rectangles, and lines. Most images can be expressed as a collection of geometrical shapes as I will demonstrate here.

The default implementation of the Index.cshtml file contains an empty div in the body. Change this to an svg element. Notice that as you change the opening tag, the ending tag is automatically changed. Add the attributes shown in bold to the svg element:

```
<svg xmlns:svg="http://www.w3.org/2000/svg" version="1.2"
    width="100px" height="230px">
</svg>
```

■ **Note**   The `width` and `height` attributes define the element's intrinsic dimensions. In IE9, you can omit these and the page will render correctly based on the actual space used. With other browsers, if the `width` and `height` are not specified the image will be clipped to some default size.

Inside the `svg` element add the following elements. These are just simple shapes; mostly `circle` elements with a rectangle (`rect`), `line`, and `polygon`.

```
<circle class="body" cx="50" cy="171" r="40" />
<circle class="body" cx="50" cy="103" r="30" />
<circle class="body" cx="50" cy="50" r="25" />
<line class="hat" x1="30" y1="25" x2="70" y2="25" />
<rect class="hat" x="40" y="10" width="20" height="15" />
<circle class="button" cx="50" cy="82" r="4" />
<circle class="button" cx="50" cy="100" r="4" />
<circle class="button" cx="50" cy="118" r="4" />
<circle class="eye" cx="42" cy="42" r="4" />
<circle class="eye" cx="58" cy="42" r="4" />
<polygon class="nose" points="45,60 45,50 60,55" />
```

A `circle` is expressed as a center point, `cx` and `cy`, and a radius, `r`. A `line` is specified as a beginning point, `x1` and `y1`, and an endpoint, `x2` and `y2`. A rectangle (`rect`) element is described by the top-left corner location, `x` and `y`, a `width`, and a `height`. A `polygon` is defined by a set of points in the form of `x1,y1 x2,y2 x3,y3`. You can specify any number of points. It is rendered by drawing a line segment between each of these points and a line segment from the last point, back to the first point.

Save your changes and press F5 to view the web page, which should look like Figure 9-2.

Figure 9-2. *The initial SVG image without styling*

Adding Styles

The default style for these elements is a solid black fill and because some of these shapes are on top of each other, several are not currently visible. Notice that you assigned a `class` attribute to each element. Now you'll apply styles for these elements using the `class` attribute. Add the code shown in Listing 9-1 inside the `svg` element, just before the elements you added earlier.

Listing 9-1. Adding SVG styles

```
<style type="text/css" >
    <![CDATA[
        .body
        {
            fill: white;
            stroke: gray;
            stroke-width: 1px;
        }

        .hat
        {
            fill: black;
            stroke: black;
            stroke-width: 3px;
        }

        .button
        {
            fill: black;
        }

        .eye
        {
            fill: black;
        }

        .nose
        {
            fill: orange;
        }

    ]]>
</style>
```

▓ **Note**   The `style` element needs to be inside the `svg` element and you can't use an external style sheet. Notice the `[CDATA[` tag around the style rules. This is necessary to prevent the XML parser from treating this as part of the HTML document.

Save these changes and press F5 to view the web page, which should look like Figure 9-3.

Figure 9-3. *The SVG images with styling applied*

Using SVG Image Files

In addition to embedding an svg element, you can also save this as a standalone image file with an .svg extension. This file can then be used just like other graphic images. I'll show you how to create a standalone SVG image and then use it on a page.

Creating an SVG Image

I'll first show you how to create a standalone .svg file and then use as a background image. This will also demonstrate the scalability of SVG images.

EXERCISE 9-2. CREATING AN SVG IMAGE

1. In the Solution Explorer, right-click the Chapter9 project and click the Add ➤ New Folder links. Enter **Images** for the folder name.

2. From the File menu, select the New ➤ File links. In the New File dialog box, select Text File from the General category, and click the Open button.

3. Enter the following markup instructions:

```
<?xml version="1.0" standalone="no"?>
<!DOCTYPE svg PUBLIC "-//W3C//DTD SVG 1.2//EN"
"http://www.w3.org/Graphics/SVG/1.2/DTD/svg12.dtd">
```

4. Copy and paste the entire svg element from the Index.cshtml file, including the style element to the new text file.

5. Click the Save button. In the "Save File As" dialog box, navigate to the Chapter9\Images folder and enter **snowman.svg** for the filename.

6. To test your image, using Windows Explorer, browse to this file and open it. This should launch a browser and display the snowman image.

7. In the Solution Explorer, right-click the Images folder and select the Add ➤ Existing Item links. Select the `snowman.svg` file and click the Add button.

Using an SVG Background

Now you have an image file that you can use just like other images. To demonstrate this, you'll add a `div` element to your page and use the `snowman.svg` as the background image. You'll also adjust the `div` size so you can see how the image looks when resized.

```
EXERCISE 9-3. ADDING A BACKGROUND IMAGE
```

1. In the `Index.cshtml` file, add the following code in the `body` element, after the `svg` element:

   ```
   <div id="container"></div>
   ```

2. This simply defines a `div` element. Now you'll use CSS to configure it. Add the following `style` element inside the `head` element:

   ```css
   <style type="text/css">
       #container {
           height: 1000px;
           width: 450px;
           background-image: url("Images/snowman.svg");
           background-size: contain;
       }
   </style>
   ```

3. In order for IIS to recognize the `.svg` file, you'll need to define the mime map. Open the `web.config` file in the root folder (not the one in the Views folder). Add the following entry shown in bold inside the `system.webServer` node:

   ```xml
   <system.webServer>
     <validation validateIntegratedModeConfiguration="false" />

     <staticContent>
       <mimeMap fileExtension=".svg" mimeType="image/svg+xml"/>
     </staticContent>

   </system.webServer>
   ```

4. Press F5 to debug your application. In addition to the small image, you should also see a larger version of your image as shown in Figure 9-4. Notice that there is no loss of image quality when expanding the size of the image.

Figure 9-4. The page with the snowman background

Reviewing SVG Support

As of this writing there were a few limitations in the current browsers. Only IE 9 and up and Chrome support the features demonstrated in this chapter:

- Opera – SVG support in Opera is limited. Embedding SVG elements in the HTML document does not work well. It will display the shapes but does not apply the styles correctly. It does display SVG image files, however.

- Firefox, Opera, and Safari – These browsers support SVG elements as well as the SVG images. However, the image is converted to a bitmap and then scaled as needed so you'll see a fuzzy image.

- Internet Explorer and Chrome – IE (9 and up) and Chrome supports SVG elements and SVG images and scales images correctly with no loss of quality.

- IE8 and below – IE, prior to version 9, does not support SVG.

Creating an Interactive Map

Drawing pictures of snowman may be fun but let's move on to some more practical uses of SVG. You will create a map of the United States with each state represented by a separate SVG *path* element, which I'll explain later.

You'll store the path definitions in an SQL Server database. I'll show you how to access the database using a model class and then display it using a view definition. Once you have the map displayed, I'll show you some CSS tricks to style the map using both static and dynamic styles. Finally, you'll add some animation to add a little flair to your web page.

Using Path Elements

The path element is the most versatile of all SVG elements. It is a collection of *MoveTo*, *LineTo*, and various *CurveTo* commands. The shape is drawn by following the path commands. Each command starts from the current position and either moves to a new position or draws a line to the next position. For example:

- Move to 25, 50
- Draw a line to 50, 50
- Draw a line to 50, 25
- Draw an arc to 25, 50

This is expressed as:

```
<path d="M25,50 L50,50 L50,25 A25,25 0 0,0 25,50 z" />
```

The "move to" and "line to" commands are pretty straightforward. The "arc to" command, as well as all the other curve commands, is more complicated because you need to provide additional control points that describe how the curve should be drawn. Each command uses a single letter as shown in Table 9-1.

Table 9-1. *The available path commands*

Command	Abbr.	Description
Move to	M	Move to the specified position
Line to	L	Draw a line to the specified position
Horizontal line to	H	Draw a horizontal line to the specified x coordinate
Vertical line to	V	Draws a vertical line to the specified y coordinate
Arc to	A	Draws an arc to the specified position
Curve to	C	Draws a cubic Bezier curve
Shorthand curve to	S	Draws a simplified cubic Bezier curve
Quadratic curve to	Q	Draws a quadratic Bezier curve
Shorthand quadratic curve to	T	Draws a simplified quadratic Bezier curve
Close path	Z	Close the figure by drawing a line to the starting position

For each of these commands, an uppercase letter is used when absolute coordinates are used. You can also specify relative coordinates and use a lowercase letter to indicate the values are relative to the current position. For more information about constructing a path element, see the article at http://www.w3.org/TR/SVG/paths.html#PathData.

As you can probably envision, drawing a complex shape like the state of Alaska will take a lot of commands. You won't want to edit this by hand. Fortunately, there are tools available to help build a path definition. For example, a free web-based tool is available at http://code.google.com/p/svg-edit. Just for grins, the path element for Alaska is shown in Listing 9-2.

Listing 9-2. The path element definition for Alaska

```
<path d="M 158.07671,453.67502 L 157.75339,539.03215 L 159.36999,540.00211 L
162.44156,540.16377 L 163.8965,539.03215 L 166.48308,539.03215 L 166.64475,541.94205 L
173.59618,548.73182 L 174.08117,551.3184 L 177.47605,549.37846 L 178.1227,549.2168 L
178.44602,546.14524 L 179.90096,544.52863 L 181.0326,544.36697 L 182.97253,542.91201 L
186.04409,545.01361 L 186.69074,547.92352 L 188.63067,549.05514 L 189.7623,551.48006 L
193.64218,553.25833 L 197.03706,559.2398 L 199.78529,563.11966 L 202.04855,565.86791 L
203.50351,569.58611 L 208.515,571.36439 L 213.68817,573.46598 L 214.65813,577.83084 L
215.14311,580.9024 L 214.17315,584.29729 L 212.39487,586.56054 L 210.77826,585.75224 L
209.32331,582.68067 L 206.57507,581.22573 L 204.7968,580.09409 L 203.98849,580.9024 L
205.44344,583.65065 L 205.6051,587.36885 L 204.47347,587.85383 L 202.53354,585.9139 L
200.43195,584.62061 L 200.91693,586.23722 L 202.21021,588.0155 L 201.40191,588.8238 C
201.40191,588.8238 200.59361,588.50048 200.10863,587.85383 C 199.62363,587.20719
198.00703,584.45895 198.00703,584.45895 L 197.03706,582.19569 C 197.03706,582.19569
196.71374,583.48898 196.06709,583.16565 C 195.42044,582.84233 194.7738,581.71071
194.7738,581.71071 L 196.55207,579.77077 L 195.09712,578.31582 L 195.09712,573.30432 L
194.28882,573.30432 L 193.48052,576.6992 L 192.34888,577.1842 L 191.37892,573.46598 L
190.73227,569.74777 L 189.92396,569.26279 L 190.24729,574.92094 L 190.24729,576.05256 L
188.79233,574.75928 L 185.23579,568.77781 L 183.13419,568.29283 L 182.48755,564.57462 L
180.87094,561.66472 L 179.25432,560.53308 L 179.25432,558.26983 L 181.35592,556.97654 L
180.87094,556.65322 L 178.28436,557.29986 L 174.88947,554.87495 L 172.30289,551.96504 L
167.45306,549.37846 L 163.41152,546.79188 L 164.70482,543.55866 L 164.70482,541.94205 L
162.92654,543.55866 L 160.01664,544.69029 L 156.29843,543.55866 L 150.64028,541.13375 L
145.14381,541.13375 L 144.49717,541.61873 L 138.03072,537.73885 L 135.92912,537.41553 L
133.18088,531.59573 L 129.62433,531.91905 L 126.06778,533.374 L 126.55277,537.90052 L
127.68439,534.99062 L 128.65437,535.31394 L 127.19941,539.67879 L 130.43263,536.93055 L
131.07928,538.54716 L 127.19941,542.91201 L 125.90612,542.58869 L 125.42114,540.64875 L
124.12785,539.84045 L 122.83456,540.97208 L 120.08632,539.19381 L 117.01475,541.29541 L
115.23649,543.397 L 111.8416,545.4986 L 107.15342,545.33693 L 106.66844,543.23534 L
110.38664,542.58869 L 110.38664,541.29541 L 108.12338,540.64875 L 109.09336,538.22384 L
111.35661,534.34397 L 111.35661,532.5657 L 111.51827,531.75739 L 115.88313,529.49413 L
116.85309,530.78742 L 119.60134,530.78742 L 118.30805,528.20085 L 114.58983,527.87752 L
109.57834,530.62576 L 107.15342,534.02064 L 105.37515,536.60723 L 104.24352,538.87049 L
100.04033,540.32543 L 96.96876,542.91201 L 96.645439,544.52863 L 98.908696,545.4986 L
99.717009,547.60018 L 96.96876,550.83341 L 90.502321,555.03661 L 82.742574,559.2398 L
80.640977,560.37142 L 75.306159,561.50306 L 69.971333,563.76631 L 71.749608,565.0596 L
70.294654,566.51455 L 69.809672,567.64618 L 67.061434,566.67621 L 63.828214,566.83787 L
63.019902,569.10113 L 62.049939,569.10113 L 62.37326,566.67621 L 58.816709,567.96951 L
55.90681,568.93947 L 52.511924,567.64618 L 49.602023,569.58611 L 46.368799,569.58611 L
44.267202,570.87941 L 42.65059,571.68771 L 40.548995,571.36439 L 37.962415,570.23276 L
35.699158,570.87941 L 34.729191,571.84937 L 33.112578,570.71775 L 33.112578,568.77781 L
36.184142,567.48452 L 42.488929,568.13117 L 46.853782,566.51455 L 48.955378,564.41296 L
51.86528,563.76631 L 53.643553,562.958 L 56.391794,563.11966 L 58.008406,564.41296 L
58.978369,564.08964 L 61.241626,561.3414 L 64.313196,560.37142 L 67.708076,559.72478 L
69.00137,559.40146 L 69.648012,559.88644 L 70.456324,559.88644 L 71.749608,556.16823 L
```

75.791141,554.71329 L 77.731077,550.99508 L 79.994336,546.46856 L 81.610951,545.01361 L
81.934272,542.42703 L 80.317657,543.72032 L 76.922764,544.36697 L 76.276122,541.94205 L
74.982838,541.61873 L 74.012865,542.58869 L 73.851205,545.4986 L 72.39625,545.33693 L
70.941306,539.51713 L 69.648012,540.81041 L 68.516388,540.32543 L 68.193068,538.3855 L
64.151535,538.54716 L 62.049939,539.67879 L 59.463361,539.35547 L 60.918305,537.90052 L
61.403286,535.31394 L 60.756645,533.374 L 62.211599,532.40404 L 63.504883,532.24238 L
62.858241,530.4641 L 62.858241,526.09925 L 61.888278,525.12928 L 61.079966,526.58423 L
54.936843,526.58423 L 53.481892,525.29094 L 52.835247,521.41108 L 50.733651,517.85452 L
50.733651,516.88456 L 52.835247,516.07625 L 52.996908,513.97465 L 54.128536,512.84303 L
53.320231,512.35805 L 52.026941,512.84303 L 50.895313,510.09479 L 51.86528,505.08328 L
56.391794,501.85007 L 58.978369,500.23345 L 60.918305,496.51525 L 63.666554,495.22195 L
66.253132,496.35359 L 66.576453,498.77851 L 69.00137,498.45517 L 72.23459,496.03026 L
73.851205,496.67691 L 74.821167,497.32355 L 76.437782,497.32355 L 78.701041,496.03026 L
79.509354,491.6654 C 79.509354,491.6654 79.832675,488.75551 80.479317,488.27052 C
81.125959,487.78554 81.44928,487.30056 81.44928,487.30056 L 80.317657,485.36062 L
77.731077,486.16893 L 74.497847,486.97723 L 72.557911,486.49225 L 69.00137,484.71397 L
63.989875,484.55231 L 60.433324,480.83411 L 60.918305,476.95424 L 61.564957,474.52932 L
59.463361,472.75105 L 57.523423,469.03283 L 58.008406,468.22453 L 64.798177,467.73955 L
66.899773,467.73955 L 67.869736,468.70951 L 68.516388,468.70951 L 68.354728,467.0929 L
72.23459,466.44626 L 74.821167,466.76958 L 76.276122,467.90121 L 74.821167,470.00281 L
74.336186,471.45775 L 77.084435,473.07437 L 82.095932,474.85264 L 83.874208,473.88268 L
81.610951,469.51783 L 80.640977,466.2846 L 81.610951,465.47629 L 78.21606,463.53636 L
77.731077,462.40472 L 78.21606,460.78812 L 77.407756,456.90825 L 74.497847,452.22007 L
72.072929,448.01688 L 74.982838,446.07694 L 78.21606,446.07694 L 79.994336,446.72359 L
84.197528,446.56193 L 87.915733,443.00539 L 89.047366,439.93382 L 92.765578,437.5089 L
94.382182,438.47887 L 97.130421,437.83222 L 100.84863,435.73062 L 101.98027,435.56896 L
102.95023,436.37728 L 107.47674,436.21561 L 110.22498,433.14405 L 111.35661,433.14405 L
114.91316,435.56896 L 116.85309,437.67056 L 116.36811,438.80219 L 117.01475,439.93382 L
118.63137,438.31721 L 122.51124,438.64053 L 122.83456,442.35873 L 124.7745,443.81369 L
131.88759,444.46033 L 138.19238,448.66352 L 139.64732,447.69356 L 144.82049,450.28014 L
146.92208,449.6335 L 148.86202,448.82518 L 153.71185,450.76512 L 158.07671,453.67502 z M
42.973913,482.61238 L 45.075509,487.9472 L 44.913847,488.91717 L 42.003945,488.59384 L
40.225672,484.55231 L 38.447399,483.09737 L 36.02248,483.09737 L 35.86082,480.51078 L
37.639093,478.08586 L 38.770722,480.51078 L 40.225672,481.96573 L 42.973913,482.61238 z M
40.387333,516.07625 L 44.105542,516.88456 L 47.823749,517.85452 L 48.632056,518.8245 L
47.015444,522.5427 L 43.94388,522.38104 L 40.548995,518.8245 L 40.387333,516.07625 z M
19.694697,502.01173 L 20.826327,504.5983 L 21.957955,506.21492 L 20.826327,507.02322 L
18.72473,503.95166 L 18.72473,502.01173 L 19.694697,502.01173 z M 5.9534943,575.0826 L
9.3483796,572.81934 L 12.743265,571.84937 L 15.329845,572.17269 L 15.814828,573.7893 L
17.754763,574.27429 L 19.694697,572.33436 L 19.371375,570.71775 L 22.119616,570.0711 L
25.029518,572.65768 L 23.897889,574.43595 L 19.533037,575.56758 L 16.784795,575.0826 L
13.066588,573.95097 L 8.7017347,575.40592 L 7.0851227,575.72924 L 5.9534943,575.0826 z M
54.936843,570.55609 L 56.553455,572.49602 L 58.655048,570.87941 L 57.2001,569.58611 L
54.936843,570.55609 z M 57.846745,573.62764 L 58.978369,571.36439 L 61.079966,571.68771 L

```
60.271663,573.62764 L 57.846745,573.62764 z M 81.44928,571.68771 L 82.904234,573.46598 L
83.874208,572.33436 L 83.065895,570.39442 L 81.44928,571.68771 z M 90.17899,559.2398 L
91.310623,565.0596 L 94.220522,565.86791 L 99.232017,562.958 L 103.59687,560.37142 L
101.98027,557.94651 L 102.46525,555.52159 L 100.36365,556.81488 L 97.453752,556.00657 L
99.070357,554.87495 L 101.01029,555.68325 L 104.89016,553.90497 L 105.37515,552.45003 L
102.95023,551.64172 L 103.75853,549.70178 L 101.01029,551.64172 L 96.322118,555.19827 L
91.472284,558.10817 L 90.17899,559.2398 z M 132.53423,539.35547 L 134.95915,537.90052 L
133.98918,536.12224 L 132.21091,537.09221 L 132.53423,539.35547 z" />
```

■ **Tip** This data, as well as the data for all the other states, was downloaded from
`http://en.wikipedia.org/wiki/File:Blank_US_Map.svg`. You can find a lot of similar material by going to
`http://commons.wikimedia.org` and entering **svg map** in the search criteria.

Implementing the Initial Map

You'll start by creating the initial map without any styles applied. The actual path elements will be stored in an SQL database. You will create the database, add a State table, and store the path definitions. You'll then create a model using LINQ to SQL to provide the state data. Finally, you'll create a new view that will display the map and then provide a link on the Index page to access it.

Creating the Database

The path elements can be quite long and are static (the shape of Alaska is not likely to change any time soon), so they can be stored in a database and retrieved by .NET when needed to render the page. The MVC project template that you used is already configured for a database connection. You'll need to create the State table and populate it with the appropriate path definitions.

EXERCISE 9-4. CREATING THE STATE TABLE

1. The database used by .NET is not actually created until the first time is it accessed. To manually create the database, In Visual Studio, select the Server Explorer from the View menu. In the Data Connections node you should see one called "DefaultConnection (Chapter9)". Right-click this item and select the Modify Connection link. This will display the Modify Connection dialog box shown in Figure 9-5.

Figure 9-5. *The Modify Connection dialog box*

2. The default values should all be correct; just click the OK button. Since the database has not been created yet, you'll see the dialog box shown in Figure 9-6. Click the Yes button to create the database.

Figure 9-6. *Creating the SQL database*

3. This will create a blank database with the name like aspnet-Chapter9-<datetime>.
    Now you'll add the State table and populate it. From the SQL menu, select the
    Transact-SQL Editor ➤ New Query links.

4. The "Connect to Server" dialog box shown in Figure 9-7 will be displayed. Click the
    Connect button to login to the database server.

Figure 9-7. *Authenticating with SQL Server*

5. In the query window, select the Chapter9 database from the dropdown list at the top of the form as shown in Figure 9-8. (Your database name will be different from mine.)

Figure 9-8. Selecting the Chapter9 database

■ **Tip** You also could right-click the connection in the Server Explorer and select the New Query link. This will connect to the database and default to the current database.

---

6. In the download that is available at www.apress.com, you'll find a States.sql file in the Chapter9 folder. Copy and paste the contents of this file into the query window and then execute the query by clicking the Execute icon or entering the Ctrl-Shift-E command. This will create the State table using the following script and then populate it with a record for each state.

```
CREATE TABLE State(
        StateCode nchar(10) NOT NULL,
        StateName nvarchar(50) NOT NULL,
        Path ntext NULL,
 CONSTRAINT PK_State PRIMARY KEY CLUSTERED
(
        StateCode ASC
)WITH (PAD_INDEX = OFF, STATISTICS_NORECOMPUTE = OFF, IGNORE_DUP_KEY = OFF,
  ALLOW_ROW_LOCKS = ON, ALLOW_PAGE_LOCKS = ON) ON [PRIMARY]
) ON [PRIMARY] TEXTIMAGE_ON [PRIMARY]
```

7. To verify the data was loaded correctly, open another query window using the Transact-SQL Editor ➤ New Query links from the SQL menu. After connecting, select the Chapter9 database and execute this query:

```
select * from State
```

8. You should see results similar to Figure 9-9.

	StateCode	StateName	Path
1	AK	Alaska	M 158.07671,453.67502 L 157.75339,539.03215 L 15...
2	AL	Alabama	M 631.30647,460.41572 L 629.81587,446.09422 L 62...
3	AR	Arkansas	M 593.82477,343.05296 L 589.84489,343.76966 L 58...
4	AZ	Arizona	M 144.9112,382.62909 L 142.28419,384.78742 L 141...
5	CA	California	M 144.69443,382.19813 L 148.63451,381.70951 L 15...
6	CO	Colorado	M 380.03242,320.96457 L 384.93566,234.63961 L 27...
7	CT	Connecticut	M 874.06831,178.86288 L 870.39088,163.98407 L 86...
8	DC	District of Columbia	M 805.81945,250.84384 L 803.96117,249.01967 L 80...
9	DE	Delaware	M 825.6261,228.2791 L 825.99441,226.13221 L 826....
10	FL	Florida	M 759.8167,439.1428 L 762.08236,446.4614 L 765.8...
11	GA	Georgia	M 672.29229,355.5518 L 672.29229,357.73422 L 672...

Query executed successful... | (LocalDb)\v11.0 (11.0 RTM) | INTERNAL\mark (51) | aspnet-Chapter9-201206... | 00:00:00 | 51 rows

Figure 9-9. *The contents of the State table*

Creating the Model

Creating a model that uses an SQL table is a pretty simple task. You'll use LINQ to SQL to create a model class that provides data from the specified table.

EXERCISE 9-5. CREATING A LINQ TO SQL MODEL

1. From the Solution Explorer, right-click the Models folder and select the Add ➤ New Item links. In the "Add New Item" dialog box, select the Data category and then select the "LINQ to SQL Classes" item and enter **State.dbml** name as shown in Figure 9-10.

Figure 9-10. *Creatinge a new LINQ-to-SQL model class*

2. This will display the Object Relational Designer. From the Server Explorer, expand the Tables node to show the State table as shown in Figure 9-11.

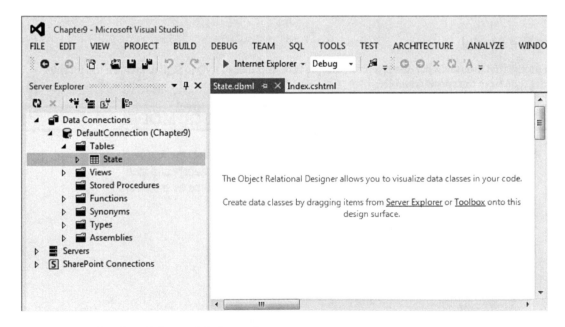

Figure 9-11. *The Object Relational design surface*

■ **Tip** If the State table is not shown, right-click the Tables node and select the Refresh link.

---

3. Drag the State table from the Server Explorer onto the Object Relational Designer pane. This will define the State.dbml class as shown in Figure 9-12.

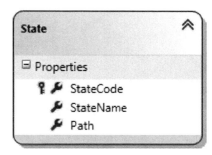

Figure 9-12. *The State.dbml design*

4. You now have a model that you can use to provide the state details for the map. Press F6 to rebuild the project. This will make the model available for linking to a view.

Creating the Map View

With a model already defined, you'll now create the view that will display the model elements.

EXERCISE 9-6 CREATING THE MAP VIEW

1. Right-click the Views\Home folder and select the Add ➤ View links.

2. In the Add View dialog box, enter the name **Map**. Select the "Create a strongly-typed view" checkbox and select the State class in the Model class dropdown list. Unselect the other check boxes and select the List template as shown in Figure 9-13.

Figure 9-13. *Creating the Map view*

3. Notice in the Map.cshtml file that the referenced model is specified like this since it is expecting to receive a collection of State classes. This happened because you choose the List template when creating the view.

    ```
    @model IEnumerable<Chapter9.Models.State>
    ```

4. Add this using statement just after the model reference. This will enable you to access the State properties through IntelliSense.

    ```
    @using Chapter9.Models
    ```

5. Replace the default contents of the body element with the following code. This defines an svg element just like you did earlier. It then uses a foreach loop to create a path element for each State defined in the model. Notice that it is storing the StateCode column in the id attribute and the StateName column in the class attribute.

```
<svg xmlns:svg = "http://www.w3.org/2000/svg" version = "1.2"
    width = "959" height = "593" id = "map">

    @foreach (State s in Model)
    {
        <path id = "@s.StateCode.Trim()" class="@s.StateName.Trim()" d="@s.Path" />
    }
</svg>
```

6. Now you'll need to implement a controller action that will display the map view.
    Open the HomeController.cs class and add the following namespace.

    ```
    using Chapter9.Models;
    ```

7. Then add the following method to the HomeController class. This executes a LINQ
    query to extract all the records from the State table and provide it to the view.

    ```
    public ActionResult Map()
    {
        StateDataContext DC = new StateDataContext();
        var states = from s in DC.States select s;

        return View(states);
    }
    ```

8. Now you'll add a link on the Index.cshtml page that will display the map page.
    Go to the Index.cshtml file and add the following line at the beginning of the body
    element (just before the svg element):

    ```
    @Html.ActionLink("Go to map", "Map", "Home")
    ```

9. Press F5 to build and run the application. The index page will be displayed. Click the
    "Go to map" link. You should see a map of the United States and all of the states are
    filled with the default color (black).

Styling the State Elements

Now that all the mechanical work is done you can have some fun styling the path elements. As I demonstrated
earlier with the snowman image, each element can be styled using a special style sheet. You can also style them
dynamically using JavaScript. I will show you how to use solid-color fills, gradients, and background images to
format each element.

Using Basic Fill Colors

You'll start by adding some simple fill rules. Using a simple element selector you'll set the stroke color to black
and khaki for the fill color. Then, to add some variety and to demonstrate using attribute selectors, you'll
change the fill color based on the state code. The id attribute contains the two-letter state code and the class
attribute contains the state name. Using the first letter of the id attribute you'll set the fill color as follows:

- A – red
- N – yellow
- M – green
- C – blue
- O – purple
- I – orange

Enter the style element shown in Listing 9-3 inside the svg element before the foreach loop.

Listing 9-3. Adding basic fill definitions

```
<style type="text/css" >
  <![CDATA[
    path
    {
    stroke: black;
    fill: khaki;
    }

    path[id^="A"]
    {
        fill: red;
    }
    path[id^="N"]
    {
        fill: yellow;
    }
    path[id^="M"]
    {
        fill: green;
    }
    path[id^="C"]
    {
    fill: blue;
    }
    path[id^="O"]
    {
        fill: purple;
    }
    path[id^="I"]
    {
    fill: orange;
    }

  ]]>
</style>
```

Press F5 to start the application and then click the "Go to map" link. The map should now look like Figure 9-14.

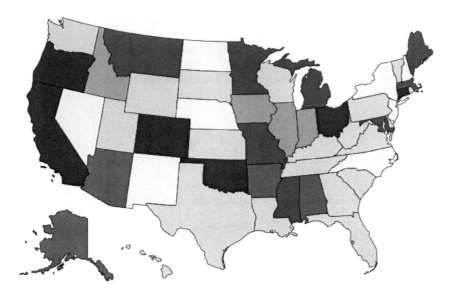

Figure 9-14. *The map with some basic styling*

As you're moving the mouse around the map it would be nice to highlight the state that the mouse is currently pointing to. Add the following rule to the style element after the existing rules.

```
path:hover
{
    opacity: .5;
}
```

Using Gradient Fills

You can use gradient fills with SVG elements but they are implemented differently than typical HTML elements. You first have to define the gradient and then reference using a url.

Add the following defs element inside the svg element but before the style element:

```
<defs>
    <linearGradient id = "blueGradient"
                    x1 = "0%"  y1 = "0%"
                    x2 = "100%"  y2 = "100%"
                    spreadMethod = "pad">
      <stop offset = "0%"    stop-color = "#ffffff" stop-opacity = "1"/>
      <stop offset = "50%" stop-color = "#6699cc" stop-opacity = "1"/>
      <stop offset = "100%" stop-color = "#4466aa" stop-opacity = "1"/>
    </linearGradient>
</defs>
```

The defs element is used to define something that can be referred to later in the document. It doesn't do anything until it is actually referenced. Here you are defining a linearGradient element and giving it the id blueGradient. You will reference it using the id attribute.

The attributes are different from the gradients you used in Chapter 4 but accomplish basically the same thing. The x1, y1, x2, and y2 attributes define a vector that specifies the direction of the gradient. In this case, it will start from the top-left corner and go to the bottom-right corner. This specifies three color values that define the gradient color at the beginning, end, and midpoint.

Now add the following path rule at the end of the style element. This will use the new gradient for the state of Wyoming.

```
path[id="WY"]
{
    fill: url(#blueGradient);
}
```

Press F5 to start the application and then go to the map page. You should see a gradient fill for Wyoming as shown in Figure 9-15.

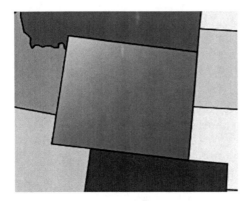

Figure 9-15. *Using a gradient fill*

Using a Background Image

You can also use an image file for the shape background. You will need to first define this as a pattern in the defs element and then reference it just like you did with the gradient. For this exercise you'll use an image of the state flag of Texas and make this the background for that state.

EXERCISE 9-7. USING A BACKGROUND IMAGE

1. In the source code download for Chapter 9 there is a TX_Flag.jpg file; copy this to the Chapter9\Images folder.

2. In the Solution Explorer, right-click the Images folder and select the Add ➤ Existing Item links. Select the TX_Flag.jpg file from the Images folder and click the Add button.

3. Add the following code to the defs element to define the background image. This specifies that the pattern should use the TX_Flag.jpg image file and stretch it to 377 x 226 pixels. This will make it large enough to cover the path element without needing to repeat.

```
<pattern id="TXflag" patternUnits="objectBoundingBox" width="1" height="1">
    <image xlink:href="~/Images/TX_Flag.jpg" x="0" y="0"
            width="377" height="226" />
</pattern>
```

4. Add the following path rule, which will use the new pattern for the state of Texas.

```
path[id="TX"]
{
    fill: url(#TXflag);
}
```

5. Press F5 to start the application and go to the map page. You should see the background image as shown in Figure 9-16.

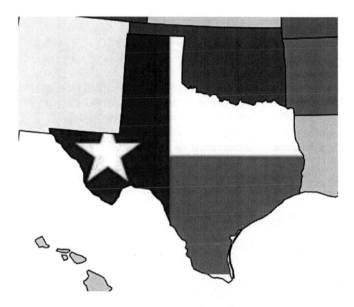

Figure 9-16. *Using a background image*

Since this is a chapter on SVG I felt a little funny about using a bitmap image. You can see the degraded image quality when the image is stretched. The state flag of Texas is one of the easiest to draw with SVG but I wanted to demonstrate that bitmapped images can be used within an SVG definition. But just for the record, here is the flag expressed in SVG (this was downloaded from the same Wikimedia Commons site I mentioned earlier and reformatted slightly).

Listing 9-4. The Texas state flag in SVG

```
<rect width="1080" height="720" fill="#fff"/>
<rect y="360" width="1080" height="360" fill="#bf0a30"/>
<rect width="360" height="720" fill="#002868"/>
<g transform="translate(180,360)" fill="#fff">
```

```
<g id="c">
    <path id="t" d="M 0,-135 v 135 h 67.5"
          transform="rotate(18 0,-135)"/>
    <use xlink:href="#t" transform="scale(-1,1)"/>
</g>
<use xlink:href="#c" transform="rotate(72)"/>
<use xlink:href="#c" transform="rotate(144)"/>
<use xlink:href="#c" transform="rotate(216)"/>
<use xlink:href="#c" transform="rotate(288)"/>
</g>
```

Notice that the group element, g, is used to define a single path. This is rotated with five different angles to create a five-pointed star.

Altering Styles with JavaScript

One of the primary uses of this kind of application is to dynamically style each element based on some external data. For example you might want to highlight states where you have sales locations. Or perhaps you want to set the colors based on some type of demographics such as population. So far you have used only static styles but you can just as easily set the styles using JavaScript.

In this example, you will first set the fill attribute on all path elements to khaki using JavaScript. This will replace the CSS property that sets the default color. This code will then set the fill color of the path element for Virginia. In a real application you would normally define the style based on external data.

This exercise will also show you how to use JavaScript to respond to the onmouseover and onmouseout events. You will replace the path:hover rule and accomplish this using these event handlers.

EXERCISE 9-8. ADJUSTING STYLES USING JAVASCRIPT

1. Add the following script element in the head element of the map.cshtml file.

    ```
    <script type="text/javascript">
        function adjustStates() {
            var paths=document.getElementsByTagName("path");
            for (var i=0; i<paths.length; i++) {
                paths[i].setAttributeNS(null, "fill", "khaki");
            }

            var path=document.getElementById("VA");
            path.setAttributeNS(null, "fill", "teal");
        }
    </script>
    ```

2. In the body element add the onload attribute using the code shown in bold:

    ```
    <body onload="adjustStates()">
    ```

3. In the style element, remove the default khaki fill like this:

```
path
{
stroke: black;
/*fill: khaki; */
}
```

4. Press F5 to start the application and go to the map page. Virginia should no longer use the default color as shown in Figure 9-17.

Figure 9-17. *Virginia styled with JavaScript*

5. Now you'll also use JavaScript to implement the hover style. You can use the `event.target` property to get the `path` element that triggered the event. You can then determine the state code by accessing its `id` attribute. Add the following methods to the existing `script` element.

```
function hoverState(e) {
    var event = e || window.event;
    var state = event.target.getAttributeNS(null, "id");
    var path = document.getElementById(state);
    path.setAttributeNS(null, "fill-opacity", "0.5");
}

function unhoverState(e) {
    var event = e || window.event;
    var state = event.target.getAttributeNS(null, "id");
    var path = document.getElementById(state);
    path.setAttributeNS(null, "fill-opacity", "1.0");
}
```

6. Then bind the `mouseover` and `mouseout` event handlers by adding the code shown in bold to the `adjustStates()` function. This uses the `addEventListener()` method to bind `hoverState()` and `unhoverState()` event handlers to each `path` element.

```
function adjustStates() {
    var paths = document.getElementsByTagName("path");
    for (var i=0; i<paths.length; i++) {
        paths[i].setAttributeNS(null, "fill", "khaki");
```

```
                   paths[i].addEventListener("mouseover", hoverState, true);
                   paths[i].addEventListener("mouseout", unhoverState, true);
               }

               var path = document.getElementById("VA");
               path.setAttributeNS(null, "fill", "teal");
       }
```

■ **Caution** In Internet Explorer, the `event` object is not passed to the event handler. Instead, it is made available through the global `window.event` property. The event handlers can be coded to work with either model by setting the event variable like this: `var event = e || window.event` so it will use the object passed in, if available, and if not, it will use the global `window.event` object. For this to work, however, you must register the event handlers by using the `addEventListener()` method. You cannot simply set the `onmouseover` attribute.

---

7. Remove the `path:hover` style rule like this:

    ```
    /*path:hover
    {
        opacity: .5;
    }*/
    ```

8. Press F5 to start the application and go to the map page. As you move the mouse around, the states should highlight just like they did with the `path:hover` style.

Adding Animation

A typical application of a map like this will allow the user to select a region and then something will happen as a result of that selection. The page would display some information based on the item that was selected. To demonstrate that, you'll add some animation when the user clicks a state. This will be using 3D transforms that are not supported by IE9 so I'll be using Chrome for this demonstration.

The CSS animation that I showed you in Chapter 4 does not work on SVG elements. Instead you'll implement the animation using JavaScript. When a state is selected, you'll first make a copy of the selected element. Then you'll use a timer to gradually change its rotation angle. You need to make a copy so that as the image rotates around it doesn't leave a hole in the map. Also, the new element will be on top of all the others so you don't have to worry about it being hidden by the other elements.

   Once the copy of the element has completed its animation, you'll remove it from the document. Then you'll display an alert showing the state code and state name of the path that was selected.

EXERCISE 9-9. ADDING ANIMATION

1. Because this uses a 3D transform, you'll need to set some of the transform properties on the `path` elements. Add the following rule to the `style` element:

```
path
{
    -webkit-perspective: 200px;
    -webkit-transform-style: preserve-3d;
}
```

2. Then add the code shown in Listing 9-5 to the script element.

Listing 9-5. Adding function to support animation

```
// Setup some global variables
var timer;
var stateCode;
var stateName;
var animate;
var angle;

function selectState(e) {
    var event = e || window.event;

    // Get the state code and state name
    stateCode = event.target.getAttributeNS(null, "id");
    stateName = event.target.getAttributeNS(null, "class");

    // Get the selected path element and then make a copy of it
    var path = document.getElementById(stateCode);
    animate = path.cloneNode(false);

    // Set some display properties and add the copy to the document
    animate.setAttributeNS(null, "fill-opacity", "1.0");
    animate.setAttributeNS(null, "stroke-width", "3");
    document.getElementById("map").appendChild(animate);

    angle = 0;

    // Setup a timer to run every 10 msec
    timer = setInterval(function () { animateState(); }, 10);
}

function animateState() {
    angle += 1;

    // If we've rotated 360 degress, stop the timer, destroy the copy
    // of the element, and show an alert
    if (angle > 360) {
        clearInterval(timer);
        animate.setAttributeNS(null, "visibility", "hidden");
        var old = document.getElementById("map").removeChild(animate);

        alert(stateCode +" - "+ stateName);
```

```
            return;
        }

        // Change the image rotation
        animate.style.webkitTransform = "rotateY(" +Math.round(angle) + "deg)";
    }
```

The selectState() function gets the state code and state name from the selected path element. It then gets the path element and uses its cloneNode() method to make a copy of it. Because the mouse is currently over the selected path, it will have the opacity set to 50%. So this code changes the opacity of the copy to 100%. It also sets the stroke width to give this element a wider border. The copy is then added to the document and a timer is started to cause the animation.

Every 10 milliseconds, the animateState() function is called, which increments the angle and redraws the image. If the rotation has reached 360 degrees, this method cancels the timer and removes the copy of the path element. It also raises an alert to display the state code and state name.

3. Add another event handler by adding the code shown in bold to the adjustStates() function. This will call the selectState() method when the user clicks a path element.

```
function adjustStates() {
    var paths = document.getElementsByTagName("path");
    for (var i=0; i<paths.length; i++) {
        paths[i].setAttributeNS(null, "fill", "khaki");

        paths[i].addEventListener("mouseover", hoverState, true);
        paths[i].addEventListener("mouseout", unhoverState, true);

        paths[i].addEventListener("click", selectState, true);
    }

    var path = document.getElementById("VA");
    path.setAttributeNS(null, "fill", "teal");
}
```

4. Change the debug browser to Chrome. Press F5 to start the application and go to the map page. Click on a state and you should see it fly off the page as shown in Figure 9-18.

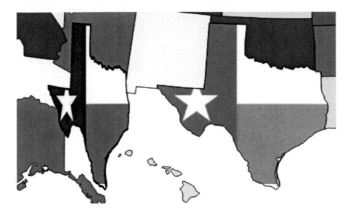

Figure 9-18. *Animating the selected state*

5. The image will then fly back into place and an alert will appear as shown in Figure 9-19.

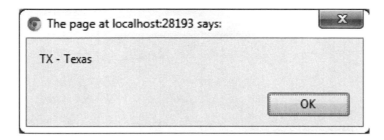

Figure 9-19. *The alert showing the name of the selected state*

Summary

In this chapter I introduced SVG with a couple of fairly simple applications. An SVG image is made up of multiple elements, which can be simple elements such as lines, circles, and rectangles or more complex options like polygons and paths. The key feature of SVG is that each individual element can be styled independently both statically and dynamically. This enables much greater control and interaction. Also, because the image is based on an expression, the images can be scaled without affecting the image quality.

In the exercises in this chapter you:

- Designed an image using simple geometric shapes
- Created a standalone .svg image file
- Displayed a map as a collection of path elements
- Implemented animation on an SVG element

You also used LINQ to SQL to implement a model class that accesses a SQL Server database and then designed a view that creates an SVG image using the model elements.

In the next chapter I'll show you how to use the canvas element to construct graphical elements in HTML5.

CHAPTER 10

Canvas

In this chapter I'll show how to use the canvas element in HTML5 to create some fun graphics. As you'll see, it is very different from SVG, which you explored in the previous chapter. I will discuss the differences in more detail later but the main thing you'll notice is that canvas is completely implemented in JavaScript. The only part that is in the markup is a simple element definition like this:

```
<canvas id="myCanvas" width="400" height="400">
    Canvas is not supported on this browser
</canvas>
```

Instead, you'll define the content by calling the various drawing methods using JavaScript. Just like with the audio and video elements, the markup within the canvas element is used when the browser does not support canvas. You can use this to provide the appropriate fallback content.

Through the exercises in the chapter, you will create three different canvas implementations that, collectively, will demonstrate the capability of canvas. You will create:

- A chess board with moving chess pieces

- A simple model of our solar system

- A page that demonstrates the various ways shapes can be composited.

Of course, you can use your imagination to apply these principles in any number of fun and compelling graphical applications.

Creating a Chess Board

In the first application you'll draw a chess board, which is just a series of squares with alternating colors. I'll show you how to use a gradient to make the board a little more interesting. You'll use image files to draw the chess pieces in the appropriate squares. Finally you'll apply a little bit of animation to move the pieces around the board. This will give you a good sense of how basic drawing techniques are used before getting into more advanced topics.

Creating the Visual Studio Project

You'll start by creating a Visual Studio project using the same Basic MVC template that you have used in previous chapters.

EXERCISE 10-1. CREATING THE VISUAL STUDIO PROJECT

1. Start Visual Studio 2012. In the Start Page, click the New Project link.

2. In the New project dialog box, select the "ASP.NET MVC4 Web Application" template. Enter the project name **Chapter10** and select a location for this project as shown in Figure 10-1.

Figure 10-1. *Creating the Chapter9 project*

3. In the next dialog box, select the Basic template and make sure the Razor view engine is selected. Click the OK button and the project will be created.

4. Right-click the Controller folder in the Solution Explorer and select the Add ➤ Controller links. Enter the name **HomeController** and select the Empty MVC Controller template. Click the Add button to create the controller.

5. Right-click the View folder and select the Add ➤ New Folder links. Enter the name **Home**.

6. Right-click the new Home folder and select the Add ➤ View links. In the Add View dialog box, enter the name **Index**, make sure the Razor view engine is selected, unselect all the check boxes, and click the Add button.

The canvas element is appropriately named as it provides an area that you can use to draw on. When you create a canvas element you define its size using the height and width attribute. You can specify other attributes through markup or CSS to specify the margin, padding, and border. These attributes affect where the element is positioned within the page. However you cannot modify any of the content within the element. The canvas element itself simply defines a blank area on which you can create your masterpiece.

When you create a canvas element in HTML you will generally assign an id attribute so you can access in JavaScript using the getElementById() method. You don't have to; you can access it using the getElementsByTagName() method or use the new query selectors that I described in Chapter 5.

Once you have the canvas element, you'll then get its drawing context by calling getContext(). You must specify which context to use. The context specifies a set of API functions and drawing capabilities. The only one that is generally available is "2d" and we will be using that exclusively in this chapter. There is work being done to define a "3d" context.

Drawing Rectangles

Unlike SVG, the only shape that you can draw directly is a rectangle. You can draw more complex shapes using paths, which I'll explain later. There are three methods that you can use to draw rectangles:

- clearRect() – clears the specified rectangle
- strokeRect() – draws a border around the specified rectangle with no fill
- fillRect() – draws a filled-in rectangle

Each of these methods takes four parameters. The first two define the x and y coordinates of the top-left corner of the rectangle. The last two parameters specify the width and height, respectively. The drawing context has the strokeStyle and fillStyle properties that control how the border or fill will be drawn. You set these before drawing the rectangle. Once set, all subsequent shapes are drawn with these properties until you change the properties.

■ **Tip**   Just like SVG, in canvas, the top-left corner of the canvas element has the x and y coordinates of 0, 0.

To demonstrate drawing rectangles, you'll start by drawing the chess board, which contains eight rows of eight squares each.

EXERCISE 10-2. DRAWING A SIMPLE CHESS BOARD

1. Add a canvas to the index.cshtml page by inserting the following markup in the blank div that was created by the project template:

```
<canvas id="board" width="600" height="600">
    Not supported
</canvas>
```

2. Then add a script element after the div but still inside the body element using the code shown in Listing 10-1.

Listing 10-1. Drawing a simple chess board

```
<script id="chess board" type="text/javascript">
    // Get the canvas context
    var chessCanvas = document.getElementById("board");
    var chessContext = chessCanvas.getContext("2d");

    drawBoard();

    // Draw the chess board
    function drawBoard() {
```

```
            chessContext.clearRect(0, 0, 600, 600);

            chessContext.fillStyle = "red";
            chessContext.strokeStyle = "red";

            // Draw the alternating squares
            for (var x = 0; x < 8; x++) {
                for (var y = 0; y < 8; y++) {
                    if ((x + y) % 2) {
                        chessContext.fillRect(75 * x, 75 * y, 75, 75);
                    }
                }
            }

            // Add a border around the entire board
            chessContext.strokeRect(0, 0, 600, 600);
        }
    </script>
```

3. Save your changes and press F5 to start the application. The page should look like Figure 10-2.

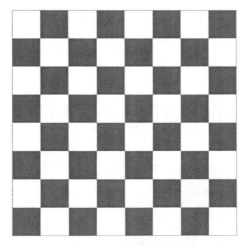

Figure 10-2. The initial chess board

The drawBoard() function first clears the area on which it will be drawing. It then uses nested for loops to draw the squares. Notice that it only draws the red squares. Since the entire area was cleared first, any area not drawn on will be white. This code uses nested for loops to iterate through the eight rows and eight columns. The red squares are the ones where the sum of row and column is odd. For even numbered rows (0, 2, 4, and 6) the odd columns (1, 3, 5, and 7) will be red. For odd-numbered rows, the even-numbered columns will be red. To clean-up the edge squares, a red border is drawn around the entire board.

Using Gradients

You can also use a gradient to fill a shape instead of a solid color. To do that you must first create a gradient object using the drawing context's `createLinearGradient()` method. This method takes four parameters, which are the x and y coordinates of the beginning and ending points of the gradient. This allows you to specify if the gradient should go from top-to-bottom, left-to-right, or corner-to-corner. The gradient is computed across the entire canvas. You cannot define gradients for individual elements.

You must then define the color stops. Each color stop defines a position along the gradient and a color. At a minimum, you'll need a color stop at 0 and 1, which define the beginning and ending colors. You can also add color stops in between these if you want to control the transition. For example, if you want to define the color at the halfway point, use 0.5.

Finally, you'll use this gradient to specify the `fillStyle` property. To try it out, add the following code shown in bold:

```
function drawBoard() {

    chessContext.clearRect(0, 0, 600, 600);

    var gradient = chessContext.createLinearGradient(0, 600, 600, 0);
    gradient.addColorStop(0.0, "#D50005");
    gradient.addColorStop(0.5, "#E27883");
    gradient.addColorStop(1.0, "#FFDDDD");

    chessContext.fillStyle = gradient;
    chessContext.strokeStyle = "red";
```

Save your changes and press F5 to start the application. The page should now look like Figure 10-3. Notice that the color transitions across the canvas, not across each square.

Figure 10-3. *The board using a gradient fill*

Using Images

Now you're ready to add the chess pieces, which will be drawn using image files. It is really easy to add an image to a canvas. You create an Image object, set its `src` property, and then call the drawing context's `drawImage()` method like this:

```
var myImage = new Image();
myImage.src = "Images/sample.jpg";
context.drawImage(myImage, 0,0, 50, 100);
```

The first parameter of the drawImage() method specifies the image that will be drawn. This can be an Image object, as I've shown here. Alternatively, you can also specify an img, video, or canvas element that is already on the page. The next two parameters specify the x and y location of the top-left corner of the image. The fourth and fifth parameters are optional and specify the width and height, respectively, that the image will be scaled to fit into. If you don't specify these parameters the image will be drawn using its intrinsic size.

The drawImage() method also allows you to supply four additional parameters. These are used to specify only the portion of the image that should be displayed on the canvas. These additional parameters include an x and y coordinate and a width and height to define the specified portion. Use the last four parameters if you only want a portion of the image to be drawn. If these are omitted, the entire image will be included.

In this application you will be drawing 32 pieces using 12 different images. Also, later in this chapter you will be adding code to move the pieces around. To facilitate this, you'll add some structure to your application. You will define a class that will store attributes about a chess piece such as the image to use and its location on the board. Then you'll implement a generic drawing function that uses the details from these attributes.

EXERCISE 10-3. DRAWING CHESS PIECES

1. In the Solution Explorer, right-click the Chapter10 project and select the Add ➤ New Folder links. Enter **Images** for the folder name.

2. The images for the chess pieces are included in the source code download file. You'll find these in the Chapter10\Images folder. Drag all 12 files to the Images folder in the Solution Explorer.

3. Add the variable declarations shown in bold in Listing 10-2 to your script element. This will define a variable to reference an Image object for each of the twelve image files. It will also define an array that you will be using to store the chess pieces.

Listing 10-2. Defining the image variables

```
<script type="text/javascript">
    // Get the canvas context
    var chessCanvas = document.getElementById("board");
    var chessContext = chessCanvas.getContext("2d");

    // Define the chess piece images
    var imgPawn = new Image();
    var imgRook = new Image();
    var imgKnight = new Image();
    var imgBishop = new Image();
    var imgQueen = new Image();
    var imgKing = new Image();
    var imgPawnW = new Image();
    var imgRookW = new Image();
    var imgKnightW = new Image();
    var imgBishopW = new Image();
    var imgQueenW = new Image();
    var imgKingW = new Image();
```

```
// Define an array to store 32 pieces
var pieces = new Array(32);

drawBoard();
```

4. Add the `loadImages()` function, shown in Listing 10-3, to your `script` element after the existing `drawBoard()` function.

Listing 10-3. Loading the image files

```
function loadImages() {
    imgPawn.src = "Images/pawn.png";
    imgRook.src = "Images/rook.png";
    imgKnight.src = "Images/knight.png";
    imgBishop.src = "Images/bishop.png";
    imgQueen.src = "Images/queen.png";
    imgKing.src = "Images/king.png";
    imgPawnW.src = "Images/wpawn.png";
    imgRookW.src = "Images/wrook.png";
    imgKnightW.src = "Images/wknight.png";
    imgBishopW.src = "Images/wbishop.png";
    imgQueenW.src = "Images/wqueen.png";
    imgKingW.src = "Images/wking.png";
}
```

5. Now you're ready to define the chess pieces. You'll use a class definition that will store the attributes needed to draw the chess piece. The `image` property contains a reference to the appropriate `Image` object. The x and y properties specify the square that the piece is in, from 0 to 7, left-to-right and top-to-bottom. The `height` and `width` properties indicate the size of the image, which will vary depending on the type of piece. The `killed` property is used to indicate if the piece has been captured. Captured images are not displayed. Add the following code to the end of the script element.

```
// Define a class to store the piece properties
function ChessPiece() {
    this.image = null;
    this.x = 0;
    this.y = 0;
    this.height = 0;
    this.width = 0;
    this.killed = false;
}
```

6. Add the code shown in Listing 10-4 to the end of your `script` element. This implements the `drawPiece()` function that draws a single chess piece based on the class properties. Finally, it provides a `drawAllPieces()` function that will draw each of the pieces defined in the array.

Listing 10-4. Drawing the chess pieces

```
// Draw a chess piece
function drawPiece(p) {
    if (!p.killed)
        chessContext.drawImage(p.image,
                                (75 - p.width) / 2 + (75 * p.x),
                                73 - p.height + (75 * p.y),
                                p.width,
                                p.height);
}

// Draw all of the chess pieces
function drawAllPieces() {
    for (var i = 0; i < 32; i++) {
        if (pieces[i] != null) {
            drawPiece(pieces[i]);
        }
    }
}
```

7. Now you need to create 32 instances of the ChessPiece class and specify all of the appropriate properties. Add the createPieces() function shown in Listing 10-5. This function creates the instances of the ChessPiece class storing them in the pieces array and sets the properties of each one.

■ **Tip** Since this is rather long and tedious, I made this function available in the source code download as a separate file. If you prefer, instead of typing the function from Listing 10-5, you can find the createPieces.js file in the Chapter10 folder and drag this to the Scripts folder in the Solution Explorer. Then add this reference in the head section:

```
<script src = "~/Scripts/createPieces.js"></script>
```

Listing 10-5. Implementing the createPieces() function

```
function createPieces() {
    var piece;

    // Black pawns
    for (var i = 0; i < 8; i++) {
        piece = new ChessPiece();
        piece.image = imgPawn,
        piece.x = i;
        piece.y = 1;
        piece.height = 50;
        piece.width = 28;

        pieces[i] = piece;
    }
```

```
// Black rooks
piece = new ChessPiece();
piece.image = imgRook;
piece.x = 0;
piece.y = 0;
piece.height = 60;
piece.width = 36;
pieces[8] = piece;

piece = new ChessPiece();
piece.image = imgRook;
piece.x = 7;
piece.y = 0;
piece.height = 60;
piece.width = 36;
pieces[9] = piece;

// Black knights
piece = new ChessPiece();
piece.image = imgKnight;
piece.x = 1;
piece.y = 0;
piece.height = 60;
piece.width = 36;
pieces[10] = piece;

piece = new ChessPiece();
piece.image = imgKnight;
piece.x = 6;
piece.y = 0;
piece.height = 60;
piece.width = 36;
pieces[11] = piece;

// Black bishops
piece = new ChessPiece();
piece.image = imgBishop;
piece.x = 2;
piece.y = 0;
piece.height = 65;
piece.width = 30;
pieces[12] = piece;

piece = new ChessPiece();
piece.image = imgBishop;
piece.x = 5;
piece.y = 0;
piece.height = 65;
piece.width = 30;
pieces[13] = piece;
```

```
// Black queen
piece = new ChessPiece();
piece.image = imgQueen;
piece.x = 3;
piece.y = 0;
piece.height = 70;
piece.width = 32;
pieces[14] = piece;

// Black king
piece = new ChessPiece();
piece.image = imgKing;
piece.x = 4;
piece.y = 0;
piece.height = 70;
piece.width = 28;
pieces[15] = piece;

// White pawns
for (var i = 0; i < 8; i++) {
    piece = new ChessPiece();
    piece.image = imgPawnW,
    piece.x = i;
    piece.y = 6;
    piece.height = 50;
    piece.width = 28;

    pieces[16 + i] = piece;
}

// White rooks
piece = new ChessPiece();
piece.image = imgRookW;
piece.x = 0;
piece.y = 7;
piece.height = 60;
piece.width = 36;
pieces[24] = piece;

piece = new ChessPiece();
piece.image = imgRookW;
piece.x = 7;
piece.y = 7;
piece.height = 60;
piece.width = 36;
pieces[25] = piece;

// White knights
piece = new ChessPiece();
piece.image = imgKnightW;
piece.x = 1;
piece.y = 7;
```

```
        piece.height = 60;
        piece.width = 36;
        pieces[26] = piece;

        piece = new ChessPiece();
        piece.image = imgKnightW;
        piece.x = 6;
        piece.y = 7;
        piece.height = 60;
        piece.width = 36;
        pieces[27] = piece;

        // White bishops
        piece = new ChessPiece();
        piece.image = imgBishopW;
        piece.x = 2;
        piece.y = 7;
        piece.height = 65;
        piece.width = 30;
        pieces[28] = piece;

        piece = new ChessPiece();
        piece.image = imgBishopW;
        piece.x = 5;
        piece.y = 7;
        piece.height = 65;
        piece.width = 30;
        pieces[29] = piece;

        // White queen
        piece = new ChessPiece();
        piece.image = imgQueenW;
        piece.x = 3;
        piece.y = 7;
        piece.height = 70;
        piece.width = 32;
        pieces[30] = piece;

        // White king
        piece = new ChessPiece();
        piece.image = imgKingW;
        piece.x = 4;
        piece.y = 7;
        piece.height = 70;
        piece.width = 28;
        pieces[31] = piece;
    }
```

8. Finally, add calls to the `loadImages()`, `createPieces()`, and `drawAllPieces()` functions by adding the following code shown in bold at the beginning of the script element.

```
// Define an array to store 32 pieces
var pieces = new Array(32);

loadImages();

drawBoard();

createPieces()
drawAllPieces();

// Draw the chess board
function drawBoard() {
```

9. Save your changes and press F5 to start the application. You should now see the
    chess pieces as shown in Figure 10-4.

Figure 10-4. *The chess board with the pieces displayed*

■ **Note** When you create an Image object and set its src property, the specified image file is downloaded asynchronously. It's possible that the file has not been loaded before the drawImage() function is called. If this happens,
the image is not displayed. If one or more chess pieces is not displayed, try refreshing the page, which should take
care of this. You can implement the onload event handler for each Image object, which is called when the image has
been loaded. This is a bit complicated since you'll need to wait for all 12 images to be loaded. However, in the next
section you'll just add a pause before drawing the images, which should resolve this.

Adding Simple Animation

To demonstrate simple animation using canvas, you'll move the pieces around. The function that draws each
piece, computes the location based on the square that the piece is in. To move a piece, you just need to update
the x and/or y property and then redraw it.

When you redraw a piece in its new location, it is still visible in the old location as well. Also, if you were to capture a piece by moving a piece in the same square as another, you would end up with two pieces in the same square. You could implement some complex logic to clear the square and redraw a red or white square before moving the piece. However, for this demonstration you will simply clear the entire canvas and redraw the board and all of the pieces.

To implement the automation, you'll create a makeNextMove() function. This will adjust the x and y positions of a chess piece and then redraw the board and all of the pieces. You'll use the setInterval() function to call this repeatedly so the pieces will move in succession.

EXERCISE 10-4. ANIMATING THE CHESS PIECES

1. Add the following variables shown in bold near the beginning of the script element:

```
// Define an array to store 32 pieces
var pieces = new Array(32);

var moveNumber = -1;
var timer;

loadImages();
```

2. Implement the makeNextMove() function shown in Listing 10-6. This code "moves" a piece by adjusting its x and y properties. It keeps track of the move number and uses this to adjust the appropriate piece. The 7th move captures a piece and sets its killed property. Since this ends the animation, the 7th move also uses the clearTimer() function so no more timer events will occur. After each move, the board and all the pieces are re-drawn. After the 7th move, this function also uses the fillText() method, which is used to write text to the canvas.

Listing 10-6. The makeNextMove implementation

```
function makeNextMove() {
    function inner() {
        if (moveNumber === 1) {
            pieces[20].y--;
        }
        if (moveNumber === 2) {
            pieces[4].y += 2;
        }
        if (moveNumber === 3) {
            pieces[29].y = 4;
            pieces[29].x = 2;
        }
        if (moveNumber === 4) {
            pieces[6].y++;
        }
        if (moveNumber === 5) {
            pieces[30].x = 5;
            pieces[30].y = 5;
        }
```

```
            if (moveNumber === 6) {
                pieces[7].y++;
            }
            if (moveNumber === 7) {
                pieces[30].x = 5;
                pieces[30].y = 1;
                pieces[5].killed = true;
                clearInterval(timer);
            }

            moveNumber++;

            drawBoard();
            drawAllPieces();

            if (moveNumber > 7) {
                chessContext.font = "30 pt Arial";
                chessContext.fillStyle = "black";
                chessContext.fillText("Checkmate!", 200, 220);
            }
        }

        return inner;
    }
```

3. Go to the beginning of the `script` element and replace the call to `drawAllPieces()` with this:

    ```
    timer = setInterval(makeNextMove(), 2000);
    ```

4. Save your changes and press F5 to start the application. After a series of moves the page should look like Figure 10-5.

Figure 10-5. *The completed chess board*

■ **Caution**   The makeNextMove() function uses an often misunderstood feature of JavaScript called closure. This function defines another function called inner(), which does the actual work. The inner() function is then returned. The makeNextMove() function will be called by the window object when the timer expires. However, all of the variables that it uses, such as the array of chess pieces, will be out of scope. The inner() function will be able to access these variables so this works around the scope issue. For more information about closures, see this article: http://stackoverflow.com/questions/111102/how-do-javascript-closures-work.

Modeling the Solar System

For the next canvas you'll draw a moving model of our solar system. For the sake of time, you'll show only the earth, sun, and moon. This implementation will take advantage of two important features of canvas:

- Paths

- Transformations

Using Paths

As I mentioned earlier, the only simple shape that canvas supports is the rectangle, which you used in the previous example. For all other shapes you must define a path. The basic approach to defining paths in canvas is very similar to SVG. You use a move to command to set the starting point and then some combination of line and curve commands to draw a shape.

In canvas, you always start with a beginPath() command. After calling the desired drawing commands, the path is completed by either calling stroke() to draw an outline of the shape or fill() to fill in the shape. The shape is not actually drawn to the canvas until either stroke() or fill() is called. If you call beginPath() again, before completing the current shape (with a call to stroke() or fill()), the canvas will ignore the previous uncompleted commands. The same strokeStyle and fillStyle properties that you used with rectangles also define the color of the path.

The actual drawing commands are:

- moveTo()

- lineTo()

- arcTo()

- bezierCurveTo()

- quadraticCurveTo()

In addition, these functions can be used for drawing:

- closePath() – this performs a lineTo() command from the current position to the starting position to close in the shape. If you use the fill() command, the closePath() function is automatically called if you're not currently at the starting position.

- arc() – This draws an arc at the specified location; you don't have to move there first. However, this is still treated as a path; you need to first call beginPath() and the arc is not actually drawn until you call either stroke() or fill().

Drawing Arcs

The `arc()` command is one that you'll likely use a lot and will be important in this example. The `arc()` command takes the following parameters:

```
arc(x, y, radius, start, end, counterclockwise)
```

The first two parameters specify the x and y coordinates of the center point. The third parameter specifies the radius. The fourth and fifth parameters determine the starting and ending point of the arc. These are specified as an angle from the x axis. The 0° angle is the right-hand side of the circle; a 90° angle would be the bottom edge of the circle. The angles are specified in radians, however, not degrees.

Unless you're drawing a full circle, the direction of the arc is important. For example if you drew an arc from 0° to 90°, the arc would be ¼ of a circle, from the right-hand side to the bottom. However, using the same end points but drawing in a counter-clockwise direction, that arc would be ¾ of the circle. The final parameter, if true, indicates that the arc should be draw in a counter-clock-wise direction. This parameter is optional. If you don't specify, it will draw the arc in a clockwise direction.

Using Transformations

At first, transformations in canvas may seem a bit confusing but they can be quite helpful once you understand how they work. First, transformations have no effect on what has already been drawn on the canvas. Instead, transformations modify the grid system that will be used to draw subsequent shapes. I will demonstrate three types of transformations in this chapter:

- Translating

- Rotating

- Scaling

As I mentioned earlier, a canvas `element` uses a grid system where the origin is at the top-left corner of the canvas. So a point at 10, 20 will be 10 pixels to the right and 20 pixels down from that corner. Transformations simply adjust the grid system. For example, the following command will shift the origin 100 pixels to the right and 50 pixels down:

```
context.translate (100, 50);
```

This is illustrated in Figure 10-6.

Figure 10-6. *Translating the context origin*

So now when you move to 10, 20, since this is relative to the new origin, the actual position (relative to the canvas), will be 110, 70. You might be wondering why you would want to do this. Well, suppose you were drawing a picture of the United States flag, which has 50 stars on it. A five-pointed star is a fairly complex shape to draw, which will require a number of drawing commands. Once you have drawn the first star, you'll need to repeat the process 49 more times, with each time using different values.

By simply translating the context to the right a little, you can repeat the exact same commands using the same values. But now the star will be in a different location. Granted, you could accomplish the same thing by creating a drawStar() function that accepted x, y parameters. Then call this 50 times passing in different values. However, once you get used to using transformation you will find this easier, especially with the other types such as rotation.

The rotate transformation doesn't move the origin; instead it rotates the x and y axis by the specified amount. A positive amount is used for a clockwise rotation and a negative value is used to rotate counter-clockwise. Figure 10-7 demonstrates how a rotate transformation works.

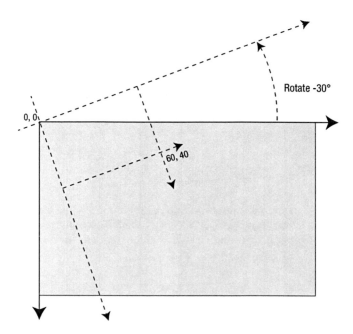

Figure 10-7. *Rotating the drawing context's grid*

■ **Note**   I indicated the rotation angle as 30° since that is what most people are familiar with. However, the rotate() command expects the value in radians. If your geometry is a little rusty, a full circle is 360° or 2π radians. In JavaScript you can use the Math.PI property to get the value of π (Pi). For example, 30° is 1/12 of a full circle so you can write this as (Math.PI*2/12).

You can use multiple transformations. For example, you can translate the origin and then rotate the x/y axis. You can also rotate the grid some more and translate again. Each transformation is always relative to the current position and orientation.

Saving the Context State

The state of a drawing context includes the various properties such as `fillStyle` and `strokeStyle` that you have already used. It also includes the accumulation of all transformations that have been applied. If you start using multiple transformations, getting back to the original state may be difficult. Fortunately, the drawing context provides the ability to save and then restore the state of the context.

The current state is saved by calling the `save()` function. Saving the state pushes the current state onto a stack. Calling the `restore()` function pops the most recently saved state off of the stack and makes that the current state. This is illustrated in Figure 10-8.

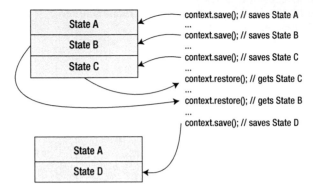

Figure 10-8. *Saving and restoring the drawing context state*

You should generally save the state before doing any transformations, especially complex ones. When you have finished drawing whatever elements needed the transformation, you can restore the state back to the way it was. Remember, changing the state by setting the `fillStyle` or performing a transformation does not affect what has already been drawn.

Drawing the Solar System

With these features at your disposal, let's draw a simple model of the solar system.

EXERCISE 10-5. MODELING THE SOLAR SYSTEM

1. Open the `index.cshtml` file and add the `canvas` element shown in bold just after the existing `canvas` element:

```
<div>
    <canvas id = "board" width = "600" height = "600">
        Not supported
    </canvas>
    <canvas id = "solarSystem" width = "450" height = "400">
        Not supported
    </canvas>

</div>
```

2. Add a new script element in the body element just after the existing script element using the code shown in Listing 10-7.

Listing 10-7. Initial solar system implementation

```
<script id = "solar system" type = "text/javascript">

    var ss = document.getElementById('solarSystem')
    var ssContext = ss.getContext('2d');

    setInterval(animateSS, 100);

    function animateSS() {
        var ss = document.getElementById('solarSystem')
        var ssContext = ss.getContext('2d');

        // Clear the canvas and draw the background
        ssContext.clearRect(0, 0, 450, 400);
        ssContext.fillStyle = "#2F1D92";
        ssContext.fillRect(0, 0, 450, 400);

        ssContext.save();

        // Draw the sun
        ssContext.translate(220, 200);
        ssContext.fillStyle = "yellow";
        ssContext.beginPath();
        ssContext.arc(0, 0, 15, 0, Math.PI * 2, true);
        ssContext.fill();

        // Draw the earth orbit
        ssContext.strokeStyle = "black";
        ssContext.beginPath();
        ssContext.arc(0, 0, 150, 0, Math.PI * 2);
        ssContext.stroke();

        ssContext.restore()
    }
</script>
```

■ **Tip** In Visual Studio, you can collapse an HTML element in the editor. Since you're done with the previous script element you can collapse it, which will make it easier to see the new element that you'll be working on. While you don't need to set the id attribute of a script element, if you do, it will be displayed when the element is collapsed as demonstrated in Figure 10-9. This will make it easier to view pages with multiple script elements.

```
<!DOCTYPE html>

<html>
<head>...</head>
<body>
    <div>
        <canvas id="board" width ="600" height ="600">
            Not supported
        </canvas>
        <canvas id="solarSystem" width="450" height="400">
            Not supported
        </canvas>
    </div>
    <script id="chess board">...</script>
    <script id="solar system" type="text/javascript">

        var ss = document.getElementById('solarSystem')
        var ssContext = ss.getContext('2d');

        setInterval(animateSS, 100);
```

Figure 10-9. *Collapsing the script element*

3. This code gets the `canvas` element and then obtains the 2d drawing context, just like the previous example. It then uses the `setInterval()` function to call the `animateSS()` function every 100 milliseconds. The `animateSS()` function is what does the real work. It clears the entire area and then fills it with dark blue color. The rest of the code relies on transformations so it first saves the drawing context and then restores it when finished.

4. This `animateSS()` function uses the `translate()` function to move the origin to the approximate midpoint of the canvas. The sun and the earth orbit are drawn using the `arc()` function. Notice the center point for both is 0, 0 since the context's origin is now in the middle of the canvas. Also notice the start angle is 0 and the end angle is specified as `Math.PI * 2`. In radians, this is a full circle or 360°. The arc for the sun is filled in and the orbit is not.

5. Press F5 to start the application. So far, the drawing is not very interesting; a sun with an orbit drawn around it as shown in Figure 10-10.

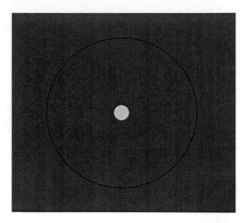

Figure 10-10. *The initial solar system drawing*

6. Now you'll draw the earth and animate it around the orbit. Normally the earth will revolve around the sun once every 365.24 days but we'll speed this up a bit and complete the trip in 60 seconds. To determine where to put the earth each time the canvas is redrawn, you must calculate the number of seconds. The amount of rotation per second is calculated as Math.PI *2 / 60. Multiply this value by the number of seconds to determine the angle where the earth should be.

7. Add the code from Listing 10-8 that is shown in bold. This code uses the rotate() function to rotate the drawing context the appropriate angle. Since the arc for the earth orbit is 150 px, this code then uses the translate() function to move the context 150 pixels to the right so the earth can be drawn at the adjusted 0,0 coordinate. The earth is then drawn using a filled arc with a center point of 0,0, the new origin of the context.

Listing 10-8. Drawing the earth

```
// Draw the earth orbit
ssContext.scale(1.1, 1);
ssContext.strokeStyle = "black";
ssContext.beginPath();
ssContext.arc(0, 0, 150, 0, Math.PI * 2);
ssContext.stroke();

// Compute the current time in seconds (use the milliseconds
// to allow for fractional parts).
var now = new Date();
var seconds = ((now.getSeconds() * 1000)+now.getMilliseconds()) / 1000;

//---------------------------------------------
// Earth
//---------------------------------------------
// Rotate the context once every 60 seconds
var anglePerSecond = ((Math.PI * 2) / 60);
ssContext.rotate(anglePerSecond * seconds);
ssContext.translate(150, 0);
```

```
// Draw the earth
ssContext.fillStyle = "green";
ssContext.beginPath();
ssContext.arc(0, 0, 10, 0, Math.PI * 2, true);
ssContext.fill();

ssContext.restore()
```

8. Save your changes and press F5 to start the application. Now you should see the earth make its way around the sun as shown in Figure 10-11.

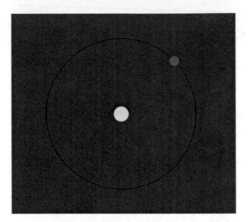

Figure 10-11. *Adding the earth to the drawing*

9. Now you'll show the moon revolving around the earth, which will demonstrate the real power of using transformations. The specific position of the moon is based on two moving objects. While it's certainly possible to compute this using some complex formulas (scientists have been doing this for centuries) with transformations, you don't have to. The drawing context was rotated the appropriate angle based on current time (number of seconds). It was then translated by the radius of the orbit so the earth is now at the origin of the context. It doesn't really matter where the earth is, we can simply draw the moon relative to the current origin.

10. You will now draw the moon just like you drew the earth. Instead of the origin being at the sun and rotating the earth around the sun, the origin is on the earth and you'll rotate the moon around the earth. The moon will rotate around the sun approximately once each month, or in other words, it will complete about 12 revolutions for each earth orbit. So you'll need to rotate 12 times faster. The `anglePerSecond` is now computed as `12 * ((Math.PI * 2) / 60)`. Add the code shown in bold in Listing 10-9.

Listing 10-9. Drawing the moon

```
// Draw the earth
ssContext.fillStyle = "green";
ssContext.beginPath();
ssContext.arc(0, -0, 10, 0, Math.PI * 2, true);
ssContext.fill();

//-------------------------------------------
// Moon
//-------------------------------------------
// Rotate the context 12 times for every earth revolution
anglePerSecond = 12 * ((Math.PI * 2) / 60);
ssContext.rotate(anglePerSecond * seconds);
ssContext.translate(0, 35);

// draw the moon
ssContext.fillStyle = "white";
ssContext.beginPath();
ssContext.arc(0, 0, 5, 0, Math.PI * 2, true);
ssContext.fill();

ssContext.restore()
```

■ **Note** There are actually about 12.368 lunar months per solar year. You can make your model more accurate by using this figure instead of 12 in the preceding code.

---

11. Save your changes and press F5 to start the application. You should now see the moon rotating around the earth as shown in Figure 10-12.

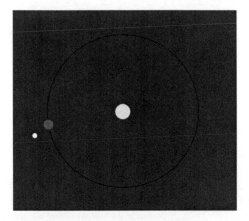

Figure 10-12. Including the moon

Applying Scaling

Before you finish up this model, there's one minor correction that you'll make. The earth's orbit is not actually a perfect circle. This attribute is known as eccentricity. (If you're curious about orbital eccentricity, check out the article at http://en.wikipedia.org/wiki/Orbital_eccentricity.) To model this in your drawing you'll stretch the orbit, making it a little bit wider than it is tall. To do this you'll use scaling.

The scale() function performs the third type of transformation. This function takes two parameters that specify the scaling along the x and y axis. A scale factor of 1 is the normal scale. A factor less than one will compress the drawing and a factor greater than 1 will stretch it. While the imperfection in the earth's orbit is extremely slight, you'll exaggerate it here and use a scale factor of 1.1 for the x axis.

Add the following code shown in bold just before the earth orbit is drawn:

```
// Draw the earth orbit
ssContext.scale(1.1, 1);
ssContext.strokeStyle = "black";
```

Press F5 to start the application, which should look like Figure 10-13.

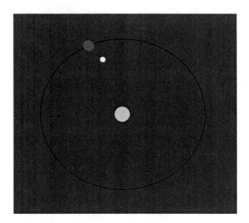

Figure 10-13. *Adding scaling*

You now have a slightly out-of-shape orbit. By simply changing the scale factor all the various drawing elements were adjusted proportionally. Also, after restoring the context, the scaling is restored to normal so subsequent elements are drawn correctly.

Clipping a Canvas

I want to cover one more feature related to paths. Earlier I said that after you call beginPath() and then the desired drawing functions, you can either call stroke() or fill(). There is one more function you can call as well: clip(). The clip() function will use the path that you just defined and will not allow anything to be drawn outside of that path. This doesn't affect what has already been drawn but any future shapes will be restricted to the clipping area defined by this path.

To demonstrate this, you'll go back to the chess board example and define a clipping path using an arc. Go to the board script element and add the code shown in bold to the drawBoard() function:

```
var gradient = chessContext.createLinearGradient(0, 600, 600, 0);
gradient.addColorStop(0, "#D50005");
gradient.addColorStop(0.5, "#E27883");
gradient.addColorStop(1, "#FFDDDD");

// Clip the path
chessContext.beginPath();
chessContext.arc(300, 300, 300, 0, (Math.PI * 2), true);
chessContext.clip();

chessContext.fillStyle = gradient;
chessContext.strokeStyle = "red";

// Draw the alternating squares
```

This defines a circle on the board and anything outside of that circle will not be visible. Press F5 to start the application, which should look like Figure 10-14.

Figure 10-14. *The chess board with a clipping path*

■ **Note** If you define the clipping path after the board is drawn, the entire board will be drawn but the pieces will be cropped so any part that is outside the clipping area will be hidden.

Understanding Compositing

With all the shapes you have drawn so far, the one drawn last overlaid, or hid, whatever preceded it. This behavior is referred to as compositing. The default behavior, called source-over, is as we've seen, to draw the current shape on top of whatever may already be on the canvas. However, there are 11 other behaviors that you can configure using the globalCompositeOperation property. These are best explained by seeing a sample of each.

In this exercise you will overlap a red square with a blue circle. You will do this 12 times, each time using a different value for the globalCompositeOperation property. To make this work correctly, you'll create 12 canvas elements, drawing the same elements on each.

EXERCISE 10-6. EXPLORING COMPOSITING

1. In the main div element, comment out the board and solarSystem canvas elements and create twelve new canvas elements using the code shown in Listing 10-10.

Listing 10-10. Creating twelve canvas elements

```
<div>
    <div>
        <canvas id = "composting1" width = "120" height = "120"></canvas>
        <br />source-over
    </div>
    <div>
        <canvas id = "composting2" width = "120" height = "120"></canvas>
        <br />destination-over
    </div>
    <div>
        <canvas id = "composting3" width = "120" height = "120"></canvas>
        <br />source-in
    </div>
    <div>
        <canvas id = "composting4" width = "120" height = "120"></canvas>
        <br />destination-in
    </div>
    <div>
        <canvas id = "composting5" width = "120" height = "120"></canvas>
        <br />source-out
    </div>
    <div>
        <canvas id = "composting6" width = "120" height = "120"></canvas>
        <br />destination-out
    </div>
    <div>
        <canvas id = "composting7" width = "120" height = "120"></canvas>
        <br />source-atop
    </div>
    <div>
        <canvas id = "composting8" width = "120" height = "120"></canvas>
        <br />destination-atop
    </div>
    <div>
        <canvas id = "composting9" width = "120" height = "120"></canvas>
        <br />xor
    </div>
    <div>
        <canvas id = "composting10" width = "120" height = "120"></canvas>
        <br />copy
    </div>
    <div>
        <canvas id = "composting11" width = "120" height = "120"></canvas>
        <br />lighter
    </div>
```

```
<div>
    <canvas id = "composting12" width = "120" height = "120"></canvas>
    <br />darker
</div>

<!-- < canvas id = "board" width = "600" height = "600">
    Not supported
</canvas>
<canvas id = "solarSystem" width = "450" height = "400">
    Not supported
</canvas>-->
</div>
```

2. Add the following `style` element in the `head` section. This will format the `canvas`
   elements into three columns so you can see all 12 examples on one screen.

```
<style>
    body div
    {
        -webkit-column-count: 3;
        column-count: 3;
    }
</style>
```

3. Collapse the solar system `script` element.

4. Add the `script` element shown in Listing 10-11 to the `body` element, just after the
   existing `script` elements.

Listing 10-11. Drawing the compositing canvases

```
<script id = "compositing" type = "text/javascript">
    for (var i = 1; i < = 12; i++) {
        var c = document.getElementById("composting"+i);
        var cContext = c.getContext("2d");

        cContext.fillStyle = "red";
        cContext.fillRect(10, 20, 80, 80);

        switch (i) {
            case 1: cContext.globalCompositeOperation = "source-over"; break;
            case 2: cContext.globalCompositeOperation = "destination-over"; break;
            case 3: cContext.globalCompositeOperation = "source-in"; break;
            case 4: cContext.globalCompositeOperation = "destination-in"; break;
            case 5: cContext.globalCompositeOperation = "source-out"; break;
            case 6: cContext.globalCompositeOperation = "destination-out"; break;
            case 7: cContext.globalCompositeOperation = "source-atop"; break;
            case 8: cContext.globalCompositeOperation = "destination-atop"; break;
            case 9: cContext.globalCompositeOperation = "xor"; break;
            case 10: cContext.globalCompositeOperation = "copy"; break;
            case 11: cContext.globalCompositeOperation = "lighter"; break;
            case 12: cContext.globalCompositeOperation = "darker"; break;
        }
```

```
            cContext.fillStyle = "blue";
            cContext.beginPath();
            cContext.arc(65, 75, 40, 0, (Math.PI * 2), true);
            cContext.fill();
        }
    </script>
```

5. This code uses a for loop to process all 12 canvas elements. It gets the corresponding element and then obtains its drawing context. It adds a red square and then sets the globalCompositeOperation property. Finally, it adds a blue circle.

6. Change the debugging browser to use Chrome as this supports all of the compositing options (as well as the multi-column support).

7. Save your changes and press F5 to start the application. The web page should look like Figure 10-15.

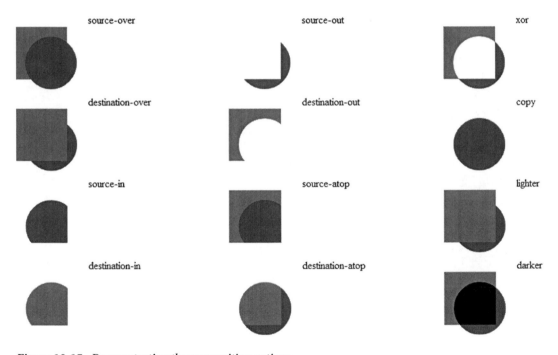

Figure 10-15. *Demonstrating the compositing options*

The compositing options are:

- source-over – This is the default operation. The source element (the element being added) is drawn on top of the destination (whatever is already in this location).

- destination-over – This is the opposite of source-over, where the source element is added underneath the existing elements.

- source-in – Only the portion of the source object that is also in a destination element is displayed. Note that none of the destination element is displayed; it is being used like a clipping shape.

- `destination-in` – Only the portion of the destination object that is also in the source element is displayed.

- `source-out` – Only the portion of the source element that does not overlap the destination element is displayed.

- `destination-out` – Only the portion of the destination element that does not overlap the source element is displayed.

- `source-atop` – The source is displayed on top of the destination element but the entire shape is clipped by the destination element.

- `destination-atop` – The source is displayed beneath the destination element but the entire shape is clipped by the source element.

- `xor` – Only the portions of the source and destination elements that do not overlap are displayed.

- `copy` – The name is misleading. This draws the source elements and clears everything else.

- `lighter` – This draws both the source and destination elements and the overlapping area is displayed in a lighter color. The actual color is determined by adding the color values of the source and destination elements.

- `darker` – draws both the source and destination elements and the overlapping area is displayed in a darker color. The actual color is determined by subtracting the color values of the source and destination elements.

▓ **Tip** Some of the names of these compositing options may not be very intuitive. I suggest that you keep this figure handy to refer to later in case you don't remember what copy does, for example.

Summary

In this chapter, you used the canvas element to create some graphical web pages. You used rectangles and paths to draw shapes on the canvas. You also included images on your the canvas. One of the really powerful features of canvas is the ability to apply transformations. The appropriate use of transformations can really simplify some complex drawing applications.

Canvas is fundamentally very different from SVG. In SVG, each shape is a separate DOM node. This provides two important features that you cannot do with canvas:

1. Attach event handlers to individual shapes

2. Individual shapes can be manipulated. A good example of this is defining the `:hover` pseudo rule, which allows the shape's attributes to be changed when the mouse is hovered over it.

In contrast to SVG, canvas is pixel based, which means it is resolution dependent. Notice that all of the drawing commands used pixel locations or sizes. When you draw a shape on a canvas element, the pixels of that canvas are adjusted as appropriate and all that is remembered in the resulting pixel content.

Canvas will tend to be more efficient because of its raw pixel manipulation. SVG on the other hand must perform a lot of rendering (and re-rendering). However, larger images with less dense content, such as maps, will generally perform better in SVG.

PART 4

■ ■ ■

Digging Deeper

In this part, I will explain several miscellaneous features that enable some advanced capabilities using JavaScript. Chapter 11 demonstrates how to use Indexed DB to create and access client-side persistent databases. In Chapter 12, you'll use the geolocation support in HTML5 to determine the user's current position. You then use Bing Maps to display this location along with a number of points of interest.

In Chapter 13, you'll use websockets to implement a multi-client chat solution. This includes creating the socket server using Visual Studio 2012. Finally in Chapter 14 I'll show you how to use the drag-and-drop feature to create user experiences that rival desktop solutions.

CHAPTER 11

■ ■ ■

Indexed DB

As browser technology has evolved, providing more and more functionality on the client device, the need to store and manipulate data locally has increased as well. To address this need, two competing technologies have emerged:

- Web SQL – An SQL engine hosted within the browser.

- Indexed DB – An API for storing and retrieving objects using keys and indices.

■ **Note** In November 2010, the W3C Working Group decided to stop work on Web SQL and it is no longer part of the HTML5 specifications. Several browsers still support it however, but its adoption as a cross-platform standard is unlikely.

This chapter will demonstrate how to use Indexed DB to store and use data on the client. If you are used to working with SQL databases, I will warn you, this is not an SQL database. It is quite powerful and useful once you get the hang of it but you'll need to adjust your perspective and set aside your SQL experience as you work through this chapter.

To explore the capabilities of Indexed DB you will re-write the chess board application that you created using canvas in Chapter 10. As I explain each of the exercises I will not go into much detail about canvas; however, refer to Chapter 10 if you need more information. Your new version of the application will create object stores to define the positions of each piece and then manipulate this data as the pieces are moved.

Introducing Indexed DB

Before I get started with the detailed demonstration, there are a few key points that I think will help you better understand how Indexed DB works. Like other databases, the data is placed in a persistent data store. In this case on the local hard drive. The data is permanent.

Using Object Stores

The primary storage unit is called an object store. This is aptly named as they are simply a collection of objects that are referenced by a key. You can think of this as a set of name-value pairs, the value being an object with a set of properties. You can use an *in-line* key, where one of the object properties serves as the key. For example, if the object has an id property with unique values, you can use that as the in-line key. If you use *out-of-line* keys, then you will specify a key when adding an object to the store. Alternatively, you can use a *key generator*, where the object store will assign incremental key values for you. The following code demonstrates these alternatives:

```
// Using an inline key
var typeStore = db.createObjectStore("pieceType", { keyPath: "id" });
typeStore.add(pieceType);

// Using an out-of-line key
var sampleStore = db.createObjectStore("sample", { });
sampleStore.add(sample, 5);

// Using a key generator
var pieceStore = db.createObjectStore("piece", { autoIncrement: true });
pieceStore.add(piece);
```

As its name implies, you can also create an index on an object store; in fact you can create as many indices as you want. An index enables you to find a specific object or collection of objects quickly. An index is a collection of name-value pairs, where the value is a key into the object store. For example, if you have a customer object store and wanted to search by last name you can create an index on the lastName property of the object. The database will automatically create an entry in the index for each object in the store. This entry will contain the last name and the corresponding key to that object. The following code demonstrates how to use an index:

```
// Create an index on the lastName property
customerStore.createIndex("lastName", "pos", { unique: true });

// Get the index
var index = custStore.index("lastName");
index.get(lastName).onsuccess = function();      // get the object
index.getKey(lastName).onsuccess = function();   // get the key
```

Indexed DB does not support relationships between object stores. You can't enforce a foreign key relationship for example. You can certainly use foreign keys, where a property in one object store is a key into another, as I will demonstrate later. However, the database does not enforce this constraint. Also, you can't perform joins between objects stores.

Processing Asynchronously

A key aspect of Indexed DB that may take some getting used to is its asynchronous processing; almost all database operations are done asynchronously. The general pattern is to call a method to perform a database operation such as opening a database or retrieving a set of records (objects). This will return a request object. You must then implement the onsuccess and onerror event handlers for that request object. If the request was successful, the onsuccess handler is called and the result of the method call is passed through the event object.

■ **Tip** The onerror event is bubbled up the hierarchy. For example, an error that occurs on the request object, if not handled will be raised on the transaction object. If not handled there it will be raised on the database object. In many cases, you can just use a single event handler at the database level and handle all the errors there.

For complex processing that requires several database calls, you'll need to be careful to nest the event handlers and consider when they are executed. For example, if you needed to make three database requests, your code might look like this:

```
var request = dbCall1()
request.onsuccess = function (e1) {
    f1(e1.target.result);

    dbCall2().onsuccess = function (e2) {
        f3(e2.target.result, e1.target.result);

        dbCall3().onsuccess = function (e3) {
            f5(e3.target.result, e2.target.result, e1.target.result);
        }

        f4(e2.target.result);
    }

    f2(e1.target.result);
}
request.onerror = function(e) {
    alert("The call failed")
}
```

This code calls dbCall1(), dbCall2(), and dbCall3(), in that order and they will be processed sequentially. In other words, dbCall2() will not start until dbCall1() has completed, and only if it was successful. Each call provides an onsuccess event handler, which makes the next call. If the first call fails, an alert is raised. What may be unexpected is the order that the non-database calls are executed. The database calls return immediately and the event handler is called later, when the operation has completed. As soon as the call to dbCall2() is made, the function returns and f2() will be executed. Then later, the dbCall2() completes, its event handler is called and f3() is executed.

Because of the nesting approach, the event handler has access to the event object from previous calls. For this reason, you should use unique names for the event parameter. This will avoid ambiguity. Also, notice the use of closure to access these event objects. As I mentioned, f2() is called before f3() so the event handler for dbCall1() which defines the e1 parameter, has completed and is no longer in scope by the time the event handler for dbCall2() is executed. The closure feature of JavaScript allows the subsequent event handlers to access this object. This is important because if you need to access all three object stores to complete an operation, you will need to wait until all three have completed and then access all three results.

■ **Tip**   To avoid closure, you could extract the properties that you need from the first two database calls and store them in local variables (declared prior to the dbCall1() call. Then in the f5() call you can use these variables instead of the e1 and e2 event objects. This is just a matter of preference, as either approach will work fine.

Using Transactions

All data access, both reading and writing, is done within a transaction, so you must first create a transaction object. When the transaction is created you specify its scope, which is defined by the object stores it will access.

You also specify the mode (read-only or read/write). You can then obtain an object store from the transaction and get or put data from/into the store like this:

```
var xact = db.transaction(["piece", "pieceType"], "readwrite");
var pieceStore = xact.objectStore("piece");
```

For read/write transactions, the data changes are not committed until the transaction completes. The interesting question to ask is "when does a transaction complete?" A transaction is complete when there are no more outstanding requests for it. Remember, everything is request-based. You make a request and then implement an event handler to do something when it finishes. If that event handler issues another request on that transaction then the transaction stays alive. This is another important reason for nesting the event handlers. If you end an event handler without issuing another request, the transaction will complete and all changes are committed. If you try to use the transaction after that, you will get a TRANSACTION_INACTIVE_ERR error.

Another thing to remember is that read/write transactions cannot have overlapping scopes. If you create a read/write transaction, you can create a second one as long as they don't both include some of the same object stores. If they have overlapping scopes, you must wait for the first transaction to complete before creating the second one. Read-only transactions, however, can have overlapping scopes.

Defining the Database

When you open a database you need to implement three event handlers:

- onsuccess – the database is opened, do something with it

- onerror – an error occurred, likely an access issue

- onupgradeneeded – the database needs to be created or upgraded

When opening a database, if it doesn't exist, it will be created automatically, however the onupgradeneeded event will be raised. You must implement an event handler for this event, which will create object stores and populate them with any default data. This is the only place where you are allowed to alter the database structure. The important thing to remember is that the onupgradeneeded event is fired before the onsuccess event.

The open() call also specifies a version number. If this is not the current version, the onupgradeneeded event is raises in this scenario also. Your event handler needs to handle both creating a database from scratch because none exists as well as altering the structure. You can query the database's current version to perform the necessary steps like this:

```
var request = dbEng.open("Sample", 2); // get version 2

request.onupgradeneeded = function (event) {
    alert("Configuring database - current version is " + e.oldVersion +
          ", requested version is " + e.newVersion);
}
```

Creating the Application

For this application I will be using the Firefox browser since it fully supports the current draft of the Indexed DB specification. The only browsers that support Indexed DB are Chrome and Firefox, although IE10 is expected to support it. The current version of Chrome does not implement the onupgradeneeded event however.

Creating the Visual Studio Project

You'll start by creating a Visual Studio project using the same Basic MVC template that you have used in previous chapters.

EXERCISE 11-1. CREATING THE VISUAL STUDIO PROJECT

1. Start Visual Studio 2012. In the Start Page, click the New Project link.

2. In the New project dialog box, select the "ASP.NET MVC4 Web Application" template. Enter the project name **Chapter11** and select a location for this project as shown in Figure 11-1.

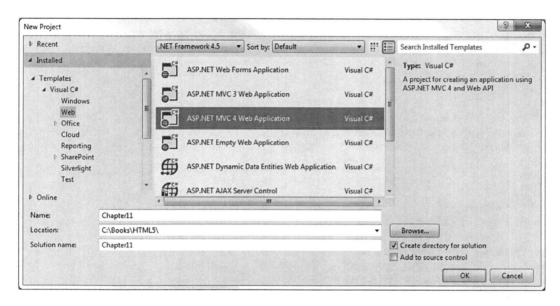

Figure 11-1. Creating the Chapter11 project

3. In the next dialog box, select the Basic template and make sure the Razor view engine is selected. Click the OK button and the project will be created.

4. Right-click the Controller folder in the Solution Explorer and select the Add ➤ Controller links. Enter the name **HomeController** and select the Empty MVC Controller template. Click the Add button to create the controller.

5. Right-click the View folder and select the Add ➤ New Folder links. Enter the name **Home**.

6. Right-click the new Home folder and select the Add ➤ View links. In the Add View dialog box, enter the name **Index**, make sure the Razor view engine is selected, unselect all the check boxes, and click the Add button.

7. In the Index.cshtml file, in the empty div that was created, add the following markup:

```
<canvas id = "board" width = "600" height = "600">
    Not supported
</canvas>
```

8. In the Solution Explorer, right-click the Chapter11 project and select the
    Add ➤ New Folder links. Enter **Images** for the folder name.

9. The images for the chess pieces are included in the source code download file.
    These are the same images used in Chapter 10. You'll find these in the Chapter10\
    Images folder. Drag all 12 files to the Images folder in the Solution Explorer.

Creating the Canvas

Now you'll design the canvas element using JavaScript. The initial design will just draw an empty board and you'll
add the chess pieces later. Refer back to Chapter 10 for more explanation about working with a canvas element.
Add a script element after the div element but inside the body element using the code from Listing 11-1.

Listing 11-1. Designing the initial canvas

```
<script>
    // Get the canvas context
    var chessCanvas = document.getElementById("board");
    var chessContext = chessCanvas.getContext("2d");

    drawBoard();

    function drawBoard() {
        chessContext.clearRect(0, 0, 600, 600);

        var gradient = chessContext.createLinearGradient(0, 600, 600, 0);
        gradient.addColorStop(0, "#D50005");
        gradient.addColorStop(0.5, "#E27883");
        gradient.addColorStop(1, "#FFDDDD");

        chessContext.fillStyle = gradient;
        chessContext.strokeStyle = "red";

        // Draw the alternating squares
        for (var x = 0; x < 8; x++) {
            for (var y = 0; y < 8; y++) {
                if ((x + y) % 2) {
                    chessContext.fillRect(75 * x, 75 * y, 75, 75);
                }
            }
        }
        // Add a border around the entire board
        chessContext.strokeRect(0, 0, 600, 600);
    }
</script>
```

Select Firefox for the debug browser. Press F5 to start the application, which should look like Figure 11-2.

Figure 11-2. *The initial (blank) chess board*

Configuring the Images

You will be using image files to represent the chess pieces. Before adding them to the canvas you'll need to create an Image object for each one and specify its `src` attribute. You'll also put these into an array to make it easier to programmatically select the desired image. Add the code shown in Listing 11-2 to the beginning of the `script` element that you just created, before the existing code.

Listing 11-2. Adding the image objects

```
// Define the chess piece images
var imgPawn = new Image();
var imgRook = new Image();
var imgKnight = new Image();
var imgBishop = new Image();
var imgQueen = new Image();
var imgKing = new Image();
var imgPawnW = new Image();
var imgRookW = new Image();
var imgKnightW = new Image();
var imgBishopW = new Image();
var imgQueenW = new Image();
var imgKingW = new Image();

// Specify the source for each image
imgPawn.src = "Images/pawn.png";
imgRook.src = "Images/rook.png";
imgKnight.src = "Images/knight.png";
imgBishop.src = "Images/bishop.png";
imgQueen.src = "Images/queen.png";
imgKing.src = "Images/king.png";
imgPawnW.src = "Images/wpawn.png";
imgRookW.src = "Images/wrook.png";
```

```
imgKnightW.src = "Images/wknight.png";
imgBishopW.src = "Images/wbishop.png";
imgQueenW.src = "Images/wqueen.png";
imgKingW.src = "Images/wking.png";

// Define an array of Image objects
var images = [
        imgPawn ,
        imgRook ,
        imgKnight ,
        imgBishop ,
        imgQueen ,
        imgKing ,
        imgPawnW ,
        imgRookW ,
        imgKnightW ,
        imgBishopW ,
        imgQueenW ,
        imgKingW
];
```

Creating the Database

Now you're ready to create and use a local Indexed DB database to configure and display the chess pieces. Initially, the data will be loaded from static data and you will simply display the starting position. Later you will animate the pieces by updating their location in object store.

Declaring the Static Data

You will need to populate the database with some data. For this application you will just declare the data as a static array and copy it to the object store. For other applications this could be downloaded from a server or entered from user input. Add the following declarations shown in Listing 11-3 to the `script` element, just after the image variables.

Listing 11-3. Declaring the static data

```
var pieceTypes = [
    { name: "pawn", height: "50", width: "28", blackImage: 0, whiteImage: 6 },
    { name: "rook", height: "60", width: "36", blackImage: 1, whiteImage: 7 },
    { name: "knight", height: "60", width: "36", blackImage: 2, whiteImage: 8 },
    { name: "bishop", height: "65", width: "30", blackImage: 3, whiteImage: 9 },
    { name: "queen", height: "70", width: "32", blackImage: 4, whiteImage: 10 },
    { name: "king", height: "70", width: "28", blackImage: 5, whiteImage: 11 }
];

var pieces = [
    { type: "pawn", color: "white", row: 6, column: 0, pos: "a2", killed: false },
    { type: "pawn", color: "white", row: 6, column: 1, pos: "b2", killed: false },
    { type: "pawn", color: "white", row: 6, column: 2, pos: "c2", killed: false },
    { type: "pawn", color: "white", row: 6, column: 3, pos: "d2", killed: false },
```

```
 { type: "pawn", color: "white", row: 6, column: 4, pos: "e2", killed: false },
 { type: "pawn", color: "white", row: 6, column: 5, pos: "f2", killed: false },
 { type: "pawn", color: "white", row: 6, column: 6, pos: "g2", killed: false },
 { type: "pawn", color: "white", row: 6, column: 7, pos: "h2", killed: false },
 { type: "rook", color: "white", row: 7, column: 0, pos: "a1", killed: false },
 { type: "rook", color: "white", row: 7, column: 7, pos: "h1", killed: false },
 { type: "knight", color: "white", row: 7, column: 1, pos: "b12", killed: false },
 { type: "knight", color: "white", row: 7, column: 6, pos: "g1", killed: false },
 { type: "bishop", color: "white", row: 7, column: 2, pos: "c1", killed: false },
 { type: "bishop", color: "white", row: 7, column: 5, pos: "f1", killed: false },
 { type: "queen", color: "white", row: 7, column: 3, pos: "d1", killed: false },
 { type: "king", color: "white", row: 7, column: 4, pos: "e1", killed: false },
 { type: "pawn", color: "black", row: 1, column: 0, pos: "a7", killed: false },
 { type: "pawn", color: "black", row: 1, column: 1, pos: "b7", killed: false },
 { type: "pawn", color: "black", row: 1, column: 2, pos: "c7", killed: false },
 { type: "pawn", color: "black", row: 1, column: 3, pos: "d7", killed: false },
 { type: "pawn", color: "black", row: 1, column: 4, pos: "e7", killed: false },
 { type: "pawn", color: "black", row: 1, column: 5, pos: "f7", killed: false },
 { type: "pawn", color: "black", row: 1, column: 6, pos: "g7", killed: false },
 { type: "pawn", color: "black", row: 1, column: 7, pos: "h7", killed: false },
 { type: "rook", color: "black", row: 0, column: 0, pos: "a8", killed: false },
 { type: "rook", color: "black", row: 0, column: 7, pos: "h8", killed: false },
 { type: "knight", color: "black", row: 0, column: 1, pos: "b8", killed: false },
 { type: "knight", color: "black", row: 0, column: 6, pos: "g8", killed: false },
 { type: "bishop", color: "black", row: 0, column: 2, pos: "c8", killed: false },
 { type: "bishop", color: "black", row: 0, column: 5, pos: "f8", killed: false },
 { type: "queen", color: "black", row: 0, column: 3, pos: "d8", killed: false },
 { type: "king", color: "black", row: 0, column: 4, pos: "e8", killed: false }
];
```

The pieceTypes[] array defines the properties needed to display each piece such as height and width. It also specifies the corresponding index in the images[] array for both the black and white images. The pieces[] array contains the same details used in the previous chapter such as row and column, and defines the starting position for each of the 32 pieces.

Opening the Database

Add the code shown in Listing 11-4 to the script object, just after the call to drawBoard() (and before the implementation of the drawBoard()function).

Listing 11-4. Opening the database

```
var dbEng = window.indexedDB ||
            window.webkitIndexedDB || // Chrome
            window.mozIndexedDB ||    // Firefox
            window.msIndexedDB;       // IE

var db;  // This is a handle to the database
```

```
if (!dbEng)
    alert("IndexedDB is not supported on this browser");
else {
    var request = dbEng.open("Chess", 1);

    request.onsuccess = function (event) {
        db = event.target.result;
    }

    request.onerror = function (event) {
        alert("Please allow the browser to open the database");
    }

    request.onupgradeneeded = function (event) {
        configureDatabase(event);
    }
}
```

Because the specification has not been finalized, the browsers will be using the vendor prefix. If you can't access the indexedDB object then the browser does not support it. For this demo you can simply use alert() to notify the user and stop further processing.

This code then uses the indexedDB object to open the Chess database, specifying that version 1 should be used. The open() method returns a DBRequest object, as I describer earlier. You will attach three event handlers for this request:

- onsuccess - This event handler simply saves the reference to the database. You will add more logic here later. Notice that the database is obtained from the event.target.result property, which is how all results are returned.

- onerror – The primary reason that the browser fails to open a database is that the browser has the IndexedDB feature blocked. This can be disabled for security reasons. In this case, the user is prompted to allow access.

- onupgradeneeded – This is raised if the database does not exist or if the specified version is not the current version. This calls the configureDatabase() function, which you'll implement now.

Defining the Database Structure

Add the code shown in Listing 11-5 to implement the configureDatabase() function.

Listing 11-5. Defining the database structure

```
function configureDatabase(e) {
    alert("Configuring database - current version is "+ e.oldVersion +
            ", requested version is "+ e.newVersion);     db = e.currentTarget.result;

    // Remove all existing data stores
    var storeList = db.objectStoreNames;
    for (var i = 0; i < storeList.length; i++) {
        db.deleteObjectStore(storeList[i]);
    }
```

```
// Store the piece types
var typeStore = db.createObjectStore
    ("pieceType", { keyPath: "name" });

for (var i in pieceTypes){
    typeStore.add(pieceTypes[i]);
}

// Create the piece data store (you'll add
// the data later)
var pieceStore = db.createObjectStore
    ("piece", { autoIncrement: true });

pieceStore.createIndex
    ("piecePosition", "pos", { unique: true });
}
```

■ **Caution**   The configureDatabase() function will be called if the database does not exists or if it is not the current version. For version changes, you can get the current version by using the db.version property and then make the necessary adjustments. Also, the event object passed to the onupgradeneeded event handler will have the e.oldVersion and e.newVersion properties. To simplify things in this project, you'll simply remove all object stores and rebuild the database from scratch. This will wipeout all existing data. That is fine for this example but in most cases you'll need to preserve the data where possible.

The objectStoreNames property of the database object contains a list of the names of all the object stores that have been created. To remove all of the existing object stores, each of the names in this list is passed to the deleteObjectStore() method.

Initially, you'll create two data stores using the createObjectStore() method:

- pieceType – contains an object for each type of piece such as pawn, rook, or king.

- piece – contains an object for each piece, 16 black and 16 white.

Specifying the Object Key

When creating an object store, you must specify a name for the store when calling the createObjectStore() method. You can also specify one or more optional parameters. Only two are supported:

- keypath – this is specified as a collection of property names. If you're using a single property, you can specify this as a string rather than a collection of strings. This defines the object property(ies) that will be used as the key. If no keypath is specified, the key must be defined out-of-line using a key generator or providing the key as explained below.

- autoIncrement – If true, this indicates that the keys are sequentially assigned by the object store.

Every object in a store must have a unique key. There are three ways to specify the key:

- Use the keypath parameter to specify one or more properties that define a unique key. As objects are added, the keypath is used to generate a key based on the object's properties.

- Use a key generator. If autoIncrement is specified, the object store will assign a key based on an internal counter.

- Provide the key value when adding the object. If you don't specify a key path or use a key generator, you must supply a key when adding an object to a store.

For the pieceType store you'll use a keypath. The name property will specify the type such as "pawn" or "knight". This will be a unique value for each object. This is also the value that will be used to retrieve an object so this is a perfect candidate for a key path. After creating the object store the data from the pieceTypes[] array is then copied to the pieceType store.

■ **Note**   While in the onupgradeneeded event handler, data can be added to an object store without explicitly creating a transaction. There is an implicit transaction created in response to the onupgradeneeded event.

Creating an Index

For the piece store there is no natural key available in the pieces data so you'll use a key generator. It will generate unique keys but the keys will have no real meaning; they're just a surrogate key used to satisfy the unique constraint. Initially when you're drawing the board you'll retrieve all of the objects so you don't need to know what the key is.

Later you'll need to retrieve a piece so you can move it. You will find the desired piece based on its position on the board. To facilitate that you'll add an index to the store based on the pos property. Since no two pieces can occupy the same space, the pos property can be used as a unique index. By specifying this as a unique index, you will get an error if you try to insert an object with the same position as an existing object.

■ **Caution**   Since the pos property is unique, you might be tempted to use it as the key. However, since you will be moving pieces, their position will change and it's considered a poor design pattern to use a key that changes often. For Indexed DB, this is especially problematic since you can't actually change a key; you must delete the current object and then add it with the new key.

When creating an index you must specify a keypath like this:

```
pieceStore.createIndex
    ("piecePosition", "pos", { unique: true });
```

In this case, the pos property is the keypath for this index. The keypath may include more than one property; in which case the index will be based on the combination of the selected properties. When an object store has an index, the index is automatically populated when an object is added to the store.

Resetting the Board

You created the piece object store but have not populated it yet. You'll do that in a separate function. To understand why, let me explain the database life cycle. The first time the web page is displayed, the database is opened, and since it doesn't exist, a new database will be created. This happens because the onupgradeneeded event is raised and you implemented this event handler to create the object stores. When the page is displayed again (or simply refreshed), this step will be skipped since the database already exists.

Later, when you start moving the pieces around as well as deleting them, you'll want to move them back to their initial position when the page is reloaded. You can use this method to do that. You'll now add a resetBoard() function to the script using the following code. This will be called, not when the database is created, but when the page is loaded.

```
function resetBoard() {

    var xact = db.transaction(["piece"], "readwrite");
    var pieceStore = xact.objectStore("piece");
    var request = pieceStore.clear();
    request.onsuccess = function(event) {
        for (var i in pieces) {
            pieceStore.put(pieces[i]);
        }
    }}
```

This code creates a transaction using the read/write mode and specifies only the piece object store, since that is the only one you'll need to access. Then the piece store is obtained from the transaction. The clear() method is used to delete all of the objects from the store. Finally, all of the objects in the pieces[] array are copied to the object store.

Now add the following code shown in bold to the onsuccess event handler. This will call the resetBoard() function after the database has been opened.

■ **Note**   The onupgradeneeded event is raised and its event handler must complete before the onsuccess event is raised. This ensures that the database has been properly configured before it is used.

```
var request = dbEng.open("Chess", 1);

request.onsuccess = function (event) {
    db = event.target.result;

    // Add the pieces to the board
    resetBoard();
}
```

▌**Tip**   In the `resetBoard()` function, you called the `put()` method (repeatedly – 32 times). However, you did not get any response objects nor implement any event handlers. This code appears to be working synchronously. Actually, these calls are processed asynchronously and a response object is returned in both cases but the return value was ignored. You could implement both `onsuccess` and `onerror` event handlers for these requests. In this case, you cheated a little. Since you don't need the result value like you would when retrieving data, you don't have to handle the `onsuccess` event. Because these calls are within a transaction, subsequent use of the store will be blocked until the updates are complete.

Drawing the Pieces

So far you have opened the database, configuring the object stores, if necessary. You have also populated the piece store with the initial positions. Now you're ready to draw the pieces. To do that you'll implement a `drawAllPieces()` function to iterate through all of the pieces and a `drawPiece()` function to display a single image. These functions will be similar to the functions you created in Chapter 10 with the same names. However, the data for these functions will be retrieved from the new database.

The `drawAllPieces()` function will use a cursor to process all of the objects in the `piece` object store. For each piece, this will extract the necessary properties and pass them to the `drawPiece()` function. The `drawPiece()` function must then access the `pieceType` store to obtain the type properties such as `height` and `width` and then display the image in the appropriate location.

Using a Cursor

When retrieving data from an object store, if you want to retrieve a single record using its key, use the `get()` method, which I will describe next. You can also select one of more objects using an index and I will explain that later in this chapter. To get all the pieces you'll need to access the entire object store, which you'll do using a cursor.

After creating the transaction and obtaining the object store, you'll call its `openCursor()` method. This returns a `DBResult` object and you'll need to provide an `onsuccess` event handler for it. When the event fires, it provides the first object only. You can obtain the next object by calling the `continue()` method. To demonstrate this, add the function shown in Listing 11-6 to the `script` element.

Listing 11-6. Drawing the pieces

```
function drawAllPieces() {

    var xact = db.transaction(["piece", "pieceType"]);

    var pieceStore = xact.objectStore("piece");
    var cursor = pieceStore.openCursor();
    cursor.onsuccess = function (event) {
        var item = event.target.result;
        if (item) {
            if (!item.value.killed) {
                drawPiece(item.value.type,
                          item.value.color,
```

```
                    item.value.row,
                    item.value.column,
                    xact);
            }
            item.continue();
        }
    }
}
```

This code creates a transaction that will use both the piece and pieceType object stores. The mode is not specified and the default value is "readonly". It then gets the piece object store and calls its openCursor() method. The onsuccess event handler gets the first object from the event object (using event.target.result). If the piece has not been captured, the drawPiece() function is called to display it, which you'll implement next. You pass in all the properties that it will need such as type, color, row, and column. You'll also pass in the transaction object so the drawPiece() function can use the same transaction to access the pieceType store.

Calling the continue() method will cause the same event to be raised again, this time supplying the next object in the event.target.result property. If there are no more objects, the result property will be null. This is how you'll know all the objects have been processed.

The openCursor() method provides some very basic capabilities to filter the objects that are returned. If no parameters are supplied it will return all the objects in the store. You can specify a key range using one of the following:

- IDBKeyRange.only() – specifies a single value and only records that match are returned.

- IDBKeyRange.lowerBound() – returns only key values greater than the value specified. By default this is inclusive so it will also return objects with keys that have an exact match as well but you can change this to only return values that are greater.

- IDBKeyRange.upperBound() – works just like lowerBound() except it returns values less than or equal to the value specified. I will demonstrate this later in the chapter.

- IDBKeyRange.bound() – allows you to specify both a lower and upper bound. You can also indicate if either of these values is inclusive.

The following example will return objects where the key is >3 and < = 7 and return them in descending order:

```
var keyRange = IDBKeyRange.bound(3, 7, false, true);
store.openCursor(keyRange, IDBCursor.PREV);
```

Retrieving a Single Object

Now you'll implement the drawPiece() function that will draw a single piece on the board. It must first access the pieceType object store to get the image details. In this case, you'll retrieve a single object using its key. The key to the pieceType object store is the type property. Add the function shown in Listing 11-7 to the script element.

Listing 11-7. Drawing a single piece

```
function drawPiece(type, color, row, column, xact) {

    var typeStore = xact.objectStore("pieceType");
    var request = typeStore.get(type);
    request.onsuccess = function (event) {
        var img;
```

```
        if (color === "black") {
            img = images[event.target.result.blackImage];
        }
        else {
            img = images[event.target.result.whiteImage];
        }

        chessContext.drawImage(img,
                    (75 - event.target.result.width) / 2 + (75 * column),
                    73 - event.target.result.height + (75 * row),
                    event.target.result.width,
                    event.target.result.height);
    }
}
```

This code uses the same transaction object, which is passed in. It obtains the pieceType object store and then calls its get() method. The onsuccess event handler gets the necessary properties and calls the canvas drawImage() method. Refer to Chapter 10 for more information about drawing images on a canvas.

Now add the call to drawAllPieces() in the onsuccess event handler for the open() call by adding the code shown in bold:

```
request.onsuccess = function (event) {
    db = event.target.result;

    // Add the pieces to the board
    resetBoard();

    // Draw the pieces in their initial positions
    drawAllPieces();
}
```

Testing the Application

Now you're ready to test the application, which will display the initial starting positions. Make sure that the debug browser is set as Firefox and press F5 to start the application. You should see an alert letting you know that the database is being configured as shown in Figure 11-3.

Configuring database - current version is 4, requested version is 5

OK

Figure 11-3. *The alert showing the database is being configured*

When you run this application again, this configuration will not be necessary. The chess board should look like Figure 11-4.

Figure 11-4. *The completed check board with static positions*

■ **Tip** If you want to remove the database from your machine, you can find the folder where they are stored and delete the corresponding subfolder. On my machine, the path is: `C:\Users\Mark.INTERNAL\AppData\Roaming\Mozilla\Firefox\Profiles\jch09kcf.default\indexedDB`. In this folder there is a subfolder for each database. The subfolder name includes the protocol (http), domain name, and port, if applicable. For my application this is `http+++localhost + 17018`. Delete this folder and restart the browser. The page should reconfigure the database since it must create a new one.

Moving the Pieces

Now you're ready to animate the board by moving the pieces around. You'll use the same canned moves that were used in Chapter 10. A piece can be moved by simply updating its position and then redrawing the board. There is one complication; however, if a move captures a piece, you need to remove it from the board. For now, you'll simply delete the object from the store but I'll show you a better way at the end of the chapter.

Defining the Moves

Since you're so database savvy now, you'll store the moves in the database as well. A move is defined by the starting and ending positions. For example, "move the piece at e2 to e3". You'll number these moves from 1 to 7 so they will be applied in the correct order. You'll need a new object store to hold the move details. To do that you'll need to specify a new version, which will raise the onupgradeneeded event. Then you'll add logic the configureDatabase() function to create the new store.

EXERCISE 11-2. ADDING THE MOVES STORE

1. Add the following code to the `script` element just after the existing static data definitions for the `pieceTypes` and `pieces` arrays:

```
var moves = [
    { id: 1, start: "e2", end: "e3" },
    { id: 2, start: "e7", end: "e5" },
    { id: 3, start: "f1", end: "c4" },
    { id: 4, start: "h7", end: "h6" },
    { id: 5, start: "d1", end: "f3" },
    { id: 6, start: "g7", end: "g6" },
    { id: 7, start: "f3", end: "f7" }
];
```

2. Add the following code shown in bold to the end of the `configureDatabase()` function. This will create and populate the move store when the database is configured.

```
pieceStore.createIndex
    ("piecePosition", "pos", { unique: true });

// Store the moves
var moveStore = db.createObjectStore
    ("move", { keyPath: "id" });

for (var i in moves) {
    moveStore.add(moves[i]);
}
}
```

3. On the `open()` call, change the version to **2** as shown in bold. This will cause the onupgradeneeded event to be raised the next time the page is loaded.

```
if (!dbEng)
    alert("IndexedDB is not supported on this browser");
else {
    var request = dbEng.open("Chess", 2);
```

Converting the Position

The objects in the `piece` store have the `row`, `column`, and `pos` properties. The `row` and `column` properties follow the same convention that was used in Chapter 10, where the top-left square is at 0,0. That is consistent with how canvas works and simplifies the `drawPiece()` implementation. In contrast, the `pos` property uses the notation widely used in Chess where the columns (files) go from "a" to "h" as you move left to right. The rows (ranks) go from "1" to "8" as you move from the bottom of the board to the top. Thus "a1" is the bottom-left square.

Before you get into the heavy work of moving the pieces you'll create a function that will convert the `pos` property into `row` and `column` properties. When a piece is moved to e3 for example, you'll need to convert "e3" into the corresponding `row` and `column` coordinates, which would be 5 (row) and 4 (column). Add the function shown in Listing 11-8 to the end of the existing `script` element.

Listing 11-8. Implementing the computeRowColumn() function

```
function computeRowColumn(oStart, end) {
    oStart.pos = end;
    switch (end.substring(0, 1)) {
        case "a": oStart.column = 0; break;
        case "b": oStart.column = 1; break;
        case "c": oStart.column = 2; break;
        case "d": oStart.column = 3; break;
        case "e": oStart.column = 4; break;
        case "f": oStart.column = 5; break;
        case "g": oStart.column = 6; break;
        case "h": oStart.column = 7; break;
    }

    oStart.row = 8 - parseInt(end.substr(1, 1));
}
```

The oStart parameter is the object from the piece store that was found at the starting position ("e2" in our example). The end parameter is the ending position, "e3", which is copied to the pos property since this will be the piece's new position.

This code then uses a switch statement to convert the "a" – "h" file notation into a "0" – "7" coordinate. This is then stored in the column property. The row property is computed by taking the last digit from the position and subtracting it from 8.

Making a Move

Just like you did in Chapter 10, you'll use a timer to make the next move every 2 seconds. You'll need a timer variable so you can clear the timer when the animation is done. You'll also need to keep track of the current move. Add the two variables shown in bold to the script element just before the drawBoard() method is called.

```
// Get the canvas context
var chessCanvas = document.getElementById("board");
var chessContext = chessCanvas.getContext("2d");

var moveNumber = 1;
var timer;

drawBoard();
```

Moving a piece will require making up to five database calls:

1. Get the next object from the move store (this defines the start and end positions).

2. Get the object at the start position.

3. Get the object at the end position (there will only be one if the move is capturing a piece).

4. Remove the object at the end position (this step will only be needed on some moves).

5. Update the object at the start position (to move it to the end position).

These calls will all be made using the same transaction. As I demonstrated at the beginning of the chapter, you'll need to nest the onsuccess event handlers for each of these calls. Add the makeNextMove() function shown in Listing 11-9 to the end of the script element.

Listing 11-9. Implementing the makeNextMove() function

```
function makeNextMove() {

    var xact = db.transaction(["move", "piece"], "readwrite");
    var moveStore = xact.objectStore("move");

    moveStore.get(moveNumber).onsuccess = function (e1) {
        var startPos = e1.target.result.start;
        var endPos = e1.target.result.end;
        var startKey = null;
        var oStart = null;

        var pieceStore = xact.objectStore("piece");
        var index = pieceStore.index("piecePosition");

        index.getKey(startPos).onsuccess = function (e2) {
            startKey = e2.target.result;

            index.get(startPos).onsuccess = function (e3) {
                oStart = e3.target.result;

                // If there is a piece at the ending location, we'll
                // need to update it to prevent a duplicate pos index
                removePiece(endPos, oStart, startKey, pieceStore);
            }
        }
    }
}
```

This function creates a transaction that will access both the move and piece store. The mode is set to "readwrite" because the objects in the piece store will be modified. It then gets the move store and calls its get() method specifying the current move, which is the key to the table. This will return a single object and the start and end positions are extracted from the result in the onsuccess event handler.

───────────────────────────────

■ **Tip** Notice that this code doesn't explicitly define a request variable. Instead the onsuccess event handler is attached directly to the database call. In the previous examples I declared a request variable and then attached the event handler to it to help you see what was happening. However, attaching the event handler directly to the method accomplishes the same thing but simplifies the code a little.

───────────────────────────────

Obtaining the Object Key

For the piece store, you used a key generator so the key is not part of the object. The code in the makeNextMove() function will use the index based on the pos property to retrieve the object at the start position (and also at the end position if there is a piece there). However, in order to update or delete an object you will need its key.

When retrieving the piece object at the start position, this code first gets the piece store from the transaction. It then gets the piecePosition index from the store. To get the key value, you'll need to call index.getkey() method which returns the key for the requested start position. This is stored in the startKey variable.

To get the desired object you'll call the index.get() method passing in the position to search for. This returns the object at the requested start position and stores it in the oStart variable.

In both cases, the data is returned in the result property. Again, the event handlers that process the results are nested.

With the necessary data obtained, the removePiece() method is called passing in the following parameters:

- end – the ending position of the piece being moved

- oStart – an object representing the piece being moved

- startID – the key to the oStart object

- pieceStore - the piece store that will be used to perform the update

Performing the Update

Now you'll implement the removePiece() function. This is perhaps misnamed since it will only remove a piece when necessary. Add the following code to the end of the script element to implement the removePiece() function.

```
function removePiece(endPos, oStart, startKey, pieceStore) {
    var index = pieceStore.index("piecePosition");
    index.getKey(endPos).onsuccess = function (e4) {
        var endKey = e4.target.result;
        if (endKey) {
            pieceStore.delete(endKey).onsuccess = function (e5) {
                movePiece(oStart, startKey, endPos, pieceStore)
            }
        }
        else
            movePiece(oStart, startKey, endPos, pieceStore);
    }
}
```

This code gets the key at the ending position. If there is a piece there, it calls the delete() method to remove it and then calls the movePiece() function in the onsuccess handler for the delete() method. Notice that it does not retrieve the object; only the key is needed to perform the delete. If there is no piece there, it just calls the movePiece() function. When calling the movePiece() function, all the data it needs is passed to it including the object, its key, the end position, and the object store that it will use.

Now you'll implement the movePiece() function that will finally perform the actual update. To update an object you call the put() method. Unlike the add() method that you used earlier to add the pieces, the put() method requires both the object and the key. If there is no object with the specified key, the object will be added. Add the movePiece() method shown in Listing 11-10 to the end of the script element.

Listing 11-10. Implementing the movePiece() function

```
function movePiece(oStart, startID, end, pieceStore) {

    computeRowColumn(oStart, end);

    var startUpdateReq = pieceStore.put(oStart, startID);
    startUpdateReq.onsuccess = function (event) {

        moveNumber++;
        drawBoard();
        drawAllPieces();

        if (moveNumber > 7) {
            clearInterval(timer);
            chessContext.font = "30pt Arial";
            chessContext.fillStyle = "black";
            chessContext.fillText("Checkmate!", 200, 220);
        }
    }
}
```

This code first computes the row and column properties using the computeRowColumn() function that you created earlier. It then updates the object. In the onsuccess event handler it increments the moveNumber variable and draws the board and all of the pieces using the existing functions. Finally, if this is the last move, the timer is cleared and the "Checkmate!" text is drawn on the canvas.

Starting the Animation

The last step is to start the timer that will cause the makeNextMove() function to be called. You'll do this in the onsuccess event handler for the open() call. Add the code shown in bold:

```
var request = dbEng.open("Chess", 2);

request.onsuccess = function (event) {
    db = event.target.result;

    // Add the pieces to the board
    resetBoard();

    // Draw the pieces in their initial positions
    drawAllPieces();

    // Start the animation
    timer = setInterval(makeNextMove, 2000);
}
```

Save your changes and press F5 to start the application. You should see the alert letting you know that the database is being configured since you changed the database version. After a series of moves you should see the completed board shown in Figure 11-5.

Figure 11-5. *The completed chess board*

Tracking the Captured Pieces

When capturing a piece you simply deleted the object and that works since the piece doesn't need to be displayed. However, if your application wants to keep track of the pieces that were captured you might want to keep the object in the store. Now I'll show you how to change this to update the object instead of deleting it. I'll also show you how to query this store to list the pieces that have been captured.

The first step is to change the removePiece() function. Instead of deleting the object at the end position, you'll update it and set the killed property. You'll also need to change the pos property since there is a unique index on this. Since the piece is not displayed, the position can be anything. To ensure it is unique, you'll prefix its unique id with an "x". Also, by prefixing these with an "x", you'll be able to query for them, as I'll explain later.

Comment out the delete() call and add the code shown in bold:

```
function removePiece(end, oStart, startID, pieceStore) {
    var index = pieceStore.index("piecePosition");
    index.getKey(end).onsuccess = function (e4) {
        var endID = e4.target.result;
        if (endID) {
            //pieceStore.delete (endID).onsuccess = function (e5) {
            //     movePiece(oStart, startID, pieceStore)
            //}

            index.get(end).onsuccess = function (e5) {
                oEnd = e5.target.result;
                oEnd.pos = 'x'+endID;
                oEnd.killed = true;
                pieceStore.put(oEnd, endID).onsuccess = function(e6){
                    movePiece(oStart, startID, end, pieceStore)
                }
            }
        }
    }
```

```
        else
            movePiece(oStart, startID, end, pieceStore);
    }
}
```

Now add the following code to the end of the script element to implement the displayCapturedPieces() function:

```
function displayCapturedPieces() {
    var xact = db.transaction(["piece"]);
    var textOut = "";

    var pieceStore = xact.objectStore("piece");
    var index = pieceStore.index("piecePosition");

    var keyRange = IDBKeyRange.lowerBound("x");
    var cursor = index.openCursor(keyRange);

    cursor.onsuccess = function (event) {
        var item = event.target.result;
        if (item) {
            textOut += " - " + item.value.color +" " +
                            item.value.type + "\r\n";
            item.continue();
        }
        else if (textOut.length > 0)
            alert("The following pieces were captured:\r\n"+textOut);
    }
}
```

This code creates a read-only transaction using only the piece store. It then gets the store and its piecePosition index. It defines a key range using a lower bound of "x". This will only return objects that begin with "x" or greater. Since the pieces on the board will have a position that starts with "a" through "h" these will be excluded. The code then iterates through the cursor and concatenates the piece details into a text string. The result is displayed using an alert() function.

■ **Caution** Be aware that the string comparisons in the key range are case sensitive. If you had used an uppercase "X", this would not have worked since a lowercase "a" comes after an uppercase "X". The W3C specification provides some details on how comparisons are supposed to work. For details, see the article at: http://www.w3.org/TR/IndexedDB/#key-construct.

Now you'll need to call this function after the animation is completed. Add the following line of code to the makeNextMove() function after the "Checkmate!" text is displayed:

```
displayCapturedPieces();
```

Save your changes and press F5 to start the application. After the animation has finished you should see the alert shown in Figure 11-6.

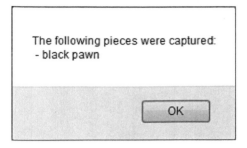

Figure 11-6. *Listing the captured pieces*

Summary

In this chapter you took a crash course in Indexed DB. Through a fairly simple application, you utilized most of the capabilities of this new technology. Probably the biggest challenge is to get used to the asynchronous processing. The sample application provides lots of examples of nesting successive calls through the onsuccess event handler. Some of the key concepts to remember include:

- Create the database and create its structure by responding to the onupgradeneeded event handler when the database is opened. Use the version to force an upgrade, if necessary.

- Objects in a store must have a unique key, which can either be defined by a key path for in-line keys, or a key generator for out-of-line keys. You can also supply the key manually when the object is added but that's not generally a practical solution.

- All data access (read and write) must be done through a transaction object. When creating the transaction you must specify the scope, which is the list of object stores that it will use as well as the type of access that is required.

- You can add one or more indices to an object store. Each index maps a key path in the object to the object's key.

- Use a cursor to process multiple objects in an object store. The objects that are selected can be filtered by specifying a key range.

- Add an object to the object store and update it later.

- Retrieve an object from an object store.

- Delete an object from an object store by specifying the object's key.

- Obtain the key for an object by using the getKey() method of the index.

- Use the put() method of an object store to add or update an object. The put() method requires both the objects and the key. This will add the object if the specified key is not found.

There is a lot that you can do with a local database like Indexed DB. Because the data is on the client, you avoid roundtrips to the server.

■ ■ ■

CHAPTER 12

Geolocation and Mapping

This chapter will demonstrate two technologies that provide powerful features that enable you to easily create some very useful web sites. Geolocation provides a standardized API that is used to determine the client's location. Mapping technology adds the ability to display this location on a map along with other points of interest. Together, these form a platform that has many useful applications.

In this chapter you'll use the geolocation API to find your current position. The accuracy of that position will vary greatly depending on available hardware and the environment. However, HTML5 defines a standard API that is used on all devices so you can provide device-independent solutions.

Just knowing your location in terms of latitude and longitude is not very helpful. To put this data to use, you'll use the Bing Maps API to display that location on a map. Then you can map additional points of interest and see them in relation to your current location.

Understanding Geolocation

While not technically part of the HTML5 specification, the WC3 has defined a standard API for accessing geolocation information, which is supported by all major current browser versions. The technology that determines the location, however, varies greatly depending on the device capabilities and the client's environment.

Surveying Geolocation Technologies

There are several technologies that can be used to determine the current location, including:

- Global Positioning Satellites (GPS) – GPS communicates with satellites to determine the current location with extremely high accuracy, particularly in rural areas. Tall buildings in an urban area can affect the accuracy but in most cases GPS provides very good results. The biggest limitation is that this doesn't work indoors very well. To use GPS, the device must have specific GPS hardware, but this is becoming increasingly common on mobile devices.

- Wi-Fi Positioning – Wi-Fi networks have a relatively short range and systems such as Skyhook Wireless maintain a large database of Wi-Fi networks and their locations. Simply being connected to a Wi-Fi network will give a pretty good idea of where you are. Often, however, you may be within range of multiple networks and the system can use triangulation to determine the location with even greater accuracy. Of course, this requires that you have a Wi-Fi enabled device and doesn't work in rural areas where there are no Wi-Fi networks.

- Cell Tower Triangulation – This uses the same principle as Wi-Fi positioning except it uses cellular telephone towers. It is not as accurate, however, because a cell tower has a much larger range. Since all cell phones will have the ability to communicate with cell towers, this technology has a broad application.

- IP Block – Every device that connects to the internet will have an IP address, which is usually provided by the ISP. Each ISP will have a block of IP addresses that it can use, which are typically assigned by geographical location. So the IP address with which you connect to the internet can provide a general location, usually a metropolitan area. There are several factors, however, that can yield incorrect results, such as NATted addresses.

Each of these technologies has different hardware requirements and provide varying levels of accuracy. With the Geolocation specification, you can easily request the current location from the browser and let it determine the best way to supply that based on the current hardware and access to external sources including satellites, cell towers, and W-Fi networks.

Using Geolocation Data

Most people think of geolocation as a device that provides turn-by-turn directions but that is only one application of this technology. Of course this requires very precise location that can only be obtained through GPS. However, even when the current location is far less accurate, your web site can still make valuable use of this information. Even if the location is determined only by the IP address, this will usually be sufficient to set the default language, for example. You may need to allow the end user to override this but most of your audience will see the initial page in their native language.

When retrieving the current location, the geolocation service also returns the estimated accuracy. Your application should use this to determine the features that will be provided. Suppose, for example, that you're creating a web page for the U.S. Postal Service that shows where the nearest post offices are. If the current location is known with very high accuracy, the web page can show a map and indicate the current location as well as the nearby post offices. In addition, it could provide the estimated driving time to each.

However, if the location is known with lesser accuracy, the page could display a map that shows where the post offices are in that general area. Presumably, the user will know where they are and can use this information to determine the best location to use. However, if the accuracy is very poor, the page should prompt for a zip code and then display the nearest post offices based on the user input. So, depending on the accuracy, the application can gracefully degrade the functionality.

Using the Geolocation API

To demonstrate how to use the Geolocation API, you'll create a simple web page that calls the API to determine your current location. Initially, this data will be displayed on the web page as text. Later you'll display this location on a map.

Creating the Visual Studio Project

You'll start by creating a Visual Studio project using the same Basic MVC template that you have used in previous chapters.

EXERCISE 12-1. CREATING THE VISUAL STUDIO PROJECT

1. Start Visual Studio 2012 and click the New Project link from the Start page.

2. In the New project dialog box, select the "ASP.NET MVC4 Web Application" template. Select a location for this project and enter the project name **Chapter12** as shown in Figure 12-1.

Figure 12-1. *Creating the Geolocation project*

3. In the next dialog box, select the Basic template and make sure the Razor view engine is selected. Click the OK button and the project will be created.

4. Right-click the Controller folder in the Solution Explorer and select the Add ➤ Controller links. Enter **HomeController** for the controller name and select the Empty MVC Controller template. Click the Add button to create the controller.

5. Right-click the View folder and select the Add ➤ New Folder links. Enter the folder name as **Home**.

6. Right-click the new Home folder and select the Add ➤ View links. In the Add View dialog box, enter the name **Index**, make sure the Razor view engine is selected, unselect all the check boxes, and click the Add button.

7. In the Index.cshtml file, replace the empty div that was created, with the following markup:

```
<div style = "width:800px; height:50px;">
    <span id = "lbl"> </span>
</div>
```

Using the Geolocation Object

The geolocation API is provided by the `geolocation` object, which you can access through the `navigator` object like this:

```
navigator.geolocation
```

If a falsy value is returned such as null or undefined, then geolocation is not supported on the current browser. You can check for support using code like this:

```
if (!navigator.geolocation) {
    alert("Geolocation is not supported");
}
else
    // do something with geolocation
```

To get the current location, use the `getCurrentLocation()` function, which takes three parameters:

1. A callback function that is executed when the call is successful.

2. An error callback function that is called when an error occurs.

3. A PositionOptions collection that contains zero or more options.

The last two parameters can be omitted. The following options are supported:

- `maximumAge` – the browser can cache previous positions and return this without actually trying to determine the location. However, the `maximumAge` attribute specifies how long (in milliseconds) a previous position can be reused without re-querying the current location.

- `timeout` – the timeout attribute specifies how long the browser should wait for a response from the `geolocation` object. This is also expressed in milliseconds.

- `enableHighAccuracy` – this is just a hint to the browser. If you don't need greater accuracy for a particular purpose, setting this to false may yield a faster response or use less power, which is a consideration for mobile devices.

If the call was successful, the position is passed to the callback function that was specified. The `Position` object includes a `coords` object that contains the following required properties:

- `latitude` (specified in degrees)

- `longitude` (specified in degrees)

- `accuracy` (specified in meters)

In addition, the following optional properties may be provided depending on the environment and the available hardware. If these are not supported they will be set to null. (The optional properties are typically available only when GPS is used.)

- `altitude` (specified in meters)

- `altitudeAccuracy` (specified in meters)

- heading (specified in degrees; north = 0, west = 90, etc.)

- speed (specified in meters/second, NaN if stationary)

These properties can be obtained by the callback function like this:

```
function successCallback(pos) {
    var lat = pos.coords.latitude;
    var long = pos.coords.longitude;
    var accuracy = pos.coords.accuracy + " meters";
}
```

If the call was not successful, the PositionError object is passed to the error callback function. This object includes a code and a message property. The error code will have one of three possible values:

- 1 – PERMISSION_DENIED

- 2 – POSITION_UNAVAILABLE

- 3 – TIMEOUT

■ **Caution**   Your application will get the location and simply display it (and later map it). However, your script could easily pass this information back to the server, which is a potential privacy issue. Since the browser cannot control what the client does with this information, for privacy reasons the browser may block the access to the geolocation object. In this case the PERMISSION_DENIED error code is returned. I will demonstrate this later.

If the client is moving and you want to continuously monitor the current location, you could call the getCurrentLocation() function repeatedly using a setInterval() function. To simplify this, the geolocation object includes a watchPosition() function. This takes the same three parameters as the getCurrentLocation() function (success callback, error callback, and options). The callback function is then invoked whenever the position changes. The watchPosition() function returns a timer handle. You can pass this handle to the clearWatch() function when you want to stop monitoring the position like this:

```
var handle = geolocation.watchPosition(callback);
...
geolocation.clearWatch(handle);
```

Displaying the Location

Now you'll add code to your application to get the current location and display it. The web page has a span element with an id of "lbl". You'll get the geolocation object and call its getCurrentLocation() function. Both the success and error callback functions will display the appropriate results in the span element.

EXERCISE 12-2. DISPLAYING THE LOCATION

1. Add the `script` element shown in Listing 12-1 to the end of the body element.

   Listing 12-1. Displaying the location

```
<script type = "text/javascript">

    var lbl = document.getElementById("lbl");

    if (navigator.geolocation) {
        navigator.geolocation
            .getCurrentPosition(showLocation,
                                errorHandler,
                                {
                                    maximumAge: 100,
                                    timeout: 6000,
                                    enableHighAccuracy: true
                                });
    }
    else {
        alert("Geolocation not suported");
    }

    function showLocation(pos) {
        lbl.innerHTML =
            "Your latitude: " + pos.coords.latitude +
            " and longitude: " + pos.coords.longitude +
            " (Accuracy of: " +  pos.coords.accuracy + " meters)";

    }

    function errorHandler(e) {
        if (e.code === 1) { // PERMISSION_DENIED
            lbl.innerHTML = "Permission denied. - " + e.message;
        } else if (e.code === 2) { //POSITION_UNAVAILABLE
            lbl.innerHTML = "Make sure your network connection is active and " +
                "try this again. - " + e.message;
        } else if (e.code === 3) { //TIMEOUT
            lbl.innerHTML = "A timeout ocurred; try again. - " + e.message;
        }
    }

</script>
```

2. Press F5 to start the application. The first time a site tries to access the geolocation object you will get a prompt like the one shown in Figure 12-2.

| **localhost** wants to track your physical location. | Allow once | Options for this site ▼ | ✕ |

Figure 12-2. Prompting for geolocation access

▓ **Note** I'm using IE 9 for this demonstration. If you're using a different browser this prompt may work a little differently.

3. To test the error handler, expand the "Options for this site" drop down and select the "Always deny and don't tell me" option. The page should display an error message like the one shown in Figure 12-3.

Permission denied. - This site does not have permission to use the Geolocation API.

Figure 12-3. Displaying the access denied error

4. Once you have set this option, IE will no longer prompt you anymore but will always deny the access. To clear this, select the Tools menu and then select Internet Options. In the middle of the Privacy tab there are options to control the geolocation access. Click the Clear Sites button shown in Figure 12-4.

Figure 12-4. *Clearing the site access choices*

5. Click the OK button to close this dialog box. Refresh the web page. It should now prompt you again. This time select the "Always allow" option. Your current location should be displayed as shown in Figure 12-5.

Your latitude: 40.7142 and longitude: -74.0064 (Accuracy of:80467 meters)

Figure 12-5. *Displaying the current location*

I'm using a normal LAN-connected machine without cell or GPS support so it is using the IP to determine the location. Consequently, the accuracy estimate is 80 km (about 50 miles).

■ **Note**　Geolocation works on all current browsers. However, if you try this application on an older browser such as IE8, you'll see the alert that geolocation is not supported.

Using Mapping Platforms

Simply displaying the latitude and longitude is not very interesting (or helpful). However, showing your location relative to other points of interest is much more useful. And displaying them on a map with roads and other reference points can really put this information to work. Fortunately, mapping technology has become so sophisticated and accessible that this is really easy to do.

■ **Note**　For the demonstration in this chapter I will be using Bing Maps. There are other mapping platforms available. If you're interested, check out the article at `http://en.wikipedia.org/wiki/Comparison_of_web_map_services` for an overview of the different mapping services.

Creating a Bing Maps Account

To use Bing Maps you'll need to first set up an account, which is free for developers. Once your account is created you'll receive a key that you'll need to include when accessing the mapping API. I will take you through the process of setting up an account.

EXERCISE 12-3. CREATING A BING MAPS ACCOUNT

1. Go to the Bing Maps site at this address: `https://www.microsoft.com/maps/developers/web.aspx`. Click the "Get an account" link.

2. In the next page, you'll need to log in with a Windows Live ID. If you don't have one, click the Create button to create an account.

3. Once you have signed in you should see the "Create an account" page shown in Figure 12-6.

Create an account

You need an account to create keys or upload map apps.

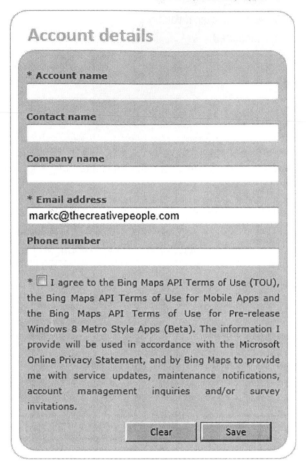

Figure 12-6. The Create an account page

4. Enter an account name. This is just for you to identify it if you have multiple accounts; **Testing** is fine. The e-mail address should default in from your Windows Live account. Make sure you select the check box agreeing to the terms of use. Click the Save button to create the account.

5. The "Maps Account Center" page, shown in Figure 12-7, should then be displayed showing your account details. Click the "Create or view keys" link on the left side of the page.

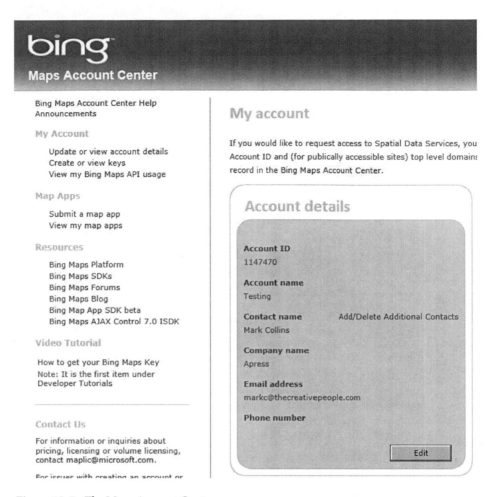

Figure 12-7. *The Maps Account Center page*

6. In the Create key page, enter an application name such as **HTML5 Test**. For the URL enter **http://localhost** and select Developer for the Application type as shown in Figure 12-8. Enter the characters that are displayed at the bottom of the form and click the Submit button.

Figure 12-8. *Creating a key*

■ **Note** Bing Maps monitors the use of your key. However, since you're not actually deploying this to a public-facing web site, this is not really applicable. If you are developing a commercial application, you can use a free key for development purposes but you will need to purchase a key for the live web site.

---

7. After the key has been generated you should see it displayed on the page. Save this as you will need it later.

Adding a Map

Now you'll add a map to your web page. You'll first add a div to the page that will contain the map. You'll also need to add a reference to the Ajax script that is used to manipulate the map. Then you'll display the map, centering it on your current location.

EXERCISE 12-4. ADDING A MAP

1. Add the code shown in bold to the body element, which will add the div that the map will be displayed in:

```
<body>
    <div style = "width:800px; height:50px;">
        <span id = "lbl"></span>
    </div>

    <div id="map" style="width:800px; height:600px;">

    </div>
```

2. Add the following reference inside the head element. This will enable your page to call the map API:

```
<script
    type = "text/javascript"
    src = "http://ecn.dev.virtualearth.net/mapcontrol/mapcontrol.ashx?v=7.0">
</script>
```

3. Add the following declaration at the top of the existing script element. This will store a reference to the map object.

```
var map = null;
```

4. Modify the showLocation() function, adding the code shown in bold in Listing 12-2. Enter your Bing Maps key where is says <use your key here>. The key should be enclosed in double quotes.

Listing 12-2. The modified showLocation() function

```
function showLocation(pos) {
    lbl.innerHTML =
        "Your latitude: " + pos.coords.latitude +
        " and longitude: " + pos.coords.longitude +
        " (Accuracy of: " +  pos.coords.accuracy + " meters)";

    // Save the current location
    var lat = pos.coords.latitude;
    var long = pos.coords.longitude;

    // Create the map
    map = new Microsoft.Maps.Map(document.getElementById("map"),
        { credentials:
            "<use your key here>" });

    // Center it on the current location
    map.setView({ zoom: 18, center: new Microsoft.Maps.Location(lat, long) });
}
```

5. Press F5 to start the application. Depending on your location, your page should look like Figure 12-9. Notice the controls at the top-left corner of the page. You can use this to zoom in or out and pan in any direction. The Automatic mode will switch to the satellite view if the map is zoomed in sufficiently.

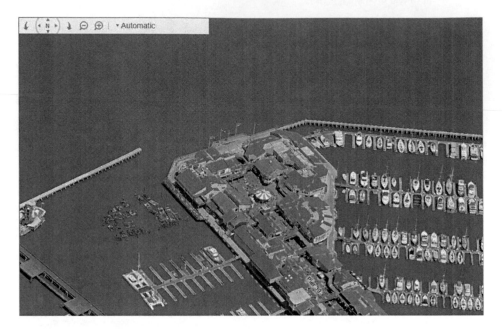

Figure 12-9. *Displaying the initial map*

When calling the setView() function to specify the center location, this code also set the zoom to 18. Depending on your application you may not want to zoom in that far, initially. Try this code using 15 or 16 to see how that looks. Of course the user can also adjust the zoom once the map is displayed.

Adding Pushpins

Now you'll display some pushpins on the map. To add a pushpin, you first create a Pushpin object, specifying its location. Then add it to the map's entities collection. First, you will add a default pushpin at the current location. Later, you'll add custom pushpins to indicate points of interest.

Add the code shown in bold to the end of the showLocation() function:

```
// Center it on the current location
map.setView({ zoom: 18, center: new Microsoft.Maps.Location(lat, long) });

// Mark the current location
var pushpin = new Microsoft.Maps.Pushpin
    (new Microsoft.Maps.Location(lat, long), null);
map.entities.push(pushpin);
```

The lat and long variables contain the same values used to center the map. Press F5 to start the application. You should see a pushpin indicating the current location as shown in Figure 12-10.

Figure 12-10. Adding a pushpin in the current location

One of the most common uses of maps in a web page is to show where there are nearby locations. For example, you might have multiple store locations and you'll want to show where each one is. Or perhaps you are in a police department and want to map out where certain crimes have been committed. You could have a public transit system and want to show where all the bus or train stops are.

Each of these scenarios is basically the same; you have a collection of locations that you want to show on a map. You can add as many locations as you want. For each, just create a Pushpin object and add it to the entities collection. If you have more than one location you should make the pushpins look different so the user can easily distinguish between them.

For this demonstration, you will indicate where there are nearby restrooms. Instead of a standard pushpin you will use an image with a familiar restroom icon. Normally you would query the server to get a list of locations based on the where the client is. However, to simplify this exercise these will be hardcoded.

▨ **Caution** I am hardcoding the location of the restrooms, which are probably nowhere near where your current location is. You can either provide different restroom locations that are near you or simply override your current location to match mine. This will be consistent with the restroom locations.

EXERCISE 12-4. ADDING CUSTOM PUSHPINS

1. In the Solution Explorer, right-click the Chapter12 project and select the Add ➤ New Folder links. Enter the name **Images**.

2. The source code download contains a `restroom.gif` image file. Drag this onto the Images folder in the Solution Explorer.

3. Add the following declaration at the top of the existing `script` element. This defines the locations of the restrooms.

```
var restrooms = [
    { lat: 37.810079, long: -122.410806 },
    { lat: 37.809079, long: -122.410206 },
    { lat: 37.811279, long: -122.410446 }
];
```

4. Add the following code to the showLocation() function just before creating the map object. This will override your current location to be near where the restrooms are.

```
// Override these for testing purposes
lat = 37.811079;
long = -122.410546;
```

5. Add the following functions to the end of the script element. The markRestrooms() function iterates through this array, calling the markRestroom() function for each. The markRestroom() function adds a single pushpin. This first creates an options collection that defines the image file to use as well as the size of the image. This is passed in when creating the Pushpin object.

```
function markRestrooms() {
    for (var i in restrooms) {
        markRestroom(restrooms[i].lat, restrooms[i].long);
    }
}

function markRestroom(lat, long) {
    var pushpinOptions = {icon: '/Images/restroom.gif', width: 35, height: 35 };
    var pushpin = new Microsoft.Maps.Pushpin
        (new Microsoft.Maps.Location(lat, long), pushpinOptions);
    map.entities.push(pushpin);
}
```

6. Add this function call at the end of the showLocation() function to display the additional pushpins.

```
// Display the restroom locations
markRestrooms();
```

7. Press F5 to debug the application. You should now see pushpins where the restrooms are located as shown in Figure 12-11.

Figure 12-11. *Adding the restroom pushpins*

■ **Caution** This is purely fictional data. If you happen to be at San Francisco's Pier 39 while reading this book, don't use this map to try to find a restroom.

There is a lot more that you can do with the mapping API. For example, you can display directions for getting to a selected point of interest. You can even display where the traffic is currently heavy. Check out the interactive SDK at http://www.bingmapsportal.com/isdk/ajaxv7. You can try out each feature and the corresponding JavaScript code is displayed underneath the map.

Summary

In this chapter you combined the features of geolocation with Bing Maps to create a really useful web site. Geolocation requests are processed asynchronously. After getting the geolocation object, you call its getCurrentLocation() function and specify the success and error callback functions. The Position object is passed to the callback function when the location has been retrieved. It contains the latitude, longitude, and estimated accuracy. If the client has GPS capability, the Position object will also include the altitude, speed, and direction.

Mapping platforms such as Bing Maps are really easy to use and integrate into your web page. In this application you displayed the map and centered in on the current location. You also added pushpins to show where the nearby restrooms are.

WebSockets

As I explained back in Chapter 1, the web application pulls data from a web server. The client initiates the transfer by sending a request to the server. The response is then rendered in the browser. All web application design is based on this request/response paradigm. However, WebSocket technology opens up a whole new world, allowing server-initiated communication with client applications.

Socket technology is not new. Sockets have been used for decades as an effective protocol for point-to-point communication between applications. The exciting news, however, is that the W3C has included a WebSocket API specification as part of the HTML5 umbrella. With a standard protocol defined, and compatible browsers becoming available, you can expect to see more and more web applications taking advantage of this technology.

In this chapter you will build a solution that uses websockets to implement a multi-session chat application that enables an agent to chat with several customers at the same time. This solution will include a websocket server hosted in a console app that you will create using C# .NET. To do this you'll need to understand the websocket protocols so I will first explain this technology and then show you how to create your own custom server. You will then implement both the agent and customer client applications utilizing the native websocket support in HTML5.

■ **Caution**   As of this writing, the W3C specification was still in draft and changes are likely. It is perhaps a bit premature to jump into this wholeheartedly. However, since this is such a promising part of the HTML5 specification I wanted to introduce you to websockets. Just be aware that things can change. You can check out the current status of the W3C specification here: `http://dev.w3.org/html5/websockets`. All major current browsers support websockets except IE9, however, they don't all support the same protocol versions, which I'll address later.

Understanding WebSockets

Sockets provide a mechanism for two-way transmissions between applications, including peer-to-peer communication. WebSockets, as I will explain in this chapter, are a specific implementation of sockets, that enable a web application to communicate with a web server. The messages passed between the browser and server are illustrated in Figure 13-1. After a series of handshaking messages that establish the connection, both sides can send messages to each other.

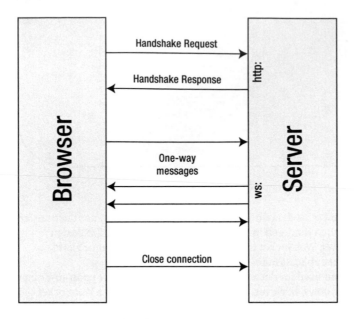

Figure 13-1. *The websockets messages*

■ **Tip**   While websockets do not provide peer-to-peer communication, as you'll see later in this chapter, the server can be implemented to route messages from one client to another. Client A can send a message to the server, which is simply forwarded to Client B. This emulates peer-to-peer messaging while providing control of the routing.

Completing a Handshake

There is a fair amount of handshaking and protocol manipulation that is required to make WebSockets work. Fortunately, the browser implements the client side protocol for you, making it really easy to write applications that use WebSockets. The handshaking messages use the HTTP protocol. Once the connection has been established, the subsequent messages are sent using the websocket protocol.

■ **Note**   Several protocol versions have been proposed and implemented by various browsers. The current version (as of this writing) is version 13, which both Chrome and Firefox support. You can review the specification of the Version 13 protocol at http://tools.ietf.org/id/draft-ietf-hybi-thewebsocketprotocol-13.txt.

The process starts when the browser sends a handshake request to the server. The handshake request will consist of multiple lines of text that will be similar to this:

```
GET /chat HTTP/1.1
Upgrade: websocket
Connection: Upgrade
Host: localhost:8100
```

```
Origin: http://localhost:29781
Sec-WebSocket-Key: <request key>
Sec-WebSocket-Version: 13
```

The request includes information about the address of the client and the protocol that it supports. You can see in this example that 13 is specified for Sec-WebSocket-Version. A request key is generated by the browser and will be different each time a connection request is made.

In return, the server will send back a response like this:

```
HTTP/1.1 101 Switching Protocols
Upgrade: websocket
Connection: Upgrade
Sec-WebSocket-Accept: <response key>
```

The response key is generated by the server and is based on the request key that was specified. I will explain the algorithm for this later in the chapter.

Building WebSocket Frames

Once the handshaking is complete and the protocols have been negotiated, messages can be exchanged between the client and server. These messages are sent using the websocket protocol. Messages are always one-way; no response is required. Of course, you can send a response but that is just another one-way message in the opposite direction. Both endpoints are always listening for messages.

A message is sent as a frame. The frame consists of a series of bytes that indicate how the message should be processed. The remainder of the message contains the actual data being sent, which is often referred to as the payload. The layout of the frame is shown in Figure 13-2.

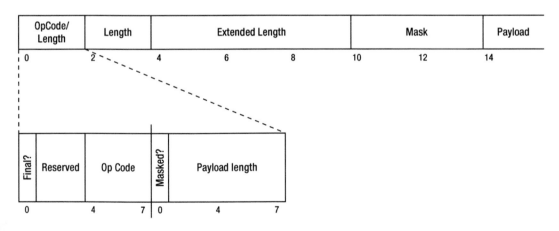

Figure 13-2. *The websocket frame*

The initial portion of the frame consists of up to 14 bytes. The first two bytes will be used on all frames. The first bit indicates if this is the final frame. A message can be transmitted in multiple frames and this bit should be set on the last frame to signal the message is complete. The next three bits are reserved for future use. The last half of the first byte contains an opcode that specifies what type of message this is. The values 0x3 – 0x7 and 0xB - 0xF are reserved for future control frames but the following values are currently defined:

- 0x0 indicates this is a continuation frame
- 0x1 specifies the payload contains text

- 0x2 indicates a binary payload

- 0x8 indicates the connection is being closed

- 0x9 specifies the message is a ping

- 0xA specifies the message is a pong

The first bit of the second byte indicates that masking is used. I will describe masking later. The remainder of the byte specifies the payload length. For payloads less than 126 bytes, the length is specified here. However, if the length is between 126 and 32,183 the length is set to 126 and the actual length is provided in the next two bytes. For messages longer than that, the length is set to 127 and the actual length is specified in the next eight bytes. So, depending on how long the message is, the frame will contain between 0 and 8 extra bytes.

The next four bytes contain the masking key. This is omitted if masking is not used. After that comes the actual payload.

For a simple, unmasked message containing the text "Hello", the frame would contain the following bytes:

```
0x81, 0x05, 0x48, 0x65, 0x6c, 0x6c, 0x6f
```

The first byte, 0x81, in binary is 10000001. The first bit is set indicating this is the final frame and the last bit is set to indicate the payload contains text. The next byte specifies a payload length of five characters, which follow immediately. The remaining five bytes contain the "H", "e", "l", "l", and "o" characters.

Unmasking a Frame

For security reasons, all frames from the client should be masked. *Masking* is a simple encoding scheme that uses a masking key that is different with each frame. The browser will take care of this for you; however, the server will need to unmask the data. Frames sent to the client should not be masked.

The masking key is provided in the four bytes directly following the length. The masking key is randomly generated by the client. To unmask the data, for each byte in the payload, the XOR operator is applied to the byte and the corresponding byte in the masking key. The first payload byte is XOR'ed with the first byte of the masking key, the second byte is XOR'ed with the second byte of the mask, an so on. The fifth byte is the XOR'ed with the first byte of the mask.

This can be done with the following C# expression. This assumes that payload[] contains an array of masked data and mask[] contains the 4-byte masking key.

```
for (int i=0; i<length; i++)
{
    payload[i]=(byte)(payload[i] ^ masks[i % 4]);
}
```

The i % 4 expression gets the appropriate masking byte and the ^ operator performs the XOR operation. After processing all of the bytes, the payload[] array will contain the unmasked data.

WebSocket Servers

To use websockets you will need to provide an application that will implement the server-side protocol. I will show you how to build your own using .NET and hosted in a console application. As you are probably expecting, there is a bit of bit and byte manipulation necessary (no pun intended).

■ **Note** There are a number of open-source websocket server implementations. This article provides links to several of these that you might want to consider for future reference:
`http://stackoverflow.com/questions/1530023/do-i-need-a-server-to-use-html5s-websockets`.
These are implemented on various platforms including JavaScript and PHP. Many of them support multiple protocols.

To create a websocket server you will first implement the following capabilities:

- Connection handshaking
- Listening for messages
- Decoding websocket frames
- Building and sending a message frame

Once the basic infrastructure is complete, you'll then provide the custom server features needed for your application. After all, the whole point of websockets is to allow the server to communicate with the client.

Designing the Agent Chat Application

In this chapter you'll build a server and two client applications that will allow agents to chat with multiple clients simultaneously. An agent will log in and connect to the server using the agent web application, letting the server know that the agent is ready to accept chat sessions. The agent application will be designed to handle up to four simultaneous chat sessions. Clients can then use the client web application to connect to the server. Each client is routed to an available agent and the chat session is started. From this point, the server is just forwarding messages between the client and the agent. This communication is described in Figure 13-3.

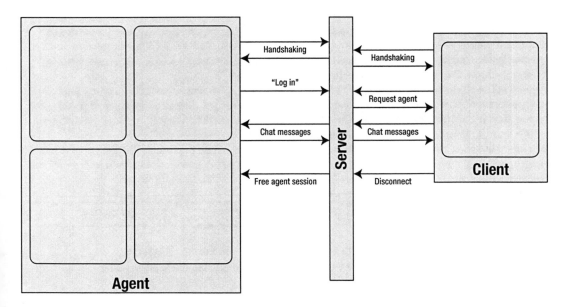

Figure 13-3. The websocket communication

To connect as an agent, the system will want to provide some authentication to ensure only authorized users can respond to clients. To simulate that, the agent application will use the standard ASP.NET web form that provides a login capability. You'll then add a custom Chat page that will allow the agent to response to four simultaneous chat sessions. However, anyone should be able to connect as a client so you'll use the Basic MVC template that you've used in previous chapters.

Both applications will connect to the websocket server using the normal handshaking protocol. Once connected, the Agent will send a message to the server that includes their name. This will signal the server that a new agent has come online. The agent's connection will be saved in a collection for future use.

The client application will also send a message to the server after the connection has been established, specifying the name of the client. The server will then find the first available agent that has an open chat session and send a message to that agent, providing the client's name. The agent page will then save the client's name on the page. At the same time, the server will send a message to the client, letting them know that an agent has been assigned to them.

At this point both the client and agent can send a message to the server, which is forwarded to the other application. Since the agent application can have four active sessions, the server will prefix the message with the client number so the agent application will know which session to update.

If the client disconnects, the server will send a message to the agent letting them know that. The agent application will then clear the corresponding chat session. If the agent disconnects, all the clients with active sessions with that agent are also notified and instructed to attempt a re-connect.

Creating a Simple Application

In this section you'll build a websocket server that handles the basic message protocols and test it using a simple web client. Initially, the server will just echo the message back to the client. You'll later add the functionality needed by the chat application. For this exercise, the server will be hosted in a console application.

Creating a WebSocket Server

To implement the websocket server you will create a WsServer class. This class creates a socket that it uses to listen for new connections. When a connection is received, it creates another socket for that connection and performs the handshaking that I described earlier. If the handshaking is successful it creates an instance of a WsConnection class that will manage the client connection.

The WsConnection class uses the new socket to listen for incoming messages on that connection. This class invokes the ReadMessage() method to process an incoming message. This handles all of the frame decoding and unmasking that may be required. The WsConnection class also provides a SendMessage() method that will send a message to the client at the other end of the connection.

The WsConnection class provides two events that are raised if handlers are provided. The first event is raised when an incoming message has been received. The second event is raised when the connection has been closed. The WsServer class will provide the event handlers for these events.

EXERCISE 13-1. CREATING A SIMPLE WEBSOCKET SERVER

1. Start Visual Studio 2012 and create a new project named **WsServer**. Select the Console Application template from the Windows category. Change the solution name to **Chapter13** as shown in Figure 13-4.

Figure 13-4. *Creating a console application project*

2. In the Solution Explorer, right-click the WsServer project and select the Add ➤ Class links. Enter **WsServer.cs** for the class name.

3. Enter the code shown in Listing 13-1 for the initial implementation of this class.

Listing 13-1. Implementing the WsServer class

```
using System;
using System.Collections.Generic;
using System.Text;

using System.Net;
using System.Net.Sockets;
using System.IO;
using System.Security.Cryptography;

namespace WsServer
{
    public class WsServer
    {
        #region Members

        // This socket listens for new connections
        Socket _listener;

        // Configurable port # that is passed in the constructor
        int _port;
```

```
            // List of connections
            List<WsConnection> _unknown;

            #endregion Members

            public WsServer(int port)
            {
                _port=port;

                // This is a list of active connections
                _unknown=new List<WsConnection>();
            }

            public void StartSocketServer()
            {
                // Create a socket that will listen for messages
                _listener=new Socket(AddressFamily.InterNetwork,
                                     SocketType.Stream,
                                     ProtocolType.IP);

                // Create and bind the endpoint
                IPEndPoint ip=new IPEndPoint(IPAddress.Loopback, _port);
                _listener.Bind(ip);

                // Listen for new connections - the OnConnect() method
                // will be invoked to handle them
                _listener.Listen(100);
                _listener.BeginAccept(new AsyncCallback(OnConnect), null);
            }

            void MessageReceived(WsConnection sender, MessageReceivedEventArgs e)
            {
                string msg=e.Message;
                Console.WriteLine(msg);
                sender.SendMessage("echo: "+msg);
            }

            void Disconnected(WsConnection sender, EventArgs e)
            {
                _unknown.Remove(sender);
                Console.WriteLine("Client has disconnected");
            }
        }
    }
```

The StartSocketServer() method is called to put the server to work. It creates a Socket object and configures it using the specified port. This method is hard-coded to use the localhost address. Once the end point is configured, the Socket object's BeginAccept() method is called. This will invoke the specified callback method (OnConnect) when a new connection is received. The MessageReceived() event handler simply writes the input message to the console and echoes the message back to the client. The WsConnection object that manages this connection is passed to the event handler. This code uses its SendMessage() method to send an echo back. The Disconnected() event handler, removes this connection from its active list and displays a message to the console window.

4. Add the PerformHandshake() method using the code shown in Listing 13-2.

Listing 13-2. Implementing the handshaking protocol

```
private void PerformHandshake(Socket s)
{
    using (NetworkStream stream=new NetworkStream(s))
    using (StreamReader reader=new StreamReader(stream))
    using (StreamWriter writer=new StreamWriter(stream))
    {
        string key="";

        // Read the input data using the stream reader, one line
        // at a time until all lines have been processed. The only
        // item that we need to get is the request key.
        string input="Empty";
        while (!string.IsNullOrWhiteSpace(input))
        {
            input=reader.ReadLine();

            if (input !=null &&
                input.Length>18 &&
                input.Substring(0, 18) == "Sec-WebSocket-Key:")
                // Save the request key
                key=input.Substring(19);
        }
        // This guid is used to generate the response key
        const String keyGuid="258EAFA5-E914-47DA-95CA-C5AB0DC85B11";
        string webSocketAccept;

        // The response key in generated by concatenating the request
        // key and the special guid. The result is then encrypted.
        string ret=key+keyGuid;
        SHA1 sha=new SHA1CryptoServiceProvider();
        byte[] sha1Hash=sha.ComputeHash(Encoding.UTF8.GetBytes(ret));
        webSocketAccept=Convert.ToBase64String(sha1Hash);

        // Send handshake response to the client using the
        // stream writer
        writer.WriteLine("HTTP/1.1 101 Switching Protocols");
        writer.WriteLine("Upgrade: websocket");
        writer.WriteLine("Connection: Upgrade");
        writer.WriteLine("Sec-WebSocket-Accept: "+webSocketAccept);
        writer.WriteLine("");
    }
}
```

The PerformHandshake() method creates a NetworkStream object passing in the Socket object to its constructor. This is the new socket that was created for this connection. It uses a StreamReader object to read the incoming data and later uses a StreamWriter to send data back. By creating these inside nested using statements you won't have to worry about disposing them. Keep in mind that the handshaking is done using http protocol so the reading and sending of data does not use the WebSocket frames.

The StreamReader object is used to read the input, one line at a time. You don't need any of this data because, for this exercise, we're assuming the correct protocol is being requested. In a more general case, however, you may need to support multiple protocols so you will need to read and interpret what is being sent in. You will need the request key, however, so this is extracted from the appropriate input line.

The response key is then concatenated with a special guid value. This is documented in the Version 13 specification (http://tools.ietf.org/id/draft-ietf-hybi-thewebsocketprotocol-13.txt). The resulting string is then encrypted using the SHA1 algorithm. Finally, the StreamWriter object is used to send back the response including the generated key.

5. Add the OnConnect() event handler using the code in Listing 13-3.

Listing 13-3. Implementing the OnConnect() event handler

```
private void OnConnect(IAsyncResult asyn)
{
    // create a new socket for the connection
    Socket socket = _listener.EndAccept(asyn);

    // Perform the necessary handshaking
    PerformHandshake(socket);

    // Create a WsConnection object for this connection
    WsConnection client = new WsConnection(socket);
    _unknown.Add(client);

    // Wire-up the event handlers
    client.MessageReceived += new MessageReceivedEventHandler(MessageReceived);
    client.Disconnected += new WsDisconnectedEventHandler(Disconnected);

    // Listen for more connections
    _listener.BeginAccept(new AsyncCallback(OnConnect), null);
}
```

The OnConnect() method gets a new Socket for this connection by calling the EndAccept() method. It calls the PerformHandshake() method and creates a WsConnection class, which you will implement next. It then connects the event handlers so the WsServer object will be notified when a message is received or the connection is closed. Finally, BeginAccept() is called again to listen for more connections.

6. In the Solution Explorer, right-click the WsServer project and select the Add ➤ Class links. Enter **WsConnection.cs** for the class name.

7. Enter the code shown in Listing 13-4 as the initial implementation for this class.

Listing 13-4. Implementing the WsConnection class

```
using System;
using System.Collections.Generic;
using System.Text;
```

```csharp
using System.Net.Sockets;

namespace WsServer
{
    // This class defines the data that is passed to the MessageReceived
    // event handler
    public class MessageReceivedEventArgs
    {
        public string Message { get; private set; }
        public int DataLength { get; private set; }
        public MessageReceivedEventArgs(string msg, int len)
        {
            DataLength = len;
            Message = msg;
        }
    }

    // Define the event handler delegates
    public delegate void MessageReceivedEventHandler
        (WsConnection sender, MessageReceivedEventArgs e);

    public delegate void WsDisconnectedEventHandler
        (WsConnection sender, EventArgs e);

    public class WsConnection : IDisposable
    {
        #region Members

        public Socket _mySocket;
        protected byte[] _inputBuffer;
        protected StringBuilder _inputString;

        // Define the events that are available
        public event MessageReceivedEventHandler MessageReceived;
        public event WsDisconnectedEventHandler Disconnected;

        #endregion Members

        public WsConnection(Socket s)
        {
            _mySocket = s;
            _inputBuffer = new byte[255];
            _inputString = new StringBuilder();

            // Begin listening - the ReadMessage() method will be
            // invoked when a message is received.
            _mySocket.BeginReceive(_inputBuffer,
                                   0,
                                   _inputBuffer.Length,
                                   0,
```

```
                                        ReadMessage,
                                        null);
            }

            protected void OnMessageReceived(string msg)
            {
                // When a message is received, call the event handler if
                // one has been specified
                if (MessageReceived != null)
                    MessageReceived(this, new MessageReceivedEventArgs(msg, msg.
Length));
            }

            public void Dispose()
            {
                _mySocket.Close();
            }
        }
    }
```

The WsConnection class has three class members:

- _mySocket – The Socket object created for this connection. This is instantiated by the WsServer class and passed into the constructor.

- _inputBuffer – This is a byte array that holds the raw frame data. This is populated by the Socket object.

- _inputString – This is a StringBuilder object that contains the incoming message after it has been processed.

The WsConnection class supports two events to notify when data has been received and when the connection with the client has been closed. The MessageReceived event uses a MessageReceivedEventArgs class to provide the received message to the event handler. The WsConnection class implements the Dispose() method, which simply closes the Socket associated with this connection.

The WsConnection class has two primary methods, which you'll implement now. These methods implement the WebSocket frame protocol.

- ReadMessage()

- SendMessage()

  8. Add the ReadMessage() method using the code shown in Listing 13-5

Listing 13-5. Implementing the ReadMessage() method.

```
protected void ReadMessage(IAsyncResult msg)
{
    int sizeOfReceivedData = _mySocket.EndReceive(msg);
    if (sizeOfReceivedData > 0)
    {
        // Get the data provided in the first 2 bytes
        bool final = (_inputBuffer[0] & 0x80) > 0 ? true : false;
        bool masked = (_inputBuffer[1] & 0x80) > 0 ? true : false;
```

```
    int dataLength = _inputBuffer[1] & 0x7F;

    int actualLength;
    int dataIndex = 0;
    byte[] length = new byte[8];
    byte[] masks = new byte[4];

    // Depending on the initial data length, get the actual length
    // and the maskingkey from the appropriate bytes.
    if (dataLength == 126)
    {
        dataIndex = 4;
        Array.Copy(_inputBuffer, 2, length, 0, 2);
        actualLength = BitConverter.ToInt16(length, 0);

        if (masked)
            Array.Copy(_inputBuffer, 4, masks, 0, 4);
    }
    else if (dataLength == 127)
    {
        dataIndex = 10;
        Array.Copy(_inputBuffer, 2, length, 0, 8);
        actualLength = (int)BitConverter.ToInt64(length, 0);
        if (masked)
            Array.Copy(_inputBuffer, 10, masks, 0, 4);
    }
    else
    {
        dataIndex = 2;
        actualLength = dataLength;
        if (masked)
            Array.Copy(_inputBuffer, 2, masks, 0, 4);
    }

    // If a mask is supplied, skip another 4 bytes
    if (masked)
        dataIndex += 4;

    // Get the actual data in the payload array
    byte[] payload = new byte[actualLength];
    Array.Copy(_inputBuffer, dataIndex, payload, 0, dataLength);

    // Unmask the data, if necessary
    if (masked)
    {
        for (int i = 0; i < actualLength; i++)
        {
            payload[i] = (byte)(payload[i] ^ masks[i % 4]);
        }
    }
}
```

```
                    // Copy the data into the input string and empty the buffer
                    _inputString.Append(Encoding.UTF8
                        .GetString(payload, 0, (int)actualLength));
                    Array.Clear(_inputBuffer, 0, _inputBuffer.Length);

                    // If this is the final frame, raise an event and clear the input
                    if (final)
                    {
                        // Do something with the data
                        OnMessageReceived(_inputString.ToString());

                        // Clear the input string
                        _inputString.Clear();
                    }

                    // Listening for more messages
                    _mySocket.BeginReceive(_inputBuffer,
                                           0,
                                           _inputBuffer.Length,
                                           0,
                                           ReadMessage,
                                           null);
            }
            // If we were not able to read the message, assume that
            // the socket is closed
            else
            {
                if (Disconnected != null)
                    Disconnected(this, EventArgs.Empty);
            }
        }
```

ReadMessage() processes a single incoming frame. It looks at the first two bytes to determine where the length is specified and if masking is used. It then gets the actual length and extracts the mask. Finally the data is unmasked. The raw data for the frame is placed in the _inputBuffer byte array by the Socket object. The processed data is stored in the _inputString member. Both of these are class members. The processed data from each frame is appended to the _inputString member. When the final frame has been processed, the entire string is passed to the OnMessageReceived() method. This allows for a single message to be transmitted in multiple frames. The OnMessageReceived() method simply invokes the event handler, if defined.

9. Add the SendMessage() method using the code in Listing 13-6.

Listing 13-6. Implementing the SendMessage() method

```
public void SendMessage(string msg)
{
    if (_mySocket.Connected)
    {
        // Create the output buffer
        Int64 dataLength = msg.Length;
        int dataStart = 0;
        byte[] dataOut = new byte[dataLength + 10];
```

```
            // Build the frame data - depending on the length, it can
            // be passed one of three ways
            dataOut[0]=0x81;

            // Store the length in the 2nd byte
            if (dataLength<256)
            {
                dataOut[1]=(byte)dataLength;
                dataStart=2;
            }
            // Store the length in the 3rd and 4th bytes
            else if (dataLength<UInt16.MaxValue)
            {
                dataOut[1]=0xFE;
                dataOut[2]=(byte)(dataLength & 0x00FF);
                dataOut[3]=(byte)(dataLength & 0xFF00);
                dataStart=4;
            }
            // Store the length in bytes 3 - 9
            else
            {
                dataOut[1]=0xFF;
                for (int i=0; i<8; i++)
                    dataOut[i+2]=(byte)((dataLength >>(i * 8)) & 0x000000FF);
                dataStart=10;
            }

            // Encode the data and store it in the output buffer
            byte[] data=Encoding.UTF8.GetBytes(msg);
            Array.Copy(data, 0, dataOut, dataStart, dataLength);

            // Send the message
            try
            {
                _mySocket.Send(dataOut,
                               (int)(dataLength+dataStart),
                               SocketFlags.None);
            }
            catch
            {
                // If we get an error, assume the socket has been disconnected
                if (Disconnected !=null)
                    Disconnected(this, EventArgs.Empty);
            }
        }
    }
```

The SendMessage() method constructs the frame header and then appends the actual text being sent. It then uses the Send() method of the Socket object to send this frame to the client.

10. With these classes implemented you can now implement the main `Program` class. Add the following code to the `Main()` method:

```
// Create the WsServer, specifying the server's address
WsServer server = new WsServer(8300);

// Start the server
server.StartSocketServer();

// Keep running until the Enter key is pressed
string input = Console.ReadLine();
```

This code creates the `WsServer` class and calls the `StartSocketServer()` method. It calls the `Console.ReadLine()` method, which will wait until the Enter key is pressed.

Creating a Web Application

With a basic server implementation you're now ready to create a web application that will use it. You will create a project using the Basic MVC4 template that you used in previous chapters. You will later modify this application to use it as the client web page.

EXERCISE 13-2. CREATING A SIMPLE CLIENT

1. In the Solution Explorer, right-click the Chapter13 solution and then select the Add ➤ New Project links.

2. In the Add New Project dialog box, select the "ASP.NET MVC4 Web Application" template. Enter the project name **Client** as shown in Figure 13-5.

Figure 13-5. Creating the Client project

3. In the next dialog box, select the Basic template and make sure the Razor view engine is selected. Click the OK button and the project will be created.

4. Right-click the Controller folder in the Solution Explorer and select the Add ➤ Controller link. Enter the name **HomeController** and select the Empty MVC Controller template. Click the Add button to create the controller.

5. Right-click the View folder and select the Add ➤ New Folder links. Enter the name **Home**.

6. Right-click the new Home folder and select the Add ➤ View links. In the Add View dialog box, enter the name **Index**, make sure the Razor view engine is selected, unselect all the check boxes, and click the Add button.

7. In the Index.cshtml file, modify the body element by adding the following markup shown in bold:

```
<body onload="connect();">
    <div>

        <pre id="output"></pre>
        <input type="text" id="input" value="" />
        <input type="submit" id="sendMsg" value="Send Message"
                onclick="send();" />

    </div>
</body>
```

8. This creates a pre element that will be used to display messages that are received as well as other debugging messages. This also defines a text box for entering the message text and a button to send it. The onload event will call the connect() function that you will implement next.

9. Now you're ready to implement the JavaScript that will communicate with your websocket server. The browser takes care of the protocol and frame manipulation so the client side is pretty easy. Add the script element shown in Listing 13-7 to the head element:

Listing 13-7. The client side JavaScript

```
<script type="text/javascript">
    var ws; // This is our socket

    function connect() {

        output("Connecting to host...");
        try {
            ws = new WebSocket("ws://localhost:8300/chat");
        } catch (e) {
            output(e);
        }
```

```
        ws.onopen = function () {
            output("connected... ");
        };

        ws.onmessage = function (e) {
            output(e.data);
        };

        ws.onclose = function () {
            output("Connection closed");
        };
    };

    function send() {
        var input = document.getElementById("input");

        try {
            ws.send(input.value);
        } catch (e) {
            output(e);
        }
    }

    function output(msg) {
        var o = document.getElementById("output");
        o.innerHTML = o.innerHTML + "<p>" + msg + "</p>";
    };

</script>
```

The onload event in the body element calls the connect() function. The connect() function creates a WebSocket object and wires up the onOpen, onMessage, and onClose() event handlers. When the Send Message button is clicked, the send() function is invoked. This gets the message from the text box and calls the websocket's send() function. The output() function simply add the specified text to the pre element.

Testing the Initial Project

You now have a basic server application and a simple client. You'll test this now to make sure websocket is working properly before adding the custom features.

EXERCISE 13-3. TESTING THE INITIAL APPLICATION

1. In the Solution Explorer, right-click the Chapter13 solution and select the "Set StartUp Projects" link.

2. In the dialog box, select the "Multiple startup projects" radio button. For both the WsServer and Client projects, change the Action to "Start". Also, use the arrows to the right of the project list so the WsServer project is started first, as shown in Figure 13-6. Click the OK button to save these options.

Figure 13-6. *Setting the startup projects*

3. In the toolbar, click the dropdown control next to the Start button and select the Browse With link. In the Browse With dialog box, select Google Chrome and then click the "Set as Default" button to make this the default browser to debug with as shown in Figure 13-7. We don't want to start browsing yet; just configure the default browser, so click the Cancel button to close the dialog box.

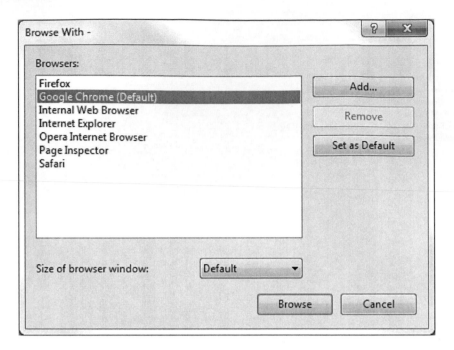

Figure 13-7. Selecting the default browser

4. Press F5 to start both the console application that hosts the websocket server and the client web page. The web page will show the "Connecting to host…" text and then "connected…".

5. Enter some text in the input box and click the Send Message button. You should see this text display in the console window and it will also be echoed on the client page as shown in Figure 13-8.

Figure 13-8. The initial client webpage

Enhancing the WebSocket Server

The solution you have developed so far implements the websocket protocol and demonstrates how data is passed between the server and client. However, using a websocket server that merely echoes the message back is not very useful. This server must manage the communication with both clients and agents. When a client sends a message to the server it will be forwarded to the appropriate agent. When the agent sends a response (back to the server) the server must route that back to the corresponding client.

To do this you will implement two more classes in the WsServer project:

- WsAgentConnection – manages the communication with an agent application

- WsClientConnection – manages the communication with a client application

Both of these classes will use an instance of the WsConnection class to send and receive messages. The WsAgentConnection class will reference up to four instances of the WsClientConnection class that represent the four clients the agent is currently chatting with. The WsClientConnection must also have a reference to the WsAgentConnection object that represents the agent supporting this client. This is described in Figure 13-9.

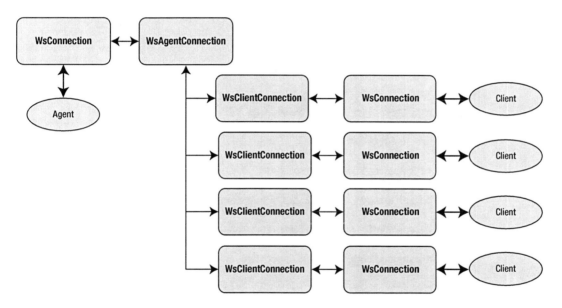

Figure 13-9. The internal server classes

When the server first receives a connection, it doesn't yet know if it is a client or an agent. It will create a WsConnection object that will listen for messages. Both applications will be coded to immediately send a message to the server identifying both the type of application (client or agent) and also the agent's or client's name. When this message is received, the server will then create either a WsAgentConnection object or a WsClientConnection object and add this to either the agent or client list.

If this is a client, the server will find an available agent and perform the necessary linkages between the WsAgentConnection and WsClientConnection objects. The server will also send a response to the client letting them know the name of the agent that they will be working with. If this is an agent, a WsAgentConnection is created and added to the agent list so it is available to respond to new clients.

When the WsConnection object is first created, it's MessageReceived and Disconnected events are handled by the WsServer object. The server will need to process the incoming message that identifies the client or agent.

However, once the specialized class is created (WsAgentConnection or WsClientConnection), this class will need to handle these events. To do this, the WsServer object must remove the event handlers, and then associate the event handlers from the new class. The specialized classes will both re-raise the Disconnected event which the WsServer object will handle.

```
┌─────────────────────────────────────────────────────────────┐
│         EXERCISE 13-4. ENHANCING THE WEBSOCKET SERVER         │
└─────────────────────────────────────────────────────────────┘
```

1. In the Solution Explorer, right-click the WsServer project and select the Add ➤ Class links. Enter **WsAgentConnection.cs** for the class name.

2. Enter the code shown in Listing 13-8 as the implementation for this class.

Listing 13-8. Implementing the WsAgentConnection class

```csharp
using System;
using System.Collections.Generic;
using System.Text;

using System.Net.Sockets;

namespace WsServer
{
    public delegate void WsDisconnectedAgentEventHandler
        (WsAgentConnection sender, EventArgs e);

    public class WsAgentConnection : IDisposable
    {
        private WsConnection _connection;
        public string _name;
        public Dictionary< int, WsClientConnection >_clients;

        public event WsDisconnectedAgentEventHandler AgentDisconnected;

        public WsAgentConnection(WsConnection conn, string name)
        {
            _connection = conn;
            _name = name;

            // Initialize our client list
            _clients = new Dictionary< int, WsClientConnection >();
            for (int i =1; i <= 4; i++)
            {
                _clients.Add(i, null);
            }
        }

        public void MessageReceived(WsConnection sender,
                                    MessageReceivedEventArgs e)
```

```
        {
            string s = e.Message.Substring(0, 1);
            int i = 0;
            if (int.TryParse(s, out i))
            {
                WsClientConnection client = _clients[i];
                if (client != null)
                {
                    client.SendMessage(e.Message.Substring(2));
                }
            }
        }

        public void SendMessage(string msg)
        {
            if (_connection != null)
                _connection.SendMessage(msg);
        }

        public void Disconnected(WsConnection sender, EventArgs e)
        {
            if (AgentDisconnected != null)
                AgentDisconnected(this, EventArgs.Empty);
        }

        public void Dispose()
        {
            if (_connection != null)
                _connection.Dispose();
        }
    }
}
```

The WsAgentConnection class uses a Dictionary to store the client connections. The key will be an integer (1–4) which will be important to the agent application so it knows which chat window to update. The constructor creates all four entries, setting the WsConnection reference to null. A null reference indicates that there is no client actively communicating in this window. The constructor also receives the associated WsConnection object. This is saved in the _connection member and is used to send a message to the agent application.

When an agent sends a message to the server it is prefixed with a number (1–4) indicating which client this should be forwarded to. The MessageReceived() event handler strips this off and then finds the corresponding WsClientConnection object in the Dictionary. The remainder of the message is then forwarded to the client using the WsClientConnection object's SendMessage() method.

The SendMessage() method simply calls the SendMessage() of the WsConnection object associated with this agent. The Disconnected() event handler raises the AgentDisconnected event, which will be handled by the WsServer class.

3. In the Solution Explorer, right-click the WsServer project and select the Add ➤ Class links. Enter **WsClientConnection.cs** for the class name.

4. Enter the code shown in Listing 13-9 as the implementation for this class.

Listing 13-9. Implementing the WsClientConnection class

```csharp
using System;
using System.Collections.Generic;
using System.Text;

using System.Net.Sockets;

namespace WsServer
{
    public delegate void WsDisconnectedClientEventHandler
        (WsClientConnection sender, EventArgs e);

    public class WsClientConnection : IDisposable
    {
        private WsConnection _connection;
        public string _name;
        public WsAgentConnection _agent;
        public int _clientID;

        public event WsDisconnectedClientEventHandler ClientDisconnected;

        public WsClientConnection(WsConnection conn,
                                  WsAgentConnection agent,
                                  int id,
                                  string name)
        {
            _connection = conn;
            _agent = agent;
            _clientID = id;
            _name = name;
        }

        public void MessageReceived(WsConnection sender,
                                    MessageReceivedEventArgs e)
        {
            if (_agent != null)
            {
                _agent.SendMessage(_clientID.ToString()+": "+e.Message);
            }
        }

        public void SendMessage(string msg)
        {
            if (_connection != null)
                _connection.SendMessage(msg);
        }

        public void Disconnected(WsConnection sender, EventArgs e)
        {
            if (ClientDisconnected != null)
                ClientDisconnected(this, EventArgs.Empty);
        }
```

```
        public void Dispose()
        {
            if (_connection != null)
                _connection.Dispose();
        }
    }
}
```

The WsClientConnection class is very similar to the WsAgentConnection class. Instead of a Dictionary of associated clients, it has a single reference to the WsAgentConnection object. This represents the agent that the client is chatting with. The constructor supplies the underlying WsConnection object, the associated WsAgentConection object, and the ID by which this client is known. This is used to prefix the message that is forwarded to the agent.

5. Open the WsServer.cs file and add the code shown in bold. This creates the collections that will store the agent and client objects.

```
#region Members

// This socket listens for new connections
Socket _listener;

// Configurable port # that is passed in the constructor
int _port;

// List of connections
List<WsConnection> _unknown;

List<WsAgentConnection> _agents;
List<WsClientConnection> _clients;

#endregion Members

public WsServer(int port)
{
    _port = port;

    // This is a list of active connections
    _unknown = new List<WsConnection>();

    _agents = new List<WsAgentConnection>();
    _clients = new List<WsClientConnection>();

}
```

6. In the WsServer class, replace the MessageReceived() event handler with the code shown in Listing 13-10.

Listing 13-10. The revised MessageReceived() event handler

```
void MessageReceived(WsConnection sender, MessageReceivedEventArgs e)
{
    string msg=e.Message;
    if (e.DataLength>14 && (msg.Substring(0, 14) == "[Agent SignOn:"))
    {
        // This is an agent signing on
        string name=msg.Substring(14, e.DataLength - 15);
        WsAgentConnection agent=new WsAgentConnection(sender, name);

        // Re-wire the event handlers
        sender.Disconnected -= Disconnected;
        sender.MessageReceived -= MessageReceived;
        sender.Disconnected += agent.Disconnected;
        sender.MessageReceived += agent.MessageReceived;

        agent.AgentDisconnected +=
            new WsDisconnectedAgentEventHandler(AgentDisconnected);

        // Move this socket to the agent list
        _unknown.Remove(sender);
        _agents.Add(agent);

        // Send a response
        agent.SendMessage("Welcome, "+name);
    }
    else if (e.DataLength>15 &&
            (msg.Substring(0, 15) == "[Client SignOn:"))
    {
        // This is a client requesting assistance
        string name=msg.Substring(15, e.DataLength - 16);

        // Find an agent
        WsAgentConnection agent=null;
        int clientID=0;
        foreach (WsAgentConnection a in _agents)
        {
            foreach (KeyValuePair<int, WsClientConnection>d in a._clients)
            {
                if (d.Value == null)
                {
                    agent=a;
                    clientID=d.Key;
                    break;
                }
            }
            if (agent != null)
                break;
        }
```

```
            if (agent != null)
            {
                WsClientConnection client =
                    new WsClientConnection(sender, agent, clientID, name);

                // Re-wire the event handlers
                sender.Disconnected -= Disconnected;
                sender.MessageReceived -= MessageReceived;
                sender.Disconnected += client.Disconnected;
                sender.MessageReceived += client.MessageReceived;

                client.ClientDisconnected +=
                    new WsDisconnectedClientEventHandler(ClientDisconnected);

                // Add this to the agent list
                _unknown.Remove(sender);
                _clients.Add(client);

                agent._clients[clientID]=client;

                // Send a message to the agent
                agent.SendMessage("[ClientName:"+clientID.ToString() +
                                  name+"]");

                // Send a response
                client.SendMessage("Hello! My name is "+agent._name +
                    ". How may I help you?");
            }
            else
            {
                // There are no agents available
                sender.SendMessage("There are no agents currently available;" +
                    "please try again later");
            }
        }
    }
```

As I explained earlier, the first message that is sent by both the client and agent applications is a sign-on message that includes their name. This will be formatted like one of these. Any other message will be ignored.

- Agent = "[Agent SignOn:<agent name>]"

- Client = "[Client SignOn:<client name>]"

The MessageReceived() event handler checks to see if the incoming message is one of these. For an agent sign-on, the name is extracted from the message. It then creates a WsAgentConnection class and sets its _name property. The MessageReceived and Disconnected events from the WsConnection object are currently mapped to the WsServer event handler. This mapping is removed and instead, these events are mapped to the WsAgentConnection object's event handers. Also, the WsAgentConnection class defines an AgentDisconnected event, which is mapped to a new event handler that you will implement later. The WsConnection object is removed from the _unknown list and the WsAgentConnection object is added to the _agents list. Finally, a welcome message is sent to the agent application.

When a client sign-on is received, very similar processing is done to create the WsClientConnection object and re-wire the event handlers. In addition, the code looks for an available agent. This iterates through the _agents list and for each agent, looks for a Dictionary entry with a null WsClientConnection reference. The search stops when the first null entry is found.

■ **Tip** You might want to improve this search to load balance between available agents. As this is currently implemented, the first agent will handle the first four clients while the other agents are idle. The search could iterate through the agents looking for the one with the fewest active clients and send the new client to them.

If an available agent was found, the WsAgentConnection object and the Dictionary key are passed to the WsClientConnection object constructor. Also, the WsClientConnection object is stored in the available Dictionary entry. A message is sent to agent application letting them know that a new client has been assigned to them. Finally, a message is sent to the client application letting the client know which agent will be assisting them. If there are no available agents, a message indicating that is sent to the client application.

7. Add the event handlers shown in Listing 13-11 to the WsServer class.

Listing 13-11. Adding the additional event handlers

```
void ClientDisconnected(WsClientConnection sender, EventArgs e)
{
    if (sender._agent != null)
    {
        sender._agent._clients[sender._clientID]=null;
        sender._agent.SendMessage("[ClientClose:" +
            sender._clientID.ToString()+"]");
    }
    _clients.Remove(sender);
    sender.Dispose();
}

void AgentDisconnected(WsAgentConnection sender, EventArgs e)
{
    foreach (KeyValuePair<int, WsClientConnection>d in sender._clients)
    {
        if (d.Value != null)
        {
            _clients.Remove(d.Value);
            d.Value.SendMessage
                ("The agent has been disconnected; please reconnect");
        }
    }
    _agents.Remove(sender);
    sender.Dispose();
}
```

These event handlers are invoked when the client or agent application is closed or otherwise disconnected. In addition to removing the connection from the appropriate list, a message is sent to the other end of the conversation so proper clean-up can be performed. If an agent is disconnected, all of the clients that were connected to it need to be notified.

Creating the Agent Application

Now you'll create the agent application that will be used by the agents responding to client requests. This will support up to four simultaneous chat sessions.

Creating the Agent Project

The Agent application will start with the standard ASP.NET web site template. This provides the ability to register and login to the site, simulating the authentication that an agent would normally use.

EXERCISE 13-5. CREATING THE AGENT PROJECT

1. From the Solution Explorer, right-click the Chapter13 solution and select the Add ➤ New Project links.

2. In the "Add New Project" dialog box, select the "ASP.NET MVC 4 Web Application" template and enter the name **Agent** as shown in Figure 13-10. Click the OK button to continue.

Figure 13-10. Creating the Agent application

3. In the next dialog box, select the Internet Application template and make sure the Razor engine is selected as shown in Figure 13-11. This template provides a login form that the agents will use to authenticate.

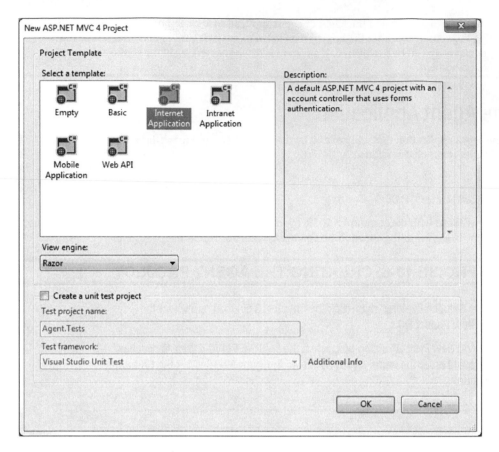

Figure 13-11. Selecting the Internet template

4. You will create a separate web page that supports the chat sessions. In the Solution Explorer, right-click the Views\Home folder and select the Add ➤ View links.

5. In the Add View dialog box, enter the name **Chat**, make sure the Razor view engine is selected, and all check boxes are unselected. Click the Add button to add the view.

6. In the Controllers folder, open the HomeController.cs file. Add the following method to the HomeController class:

```
public ActionResult Chat()
{
    ViewBag.Message = "Respond to chat";

    return View();
}
```

7. In the Views\Shared folder, open the _Layout.cshtml file. Inside the nav element you'll see three @Html.ActionLink() methods that setup the navigation options on the home page. Add the following line to this section to add a navigation link to the new chat page:

```
<li>@Html.ActionLink("Begin Chat", "Chat", "Home")</li>
```

Implementing the Chat Web Page

Now you'll implement the chat page. This will support four separate chat sessions. You'll first add the markup for the elements that you'll need and then apply a style element to make the page look better. Then you'll add JavaScript to access the websocket and communicate with the websocket server that you created.

EXERCISE 13-6. IMPLEMENTING THE CHAT PAGE

1. Open the chat.cshtml file and replace the body element with the markup shown in Listing 13-12.

Listing 13-12. Adding the page markup

```
<body onload="connect();">
    <div>
        <div>
        <p id="agentName">@User.Identity.Name</p>
        <pre id="output"></pre>
        </div>
        <div id="div1" class="client">
            <p id="client1" class="clientName">unassigned</p>
            <div id="chat1" class="chat">

            </div>
          <input type="text" id="input1" class="input" value="" />
          <input type="submit" value="Send" onclick="send('1');" />
        </div>
        <div id="div2" class="client">
            <p id="client2" class="clientName">unassigned</p>
            <div id="chat2" class="chat">

            </div>
          <input type="text" id="input2" class="input" value="" />
          <input type="submit" value="Send" onclick="send('2');" />
        </div>
        <div id="div3" class="client">
            <p id="client3" class="clientName">unassigned</p>
            <div id="chat3" class="chat">

            </div>
          <input type="text" id="input3" class="input" value="" />
          <input type="submit" value="Send" onclick="send('3');" />
```

```
            </div>
            <div id="div4" class="client">
                <p id="client4" class="clientName">unassigned</p>
                <div id="chat4" class="chat">

                </div>
                <input type="text" id="input4" class="input" value="" />
                <input type="submit" value="Send" onclick="send('4');" />
            </div>
        </div>
    </body>
```

At the top of the body element, there is a p element with the value of @User.Indentity.Name. This is Razor syntax that will display the agent's name here. Since the agent will be logged in, the web page already knows their name.

This page will use a div element for each of the chat windows. Inside this there is an empty div element that will contain the messages that are sent back and forth. Inside the outer div there is p element that will hold the client's name, which is currently set to "unassigned". There is also a textbox that is used to enter the message and a button to send it.

2. To improve the layout of the form, add the style element shown in Listing 13-13 inside the head element.

Listing 13-13. Adding the style element

```
<style>
    body
    {
        background: #f0f0f0;
        width: 900px;
    }
    .client
    {
        display: block;
        float: left;
        width: 400px;
        height: 385px;
        border: 2px solid #6699cc;
        border-radius: 5px;
        background-color: white;
    }
    .chat
    {
        height: 300px;
        font-size: smaller;
        line-height: 12px;
        overflow-y: scroll;
    }
    .input
    {
        width:330px;
    }
```

```
        .clientName
        {
            height: 20px;
            width: 380px;
            text-align: center;
            font-size: 15px;
            font-weight: bold;
        }
    </style>
```

3. Now you'll add the JavaScript code that will make all of this work. Add the `script` element shown in Listing 13-14 to the `head` element.

Listing 13-14. The JavaScript implementation

```
<script type="text/javascript">

    var ws; // This is our socket

    function connect() {

        output("Connecting to host...");
        try {
            ws=new WebSocket("ws://localhost:8300/chat");
        } catch (e) {
            output(e);
        }
        ws.onopen=function () {
            output("connected... ");

            // Send the Agent sign-on message
            var p=document.getElementById("agentName");
            ws.send("[Agent SignOn:"+p.innerHTML+"]");
        };

        ws.onmessage=function (e) {
            displayMsg(e.data);
        };

        ws.onclose=function () {
            output("Connection closed");
        };
    };

    // Send the input text to the server
    function send(i) {
        var input=document.getElementById("input"+i);
```

```
        try {
            ws.send(i+":"+input.value);
            var o=document.getElementById("chat"+i);
            o.innerHTML=o.innerHTML+"<p><b>Me:</b>"+input.value+"</p>";
            input.value="";
        } catch (e) {
            output(e);
        }
    }

    // Add text to the debug area
    function output(msg) {
        var o=document.getElementById("output");
        o.innerHTML=o.innerHTML+"<p>"+msg+"</p>";
    };

    // Handle a received message
    function displayMsg(msg) {
        var i=msg.substring(0, 1);
        var cmd=msg.substring(0, 12);

        // For the initial message from the server, save the client's name
        if (cmd === "[ClientName:") {
            displayClientName(msg.substring(12));
        }

        // If the client has disconnected, clear the chat window
        else if (cmd === "[ClientClose") {
            resetClient(msg.substring(13,14));
        }

        // Display the message in the debug area is not formatted properly
        else if (i !="1" && i !="2" && i !="3" && i !="4") {
            output(msg)
        }

        // Display the message in the chat window
        else {
            var o=document.getElementById("chat"+i);
            o.innerHTML=o.innerHTML+"<p><b>Client:</b>" +
                msg.substring(3, msg.length)+"</p>";
        }
    };

    // Display the client's name in the chat window
    function displayClientName(msg) {
        var i=msg.substring(0, 1);
        var o=document.getElementById("client"+i);
        o.innerHTML=msg.substring(1, msg.length - 1);
    }
```

```
            // Clear the chat window so it can be reused for another client
            function resetClient(i) {
                // Clear the client's name
                var o = document.getElementById("client" + i);
                o.innerHTML = "unassigned";

                // Remove the chat messages
                var o2 = document.getElementById("chat" + i);
                while (o2.hasChildNodes()) {
                    o2.removeChild(o2.firstChild);
                }
            }
        </script>
```

Just like the earlier web page that you implemented, the onload event calls the connect() function, which wires up the onopen, onmessage, and onclose event handlers. In this case, the onopen event handler sends the agent sign-on message to the server. The onmessage event handler calls the displayMsg() function. This has special logic to interpret the message. The server will send the client's name when the client is assigned and will send a message when the client has disconnected. These special cases are processed by the displayClientName() and resetClient() functions, respectively. For all other messages, the first character is expected to be 1–4, indicating which window this is for. Using this, the appropriate div element is obtained and the message is added to it. The message is prefixed with the "Client:" text.

The send() function that is called when the Send button is clicked takes a parameter that indicates which window is sending the message. It uses this to get the appropriate input element and also to prefix the message so the server will know which client this is for. It also displays the text in the div element after prefixing it with the "Me:" text. This is done so the chat window contains both incoming and outgoing messages.

The resetClient() function changes the client name back to "unassigned". It also iterates through the div, removing all of the p tags that were added.

Testing the Agent Application

Before you complete the development, let's test the form to make sure it looks OK. In the Solution Explorer, right-click the Agent project and select the Debug ➤ "Start new instance" links. This should launch the Chrome browser and display the home page. Click the Register link at the top of the page and enter your name, e-mail address, and a password as shown in Figure 13-12.

Your logo here

Register. Create a new account.

Passwords must be at least 6 characters long.

User name

Mark

Email address

markc@thecreativepeople.com

Password

••••••

Confirm password

••••••

Register

Figure 13-12. Registering the user

Now your name is displayed on the form as shown in Figure 13-13.

Hello, Mark ! Log off

Home   About   Contact   **Begin Chat**

Figure 13-13. The navigation links

■ **Tip**   The next time you open this site, you'll use the Log In link instead of the Register link. When you log in, if you select the Remember Me check box, it will automatically log you in when the application is started.

Notice also the Begin Chat link that you added. Click this link to open the chat page, which should look like Figure 13-14.

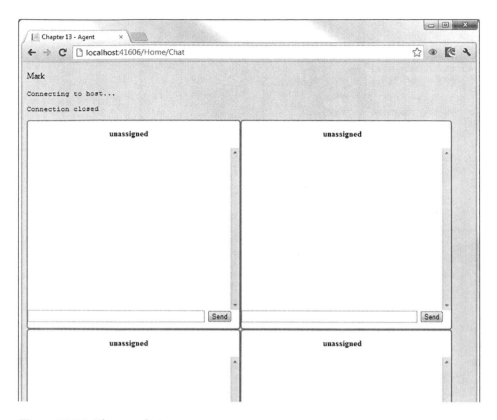

Figure 13-14. *The new chat page*

Because the server is not running, the connection could not be established and the "Connection closed" message is displayed. Close the window and stop the debugger.

Implementing the Client Application

You created the Client project earlier in the chapter to test the initial server implementation. Now you'll modify the Index.cshtml file to function as the client side of the chat solution.

EXERCISE 13-7. CREATING THE CLIENT APPLICATION

1. Open the Index.cshtml file in the Client project.

2. Replace the body element with the following markup. This adds a div element that contains a textbox for the client's name and a submit button. A second div implements the actual chat window. It includes a div that will display the chat messages, a text box for entering a new message and a submit button that will send it.

```
<body>
    <div>
        <p>Enter your name to begin chat</p>
        <input type="text" id="name" class="input" value="" />
        <input type="submit" id="connect"
                value="Chat now..." onclick="connect();" />
        <pre id="output"></pre>
    </div>
    <div id="div1" class="client">
        <p id="client1" class="clientName"></p>
        <div id="chat1" class="chat">

        </div>
        <input type="text" id="input" class="input" value="" />
        <input type="submit" value="Send" class="send" onclick="send();" />
    </div>
</body>
```

3. Add the `style` element shown in Listing 13-15 to the `head` element:

Listing 13-15. Defining the CSS styles

```
<style>
    body
    {
        background: #f0f0f0;
        width: 450px;
    }
    .client
    {
        display: block;
        float: left;
        width: 400px;
        height: 345px;
        border: 2px solid #6699cc;
        border-radius: 5px;
        background-color: white;
    }
    .chat
    {
        height: 300px;
        font-size: smaller;
        line-height: 12px;
        overflow-y: scroll;
    }
    .input
    {
        width:330px;
    }
</style>
```

4. Replace the existing `script` element with the code shown in Listing 13-16.

Listing 13-16. Adding the JavaScript

```
<script type="text/javascript">

    var ws; // This is our socket

    function connect() {

        output("Connecting to host...");
        try {
            ws = new WebSocket("ws://localhost:8300/chat");
        } catch (e) {
            output(e);
        }
        ws.onopen = function () {
            output("connected... ");
            var p = document.getElementById("name");
            ws.send("[Client SignOn:" + p.value + "]");
        };

        ws.onmessage = function (e) {
            displayMsg(e.data);
        };

        ws.onclose = function () {
            output("Connection closed");
        };
    };

    function send() {
        var input = document.getElementById("input");

        try {
            ws.send(input.value);
            var o = document.getElementById("chat1");
            o.innerHTML = o.innerHTML + "<p><b>Me:</b>" + input.value + "</p>";
            input.value = "";
        } catch (e) {
            output(e);
        }
    }

    function output(msg) {
        var o = document.getElementById("output");
        o.innerHTML = o.innerHTML + "<p>" + msg + "</p>";
    };
```

```
function displayMsg(msg) {
    var o = document.getElementById("chat1");
    o.innerHTML = o.innerHTML + "<p><b>Agent:</b>" + msg + "</p>";
};

</script>
```

This code is similar to the JavaScript on the Agent application. The connect() function gets a WebSocket and sends the initial sign-on message and then wires-up the onmessage and onclose event handlers. The send() function sends the text that was entered to the server and echoes it on the page. The displayMsg() function is the event handler for the processing incoming messages from the server, which are displayed on the page.

Testing the Solution

Earlier in the chapter, you setup the WsServer and the Client projects to both start when debugging. Now you'll need to add the Agent application as well. Then you will debug all three applications at the same time.

EXERCISE 13-8. TESTING THE SOLUTION

1. Right-click the Chapter13 solution and select the "Set StartUp Projects" link. In the dialog box, change the action for the Agent application to Start. Also move this down to be the second project loaded.

2. Press F5 to debug the applications. You should see the console app as well as two browser windows. Go to the Agent page. If not already logged in, log in now. You should only have to register once. After that you just log in.

3. Click the Begin Chat link, which should display the new chat page, and show that you are connected to the server.

4. Go to the Client page, enter a name, and click the Chat now button. You should get a response in the chat windows as illustrated in Figure 13-15.

Figure 13-15. *The client web application*

5. Enter a message and send it. From the Agent page enter a response and send it. You should see all of the messages displayed in the client's chat window as shown in Figure 13-16.

Figure 13-16. *Updating the client window with an outgoing message*

6. Create another copy of the client page and enter a different name. Enter some messages back and forth.

7. Go to the Agent window and you should see messages in two windows as shown in Figure 13-17.

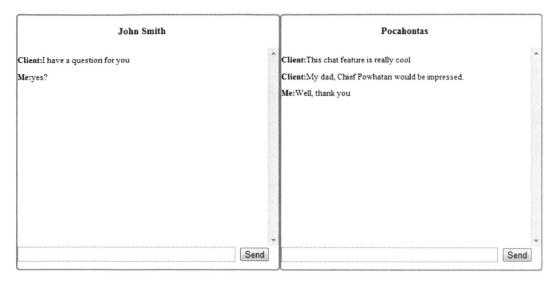

John Smith

Client:I have a question for you

Me:yes?

[Send]

Pocahontas

Client:This chat feature is really cool

Client:My dad, Chief Powhatan would be impressed.

Me:Well, thank you

[Send]

Figure 13-17. *The Agent page with multiple sessions*

Summary

In this relatively brief introduction to WebSockets you created a simple chat system that allows an agent to chat with multiple clients simultaneously. While the server implementation was pretty involved, the client side was fairly simple. After creating the WebSocket object, specifying the location of the WebSocket server, you just wire up event handlers to be notified when the connection is established, when a message is received, and when the connection has been closed.

In this demo, you created a standalone application, but in many cases you'll simply add the chat capability to your existing web application. For example, you might ask the user if they want assistance with the page they are viewing and if they do, this simple code will allow them to chat right from that page.

The server side requires a bit of protocol handling. First, the server receives handshaking messages using http. The request key is obtained and used to generate the response key. The entire response is then sent back to the client. The actual messages are sent using the ws protocol, which includes a frame header. Messages from the client are masked, which require logic in the server to unmask it. Messages from the server are not masked.

The demo application provides a chat capability. This is only one possible use of WebSockets. They can also be used any time the server needs to initiate communication with the client. Keep in mind, however, that the client must initiate the connection with the server.

CHAPTER 14

■ ■ ■

Drag and Drop

The ability to select an element and drag it to another location is an excellent example of a natural user experience. I can still remember the early Apple computers where you could delete a file by dragging it onto a trash can icon. This action, and hundreds more like it, are a key component of user experiences found on desktop applications. Web applications, however, have lagged far behind in this arena. With the drag and drop (DnD) API in HTML5, you'll find web applications rapidly catching up.

In this chapter you'll build a web application that implements a Checkers game, using the DnD API to move the pieces around the board. I will first explain the concepts and how a DnD application is structured. Then we'll dive into the code, demonstrating the various aspects. I'll finish up with some advanced features including dragging between browser windows.

Understanding Drag and Drop

Before I get into building an application I want to explain the basic concepts of the DnD API. This will help you put this in context as you start to write code. I will first explain the events that are raised; it is important to know when each is raised and on which object. Then we'll look at the dataTransfer object, which you'll use to pass information from the object being dragged to each of the events and eventually to the drop action. You can also use this to configure various aspects of the dragging operation. Finally, I'll show you how to make objects draggable.

Handling Events

As with its desktop counterpart, DnD is an event-based API. As the user selects an item, moves it and drops it, events are raised, allowing the application to control and respond to these actions. To effectively use this API, you'll need to know when these events are raised and on which element they are raised. At first, this may seem confusing but it's pretty straightforward once you see this in perspective.

In a DnD operation, there are two elements involved:

- The element that is being dragged, sometimes referred to as the source

- The element being dropped on, usually called the target

You can think of this as the source being an arrow that is being dropped onto a target, as illustrated in Figure 14-1.

- dragstart
- drag
- dragend

- dragenter
- dragover
- dragleave
- drop

Figure 14-1. *The source and target elements*

During a DnD operation, events are fired on both elements and I've indicated which events are raised on each. On the source element, the dragstart, drag, and dragend events are comparable to the mousedown, mousemove and mouseup events in a windows application. When you click on an element and start to move the mouse, the dragstart event is raised. This is immediately followed by the drag event and the drag event is also repeatedly raised with each move of the mouse. Finally, the dragend event is raised when the mouse button is released.

The events on the target element are a little more interesting. As the mouse is moved around the page, when it enters the area defined by an element, the dragenter event is raised on that element. As the mouse continues to move, the dragover event is raised on the target element. If the mouse moves outside of that element, the dragleave event is fired on the target element. Presumably, the mouse is now on a different element and a dragenter event is raised on that element. However, if the mouse button is released while over the target element, instead of a dragleave event, the drop event will be raised.

Now let's walk through a typical scenario and see the order of these events. This is illustrated in Table 14-1.

Table 14-1. *Sequence of events*

Element	Event	Notes
Source	dragstart	Raised when the mouse is clicked and starts to move
Source	drag	Raised with each mouse move
Target	dragenter	Raised when the mouse enters the target element's space
Target	dragover	Raised with each mouse move when the pointer is over the target
Source	drag	This event continues to be raised as the mouse moves
Target	dragleave	Raised when the mouse is moved past the current target
Target	dragenter	Raised when mouse moves to a new target element
Target	drop	Raised when the mouse button is released
Source	dragend	Ends the drag and drop operation

Now that you understand the events that are used, you can implement a DnD operation by providing appropriate handlers for each of these events.

Using the Data Transfer Object

There is one more DnD concept that you should understand as well. Simply dragging an element around a page is not all that useful; what we're really after is the data associated with the element. In the example I gave earlier with dragging a file to the trash can, seeing the icon swallowed up by the trash may be fun to watch, but the ultimate goal is to delete the file. In this case, you're passing a file specification to the recycle bin so it can perform the requested action in the file system.

Storing Data

In the DnD API, the `dataTransfer` object is used to store the data associated with the operation. The `dataTransfer` object is usually initialized in the `dragstart` event handler. Recall that this event is raised on the source element. The event handler can access the data from the source element and store it in the `dataTransfer` object. This is then provided to all of the other event handlers so they can use it in their specific processing. Ultimately, this is used by the `drop` event handler to take the appropriate action on this data.

The `dataTransfer` object is provided as a property of the event object that is passed to each of the event handlers. You use the `setData()` method to store data in the `dataTransfer` object. To indicate the type of data, an appropriate MIME type needs to be supplied as well. For example to add some simple text, call the method like this:

```
e.dataTransfer.setData("text/plain", "Hello, World!");
```

To access this data in a subsequent event, such as the `drop` event, use the `getData()` method like this:

```
var msg = e.dataTransfer.getData("text/plain");
```

You'll need to use the same MIME type when retrieving the data as was used when the data was stored.

Using Drop Effects

Another purpose for the `dataTransfer` object is to provide feedback to the user as to the action that will occur when the item is dropped. This is called the drop effect and there are four possible values:

- copy – the selected element will be copied in the target location
- move – the selected element will be moved to the target location
- link – a link to the selected item will be created in the target location
- none – the drop operation is not allowed

When you start dragging an item, the cursor will change to indicate the drop effect that will occur when the item is dropped on the target. This is standard Windows UI and you can try this out on most applications. For example, using the text editor in Visual Studio, select some text and then start dragging it. You should see the cursor change to either a move cursor or a "not allowed" cursor depending on where you trying to move it to. If you hold down the Ctrl key before moving it, you should see the copy cursor instead of the move cursor.

In the dragstart event handler you can specify the drop effects that are allowed based on the source element that is selected. You can specify more than one allowed effect by simply concatenating them (for example "copyMove") or specify all effects like this:

```
e.dataTransfer.effectAllowed = "all"; // "copy", "link", "move", "copyLink", "linkMove",
"copyMove"
```

Then, in the dragover event, you'll specify the drop effect that will occur if the source element is dropped there. If that drop effect is one of the allowed effects, the cursor will change to indicate that drop effect. If that effect is not allowed, however, the cursor will use the "not allowed" icon. If this is not a valid location to accept the drop, set the drop effect to "none" like this:

```
if (validLocation) {
    e.dataTransfer.dropEffect = "move";
}
else {
    e.dataTransfer.dropEffect = "none";
}
```

Enabling Draggable Elements

So now you know you can disable the drop event on an element by setting the drop effect to "none" in the dragover event. But how do you control which elements can be dragged to start with? The answer is simple: just set the draggable attribute in the markup for the element. For example, to create a div that can be dragged, enter the markup like this:

```
<div id="myDiv" draggable="true">
    <p>This div is draggable</p>
</div>
```

By default, images and links are draggable. Go to the google.com and try dragging the Google logo. You should see a somewhat muted copy of this image being dragged as you move the cursor.

If you drag this image onto a Firefox browser window, Firefox will navigate to this image. You've just seen drag and drop in action. Because using drag and drop is such a natural way of working, browsers try to accommodate this out-of-the-box as best they can. For example, if you drag some text from a text editor that appears to be a URL onto a browser, it will try to navigate to that address. If you drag an image file onto a browser it will either navigate to it or download it.

Sometimes the default action can cause issues with your custom code. I will show you later in the chapter how to disable this.

■ **Note** For more information on the DnD API, check out the W3C specification at
http://dev.w3.org/html5/spec/single-page.html#dnd.

Creating the Checkers Application

To demonstrate the DnD API, you'll create a web application that displays a typical checkers board of alternating red and white squares. You'll use image files to represent the checkers and display them in their initial starting position. Then you'll create event handlers that will allow you to move a piece to a different square. Finally, you'll add logic to disable illegal moves.

■ **Tip** Throughout this chapter you will be adding and modifying code in this project as you add features to the application. If there is any question about where each change should be made, the final code is listed in Appendix C and it is also available with the source download.

Creating the Project

You'll first need to create a Visual Studio project that is similar to ones you created previously. This will use the Basic MVC4 project template.

EXERCISE 14-1. CREATING THE VISUAL STUDIO PROJECT
---

1. Start Visual Studio 2012. In the Start Page, click the New Project link.

2. In the New project dialog box, select the "ASP.NET MVC4 Web Application" template. Enter the project name **Chapter14** and select a location for this project as shown in Figure 14-2.

Figure 14-2. Creating the Chapter14 project

3. In the next dialog box, select the Basic template and make sure the Razor view engine is selected. Click the OK button and the project will be created (this may take a few seconds).

4. Right-click the Controller folder in the Solution Explorer and select the Add ➤ Controller links. Enter the name **HomeController** and select the Empty MVC Controller template. Click the Add button to create the controller.

5. Right-click the View folder and select the Add ➤ New Folder links. Enter the name **Home**.

6. Right-click the new Home folder and select the Add ➤ View links. In the Add View dialog box, enter the name **Index**, make sure the Razor view engine is selected, unselect all the check boxes, and click the Add button.

7. Right-click the Chapter14 solution and select the Add ➤ New Folder links. Enter the name **Images**.

8. The source code download for this chapter includes an Images folder with five images. Copy all five images to the Images folder in the Solution Explorer.

Drawing the Checkers Board

To draw the board you'll use a separate div element for each square. You'll need eight rows with eight div elements each. Fortunately, this is pretty easy to do using a couple of nested for loops and the Razor syntax.

■ **Note** In Chapter 10 you drew a chess board using a canvas element. However, that won't work for this application because you need separate DOM elements for each square. You might be tempted to use SVG to create the board since each rect element is a separate DOM element, however, the SVG elements do not support the DnD API.

```
┌─────────────────────────────────────────────────────────────┐
│              EXERCISE 14-2. DRAWING THE BOARD                  │
└─────────────────────────────────────────────────────────────┘
```

1. In the empty div created by the project template, set the class attribute to "board" like this:

   `<div class="board">`

2. Add the code shown in Listing 14-1 inside this div.

   Listing 14-1. Creating the squares on the board

```
@for (int y = 0; y < 8; y++)
{
    for (int x = 0; x < 8; x++)
    {
        string id = x.ToString() + y.ToString();
        string css;
        if ((x+y) % 2 == 0)
        {
            css = "bwhite";
        }
        else
        {
            css = "bblack";
        }
        <text>
```

```
            <div id="@id" class="@css" draggable="false">

            </div>
            </text>
        }
    }
```

3. This code uses two nested `for` loops to create the `div` elements. Inside the second for loop, the `id` variable is computed by concatenating the `x` and `y` variables. The `css` variable alternates between bwhite and bblack. For even-numbered rows, the even columns are black and the odd columns are white. This reverses for odd-numbered rows. The `draggable` attribute is set to false because we don't want squares being dragged; only pieces.

4. Now you'll need to add some style rules to set the size and color of each square. Add the `style` element shown in Listing 14-2 inside the `head` element.

Listing 14-2. Adding the CSS styles

```css
<style type="text/css" >
    .board
    {
        width: 400px;
        height: 400px;
    }
    .bblack
    {
        background-color: #b93030;
        border-color: #b93030;
        border-width: 1px;
        border-style: solid;
        width: 48px;
        height: 48px;
        float: left;
        margin: 0px;
        padding: 0px;
    }
    .bwhite
    {
        background-color: #f7f7f7;
        border-color: #b93030;
        border-width: 1px;
        border-style: solid;
        width: 48px;
        height: 48px;
        float: left;
        margin: 0px;
        padding: 0px;
    }
</style>
```

5. Press F5 to preview this page, which should look like Figure 14-3.

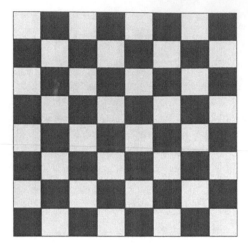

Figure 14-3. *The initial board*

6. Now you'll add the checkers by including an img element inside the appropriate div elements. Add the code shown in bold in Listing 14-3.

Listing 14-3. Adding the images

```
<text>
<div id="@id" class="@css" draggable="false">

    @if ((x + y) % 2 != 0 && y != 3 && y != 4)
    {
        string imgSrc;
        string pid;
        if (y < 3)
        {
            imgSrc="Images/WhitePiece.png";
            pid="w"+id;
        }
        else
        {
            imgSrc = "Images/BlackPiece.png";
            pid = "b" + id;
        }
        <text>
        <img id="@pid" src="@imgSrc" draggable="true" class="piece" >
        </text>
    }

</div>
</text>
```

7. To determine the appropriate squares, the first rule is that checkers are only on the black (or red in this case) squares. So the code uses the same $(x + y) \% 2 \mathrel{!=} 0$ logic that was used to compute the css variable. Then, checkers are only placed on the top 3 and bottom 3 rows, so the code excludes rows 3 and 4. If the row is less than 3, this will add a white checker and use a black checker for the other rows. The code computes the id for the img element by prefixing the id of the square with either "w" or "b". Notice that the draggable attribute is set to true.

8. The class attribute for the img elements was set to piece. Now add the following rule to the existing style element, which will add padding so the checker will be centered in the square.

```
.piece
{
    margin-left: 4px;
    margin-top: 4px;
}
```

9. Press F5 to start the application and you should now see the checkers as demonstrated in Figure 14-4.

Figure 14-4. *The initial checker board with checkers*

Adding Drag and Drop Support

The img elements were added with the draggable attribute so you should be able to select one and drag it. However, you'll notice that none of the squares will accept the drop and the cursor shows the "not allowed" icon. If you want to try some default browser functionality, try dragging an image to address bar; the browser will navigate to the image's URL. You will now add code that will enable a drop so you can start moving the pieces. Then you'll refine this code to ensure that only legal moves are allowed.

■ **Note** For the rest of this chapter I will be using Firefox to test the application. Chrome also supports DnD but has a bug that won't allow you to access the dataTransfer object except in the drag event (see this article for details - https://bugs.webkit.org/show_bug.cgi?id=23695). Opera will also work fine but IE9 doesn't support DnD at all.

Allowing a Drop

You have draggable elements and all you need to complete a drag and drop operation is an element that will accept a drop. To do that you'll need an event handler for the dragover event that sets the drop effect. By default the effectAllowed property is set to all so setting the drop effect to move, copy, or link will all be valid settings. To try this out, add a script element at the end of the body element and add the code shown in Listing 14-4.

Listing 14-4. The initial event implementation

```
<script type="text/javascript">
    // Get all the black squares
    var squares = document.querySelectorAll('.bblack');
    var i = 0;
    while (i < squares.length) {
        var s = squares[i++];
        // Add the event listeners
        s.addEventListener('dragover', dragOver, false);
    }

    // Handle the dragover event
    function dragOver(e) {
        if (e.preventDefault) {
            e.preventDefault();
        }

        e.dataTransfer.dropEffect = "move";
    }
</script>
```

This code uses the querySelectorAll() function that I described in Chapter 5 to get all of the black squares. It then iterates through the collection that is returned and adds an event handler for the dragover event. The dragover() function calls the preventDefault() function to cancel the browser's default action. It then gets the dataTransfer object and sets the dropEffect property to "move".

Press F5 to run the application and try dragging a checker. You should now get a move cursor on all the black squares but a not allowed cursor on the white squares. Try dropping the checker on an empty black square. Since you have not yet implemented a drop event handler the browser will execute its default drop action. Since the item being dragged is an image, the default action is to navigate to the image file.

Performing the Custom Drop Action

The default action is not what we're looking for here so we'll need to implement the drop event hander and provide our own logic. The drop event handler is where all the real work happens. This is where the file is deleted if it's a trash can. For this application, the drop action will create a new img element at the target location and remove the previous image.

To implement the drop, you'll also need to provide the dragstart event handler. In the dragstart event handler, you will store the id of the img element that is being dragged in the dataTransfer object. This will be used by the drop event handler so it will know which element to remove.

EXERCISE 14-3. IMPLEMENTING THE DROP

1. Add the following function to the existing script element, which will be used as the dragstart event handler. This code gets the id of the source element (remember the dragstart event is raised on the source element) which is the selected checker image. This id is stored in the dataTransfer object. This function also specifies that the allowed effects should be "move" since we'll be moving this image.

    ```
    function dragStart(e) {
        e.dataTransfer.effectAllowed = "move";
        e.dataTransfer.setData("text/plain", e.target.id);
    }
    ```

2. To provide the drop event handler add the code shown in Listing 14-5.

    Listing 14-5. Implementing the drop event handler

    ```
    function drop(e) {
        // Prevent the event from being raised on the parent element
        if (e.stopPropagation) {
            e.stopPropagation();
        }

        // Stop the browsers default action
        if (e.preventDefault) {
            e.preventDefault();
        }

        // Get the img element that is being dragged
        var droppedID = e.dataTransfer.getData("text/plain");
        var droppedPiece = document.getElementById(droppedID);

        // Create a new img on the target location
        var newPiece = document.createElement("img");
        newPiece.src = droppedPiece.src;
        newPiece.id = droppedPiece.id.substr(0, 1) + e.target.id;
        newPiece.draggable = true;
        newPiece.classList.add("piece");
        newPiece.addEventListener("dragstart", dragStart, false);
        e.target.appendChild(newPiece);

        // Remove the previous image
        droppedPiece.parentNode.removeChild(droppedPiece);
    }
    ```

3. This code first calls the `stopPropagation()` function to keep this event from bubbling up to the parent element. It also calls `preventDefault()` to cancel the browser's default action, which as we found out, is to navigate to the image file. It then gets the `id` from the `dataTransfer` object and uses this to access the `img` element. This function then creates a new `img` element and sets all the necessary properties and adds the necessary event handlers. As I explained before, the `drop` event is raised on the target element; the elements being dropped on. The `id` for the new `img` element is computed using the `id` of the new location, which is obtained from the `target` property of the `event` object. The id prefix ("b" or "w") is copied from the existing `img` element. Finally, this code removes the existing `img` element.

4. Now you'll need to wire-up the event handlers. To do that, add the following code shown in bold:

```
var squares = document.querySelectorAll('.bblack');
var i = 0;
while (i < squares.length) {
    var s = squares[i++];
    s.addEventListener('dragover', dragOver, false);

    s.addEventListener('drop', drop, false);

}

i = 0;
var pieces = document.querySelectorAll('img');
while (i < pieces.length) {
    var p = pieces[i++];
    p.addEventListener('dragstart', dragStart, false);
}
```

5. The `dragstart` event must be added to the `img` elements. This code gets all of the `img` elements using the `querySelectorAll()` function.

6. Now press F5 to start the application. You should be able to drag a checker to any red square.

Providing Visual Feedback

When dragging an element it's a good idea to provide some visual feedback indicating the object that was selected. By setting the `dropEffect` property in the `dragover` event handler the cursor indicates if a drop is allowed or not. However, you should do more than that. Both the source and target elements should stand out visually so the user can easily see that if they release the mouse button, the piece will be moved from here to there.

To do this, you'll dynamically add a `class` attribute to the source and target elements. Then you can style them with normal CSS style rules. For the source element you'll use the `dragstart` and `dragend` events to add and then remove the `class` attribute. Likewise for target element you'll use the `dragenter` and `dragleave` events.

EXERCISE 14-4. ADDING VISUAL FEEDBACK

1. You already have a `dragstart` event handler; add the following code in bold to the `dragStart()` function. This will add the "selected" class to the element.

    ```
    function dragStart(e) {
        e.dataTransfer.effectAllowed = "all";
        e.dataTransfer.setData("text/plain", e.target.id);

        e.target.classList.add("selected");

    }
    ```

2. Add the `dragEnd()` function using the following code that will simply remove the selected class when the drag operation has completed.

    ```
    function dragEnd(e) {
        e.target.classList.remove("selected");
    }
    ```

3. Add the `dragEnter()` and `dragLeave()` function using the following code. This adds the "drop" class to the element and then removes it.

    ```
    function dragEnter(e) {
        e.target.classList.add('drop');
    }

    function dragLeave(e) {
        e.target.classList.remove("drop");
    }
    ```

4. Since you've added three new event handlers, you'll need to add code to add the event listeners. Add the code shown in bold to the existing `script` element.

    ```
    var squares = document.querySelectorAll('.bblack');
    var i = 0;
    while (i < squares.length){
        var s = squares[i++];
        s.addEventListener('dragover', dragOver, false);
        s.addEventListener('drop', drop, false);

        s.addEventListener('dragenter', dragEnter, false);
        s.addEventListener('dragleave', dragLeave, false);

    }
    ```

```
    i = 0;
    var pieces = document.querySelectorAll('img');
    while (i < pieces.length){
        var p = pieces[i++];
        p.addEventListener('dragstart', dragStart, false);

        p.addEventListener('dragend', dragEnd, false);

    }
```

5. Now you'll need to make a couple of changes to the drop event handler. You add the "drop" class to the target element in the `dragenter` event and then remove it in the `dragleave` event. However, if they drop the image, the `dragleave` event is not raised. You'll also need to remove the "drop" class in the `drop` event as well. Also, when creating a new `img` element you'll need to wire up the `dragend` event handler.

6. Add the code shown in bold.

```
    // Create a new img on the target location
    var newPiece = document.createElement("img");
    newPiece.src = droppedPiece.src;
    newPiece.id = droppedPiece.id.substr(0, 1) + e.target.id;
    newPiece.draggable = true;
    newPiece.classList.add("piece");
    newPiece.addEventListener("dragstart", dragStart, false);

    newPiece.addEventListener("dragend", dragEnd, false);

    e.target.appendChild(newPiece);

    // Remove the previous image
    droppedPiece.parentNode.removeChild(droppedPiece);

    // Remove the drop effect from the target element
    e.target.classList.remove('drop');
```

7. Finally, you'll need to define the CSS rules for the "drop" and "selected" values. I've chosen to set the `opacity` attribute but you could just as easily add a border, change the background color, or any number of effects to achieve the desired purpose.

8. Add the following rules to the existing `style` element.

```
    .bblack.drop
    {
        opacity: 0.5;
    }
    .piece.selected
    {
        opacity: 0.5;
    }
```

9. Press F5 to start the application. Try dragging an image to a red square and you should see the expected visual feedback as shown in Figure 14-5.

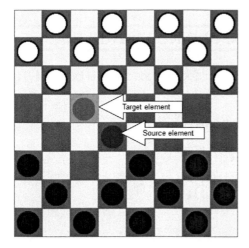

Figure 14-5. *Displaying the drag and drop visual feedback*

Enforcing the Game Rules

You've probably noticed that you can move a piece to any red square. The current implementation doesn't enforce any rules to ensure a legal move is being made. You'll now add that logic. This will be needed by the following events:

- dragover – to set the dropEffect to "none" for illegal moves
- dragenter – to change the style only for valid drop locations
- drop – to only perform the move if it's a legal move

You'll implement an isValidMove() function that will evaluate the attempted move and return false if this is an illegal move. Then you'll call this function in each of the three events listed above.

Verifying a Move

Fortunately, the rules in Checkers are fairly simple. Because the dragover event handler is not added to the white squares, dropping a piece there is already disabled, which further simplifies the work needed. The rules that you'll enforce are:

1. You cannot move to a square already occupied.
2. Pieces can only more forward.
3. Pieces can only move one space diagonally, or two spaces (diagonally) if jumping an occupied square.
4. You can only jump a piece of a different color.
5. A jumped piece must be removed from the board.

■ **Note**   You'll later add logic to handle promoting a piece to a king.

EXERCISE 14-5. ENFORCING THE RULES

1. Implement the isValidMove() function by adding the code shown in Listing 14-6 to the existing script element.

    Listing 14-6. Implementing the isValidMove() function

```
function isValidMove(source, target, drop) {
    // Get the piece prefix and location
    var startPos = source.id.substr(1, 2);
    var prefix = source.id.substr(0, 1);

    // Get the drop location
    var endPos = target.id;

    // You can't drop on the existing location
    if (startPos === endPos) {
        return false;
    }

    // You can't drop on occupied square
    if (target.childElementCount != 0) {
        return false;
    }

    // Compute the x and y coordinates
    var xStart = parseInt(startPos.substr(0, 1));
    var yStart = parseInt(startPos.substr(1, 1));
    var xEnd = parseInt(endPos.substr(0, 1));
    var yEnd = parseInt(endPos.substr(1, 1));

    switch (prefix) {
        // For white pieces...
        case "w":
            if (yEnd <= yStart)
                return false; // Can't move backwards
            break;

        // For black pieces...
        case "b":
            if (yEnd >= yStart)
                return false; // Can't move backwards
            break;
    }
```

```
        // These rule apply to all pieces
        if (yStart === yEnd || xStart === xEnd)
            return false; // Move must be diagonal

        if (Math.abs(yEnd - yStart) > 2 || Math.abs(xEnd - xStart) > 2)
            return false; // Can't move more than two spaces

        // If moving two spaces, find the square that is jumped
        if (Math.abs(xEnd - xStart) === 2) {
            var pos = ((xStart + xEnd) / 2).toString() +
                      ((yStart + yEnd) / 2).toString();
            var div = document.getElementById(pos);
            if (div.childElementCount === 0)
                return false;  // Can't jump an empty square
            var img = div.children[0];
            if (img.id.substr(0, 1).toLowerCase() === prefix.toLowerCase())
                return false; // Can't jump a piece of the same color

            // If this function is called from the drop event
            // Remove the jumped piece
            if (drop) {
                div.removeChild(img);
            }
        }
    }

    return true;
}
```

2. The parameters to the isValidMove() function include the source and target
    elements. Remember the source is an img element and its id attribute is a
    combination of the color ("w" or "b") and the x and y coordinates. The target is a
    div element and its id attribute is just the x and y coordinates. I've added lots of
    comments to this code so it should be fairly self-explanatory but I will point out a
    couple of the more interesting points.

    •   To determine if a square is occupied, you can simply check the
        childElementCount property. This will be 0 for empty squares.

    •   For white pieces, moving forward means the y coordinate is increasing but for
        black pieces the opposite is true. To handle this, the function uses a switch
        statement to apply a different rule for each.

    •   If the piece is moving two spaces then the function needs to check the square
        that is being jumped. Its location is determined by averaging the starting and
        ending positions.

    •   If the square is occupied then the code checks to see if the piece is the same
        color. The code first gets the child element, which will be the img on that
        square. The color is determined by the prefix of the id attribute. The code
        converts the prefix to lowercase before comparing. I'll explain that later.

- If a piece of a different color is being jumped, then we'll remove it since the code already has the `img` element. However, we only want to do this if this method is called from the `drop` event, which is specified by the third parameter to this function. The other two events (`dragOver` and `dragEnter`) use this method to validate the move but don't actually make the move and they will pass false for the third parameter.

3. Now you'll need to change `dragover` event to validate the move before setting the `dropEffect`. Replace the existing implementation of the `dragOver()` function with the following code. The new code gets the `id` of the `img` that is being dragged from the `dataTransfer` object and then uses the `id` to get the element. This is passed in to the `isValidMove()` function along with the target element, which is obtained from the `event` object (e.target). The `dropEffect` is set to "move" only if this is a valid move.

```
function dragOver(e) {
    if (e.preventDefault) {
        e.preventDefault();
    }

    // Get the img element that is being dragged
    var dragID = e.dataTransfer.getData("text/plain");
    var dragPiece = document.getElementById(dragID);

    if (dragPiece &&
        e.target.tagName === "DIV" &&
        isValidMove(dragPiece, e.target, false)) {
        e.dataTransfer.dropEffect = "move";
    }
    else {
        e.dataTransfer.dropEffect = "none";
    }
}
```

4. Replace the implementation of the `dragEnter()` function with the following code. This code is essentially the same as the `dragOver()` function, except it adds the "drop" class to the element instead of setting the `dropEffect`.

```
function dragEnter(e) {
    // Get the img element that is being dragged
    var dragID = e.dataTransfer.getData("text/plain");
    var dragPiece = document.getElementById(dragID);
```

```
    if (dragPiece &&
        e.target.tagName === "DIV" &&
        isValidMove(dragPiece, e.target, false)) {
        e.target.classList.add('drop');
    }
}
```

5. For the `drop()` function, wrap the code that performs the drop inside an `if` statement that validates the move by adding the code shown in bold. This time, the code is passing true for the third parameter to the `isValidMove()` function.

```
if (droppedPiece &&
    e.target.tagName === "DIV" &&
    isValidMove(droppedPiece, e.target, true)) {

    // Create a new img on the target location
    var newPiece = document.createElement("img");
    newPiece.src = droppedPiece.src;
    newPiece.id = droppedPiece.id.substr(0, 1) + e.target.id;
    newPiece.draggable = true;
    newPiece.classList.add("piece");
    newPiece.addEventListener("dragstart", dragStart, false);
    newPiece.addEventListener("dragend", dragEnd, false);
    e.target.appendChild(newPiece);

    // Remove the previous image
    droppedPiece.parentNode.removeChild(droppedPiece);

    // Remove the drop effect from the target element
    e.target.classList.remove('drop');
}
```

6. With these changes now in place, try running the application. You should only be allowed to make legal moves. If you jump a checker it should be removed from the board.

Promoting to King

In Checkers, when a piece moves all the way to the last row, it is promoted to a king. A king works just like a regular piece except that it can move backwards. You'll now add code to check if a piece needs to be promoted. To promote a piece you'll change the image that is displayed to indicate it is a king. You'll also change the prefix, making it a capital "B" or "W". Then you can allow different rules for kings.

You'll put all this logic in a single function called `kingMe()` and you'll call this every time a drop occurs. If the piece is already a king or if it's not on the last row, the function just returns. Otherwise it performs the promotion.

EXERCISE 14-6. ADDING PROMOTION

1. Add the kingMe() function shown in Listing 14-7 to the existing script element.

   Listing 14-7. Implementing the kingMe() function

```
function kingMe(piece) {

    // If we're already a king, just return
    if (piece.id.substr(0, 1) === "W" || piece.id.substr(0, 1) === "B")
        return;

    var newPiece;

    // If this is a white piece on the 7th row
    if (piece.id.substr(0, 1) === "w" && piece.id.substr(2, 1) === "7") {
        newPiece = document.createElement("img");
        newPiece.src = "Images/WhiteKing.png";
        newPiece.id = "W" + piece.id.substr(1, 2);
    }

    // If this is a black piece on the 0th row
    if (piece.id.substr(0, 1) === "b" && piece.id.substr(2, 1) === "0") {
        var newPiece = document.createElement("img");
        newPiece.src = "Images/BlackKing.png";
        newPiece.id = "B" + piece.id.substr(1, 2);
    }

    // If a new piece was created, set its properties and events
    if (newPiece) {
        newPiece.draggable = true;
        newPiece.classList.add("piece");

        newPiece.addEventListener('dragstart', dragStart, false);
        newPiece.addEventListener('dragend', dragEnd, false);

        var parent = piece.parentNode;
        parent.removeChild(piece);
        parent.appendChild(newPiece);
    }
}
```

2. The `kingMe()` function simply returns if the `id` prefix is ether "B" or "W", which indicates this is already a king. It then checks to see if this is a white piece on row 7 or a black piece on row 0. If so, a new `img` element is created with the appropriate `src` and `id` properties. If a new `img` was created the function then sets all of the properties and events, removes the existing `img` element from the `div` element and adds the new one.

3. Modify the `drop()` function to call the `kingMe()` function after a drop has been performed by adding the line shown in bold.

```
// Remove the previous image
droppedPiece.parentNode.removeChild(droppedPiece);

// Remove the drop effect from the target element
e.target.classList.remove('drop');

// See if the piece needs to be promoted
kingMe(newPiece);
```

■ **Tip** When you implemented the isValidMove() function the rule that prevents the piece from moving backwards only applies to "b" and "w" prefixes. Since a king has a capital "B" or "W" this rule doesn't apply so the king can move backwards. Also, when jumping a piece, the comparison was done after first converting to lowercase. This will allow a white piece to jump either a black piece or a black king.

---

4. Try moving the pieces around until you move one to the last row. You should see the image change to indicate this is now a king as shown in Figure 14-6.

Figure 14-6. *The check board with a king*

5. Once you have a king, try moving it backwards and also try jumping pieces with it.

Moving in Turn

You've probably noticed that the application does not enforce each player alternating turns. You'll implement this logic now. After each move is made (drop event processed), you'll set the draggable attribute to false for all the pieces of the color that just moved. That will keep you from moving a piece of the same color. However there is one exception to this rule that will require a little extra work. If you jump a piece, then that same piece can make another move as long as it is another jump.

You'll start by implementing the general rule first. This will be performed by creating a new function called enableNextPlayer(). This function will use the querySelectorAll() function to get all of the img elements. The draggable attribute will be set to either true or false depending on the id prefix. Then you'll later add special logic that will handle the jump condition.

EXERCISE 14-7. TAKING TURNS

1. Add the enableNextPlayer() function to the existing script element using the code shown in Listing 14-8.

    Listing 14-8. Implementing the enableNextPlayer() function

    ```
    function enableNextPlayer(piece) {

        // Get all of the pieces
        var pieces = document.querySelectorAll('img');

        i = 0;
        while (i < pieces.length) {
            var p = pieces[i++];

            // If this is the same color that just moved, disable dragging
            if (p.id.substr(0, 1).toUpperCase() ===
                piece.id.substr(0, 1).toUpperCase()) {
                p.draggable = false;
            }
                // Otherwise, enable dragging
            else {
                p.draggable = true;
            }
        }
    }
    ```

2. At the end of the isValidMove() function add the code shown in bold. This will call the enableNextPlay() function when a drop is being performed.

    ```
    // Set the draggable attribute so the next player can take a turn
    if (drop) {
        enableNextPlayer(source);
    }

    return true;
    }
    ```

■ **Note**   Normally it might make more sense to put this call in the drop() function. However, only the isValidMove() function knows that a jump occurred and we'll need to add the override logic here, and that needs to be after the general rule has been applied.

---

3. The `drop()` function creates a new `img` element and currently sets the `draggable` attribute to true. Now you'll need to make this conditional based on the `draggable` attribute of the existing piece. Add the code shown in bold to the `drop()` function.

```
// Create a new img on the target location
var newPiece = document.createElement("img");
newPiece.src = droppedPiece.src;
newPiece.id = droppedPiece.id.substr(0, 1) + e.target.id;

if (droppedPiece.draggable){

    newPiece.draggable = true;

}

newPiece.classList.add("piece");
newPiece.addEventListener("dragstart", dragStart, false);
newPiece.addEventListener("dragend", dragEnd, false);
e.target.appendChild(newPiece);
```

4. Now you'll need change the `dragStart` event handler to ignore this event if the element is not draggable. Add the code shown in bold to the `dragStart()` function.

```
function dragStart(e) {

    if (e.target.draggable) {

        e.dataTransfer.effectAllowed = "move";
        e.dataTransfer.setData("text/plain", e.target.id);

        e.target.classList.add("selected");

    }

}
```

5. Now you'll implement the special jump logic. If the piece just made a jump, you'll set the `draggable` attribute back to true so it will be allowed to make another move. However, you'll also add "jumpOnly" to the `classList` so you can enforce that the only move that it is allowed to make is another jump.

6. Add the code shown in bold to the `isValidMove()` function. This will look for "jumpOnly" in the `classList` and set the `jumpOnly` flag accordingly.

```
var jumpOnly = false;
if (source.classList.contains("jumpOnly")) {
    jumpOnly = true;
}

// Compute the x and y coordinates
var xStart = parseInt(startPos.substr(0, 1));
var yStart = parseInt(startPos.substr(1, 1));
```

7. Now add the code shown in bold to the `isValidMove()` function. The first part adds the rule to make sure a jump is being made if `jumpOnly` is true. The second part sets the `jumped` flag to indicate that this move is making a jump.

```
// These rule apply to all pieces
if (yStart === yEnd || xStart === xEnd)
    return false; // Move must be diagonal

if (Math.abs(yEnd - yStart) > 2 || Math.abs(xEnd - xStart) > 2)
    return false; // Can't move more than two spaces

if (Math.abs(xEnd - xStart) === 1 && jumpOnly)
    return false; // Only jumps are allowed

var jumped = false;

// If moving two spaces, find the square that is jumped
if (Math.abs(xEnd - xStart) === 2) {
    var pos = ((xStart + xEnd) / 2).toString() +
              ((yStart + yEnd) / 2).toString();
    var div = document.getElementById(pos);
    if (div.childElementCount === 0)
        return false;  // Can't jump an empty square
    var img = div.children[0];
    if (img.id.substr(0, 1).toLowerCase() === prefix.toLowerCase())
        return false; // Can't jump a piece of the same color

    // If this function is called from the drop event
    // Remove the jumped piece
    if (drop) {
        div.removeChild(img);

        jumped = true;

    }
}
```

8. At the end of the `isValidMove()` function add the code shown in bold. This will override the `draggable` attribute if a jump was made and add "jumpOnly" to the `classList`.

```
if (drop) {
    enableNextPlayer(source);

    // If we jumped a piece, we're allowed to go again
    if (jumped) {
        source.draggable = true;
        source.classList.add("jumpOnly"); // But only for another jump
    }

}
```

9. Modify the `drop()` function to also add "jumpOnly" to the `classList` when creating the new `img` element by adding the code shown in bold.

```
// Create a new img on the target location
var newPiece = document.createElement("img");
newPiece.src = droppedPiece.src;
newPiece.id = droppedPiece.id.substr(0, 1) + e.target.id;
if (droppedPiece.draggable){
    newPiece.draggable = true;

    newPiece.classList.add("jumpOnly");

}
newPiece.classList.add("piece");
```

10. Now you'll need to clear the "jumpOnly" text from the `classList` when the next move is completed. You'll do that in the `enableNextPlayer()` function by adding the code shown in bold.

```
function enableNextPlayer(piece) {

    // Get all of the pieces
    var pieces = document.querySelectorAll('img');

    i = 0;
    while (i < pieces.length) {
        var p = pieces[i++];

        // If this is the same color that just moved, disable dragging
        if (p.id.substr(0, 1).toUpperCase() ===
            piece.id.substr(0, 1).toUpperCase()) {
            p.draggable = false;
        }
            // Otherwise, enable dragging
        else {
            p.draggable = true;
        }

        p.classList.remove("jumpOnly");

    }
}
```

11. Now test the application and make sure that each player must alternate turns. Also, verify that you can make successive jumps.

■ **Note**   The draggable attribute is set to true, initially, for both the white and black pieces so either color can make the first move. If you wanted to specify which color went first, you would change the Razor syntax that creates the initial img elements to set the draggable attribute to false for one color. I did some research to see what color was supposed to go first but found mixed results. Some places indicated black goes first and others said that the white goes first. Some, however, said it's just a game, what difference does it make? I decided to implement this logic, so either can go first.

Using Advanced Features

Before I finish this chapter, there are a couple of things that I want to discuss briefly. First, I'll show you how to use a custom drag image. Then I'll demonstrate dragging elements across browser windows.

Changing the Drag Image

When you drag an element, a copy of the element follows the cursor as you move it around the page. This is referred to as the drag image. However, you can specify a different image to be used. This is done with the setDragImage() function of the dataTransfer object.

There is a smiley face image in the Images folder. Add the code shown in bold to the dragStart() function to use this as the drag image.

```
function dragStart(e) {
    if (e.target.draggable) {
        e.dataTransfer.effectAllowed = "move";
        e.dataTransfer.setData("text/plain", e.target.id);

        e.target.classList.add("selected");

        var dragIcon = document.createElement("img");
        dragIcon.src = "Images/smiley.jpg";
        e.dataTransfer.setDragImage(dragIcon, 0, 0);

    }
}
```

Try out the application and as you move pieces you should see the smiley face as shown in Figure 14-7.

Figure 14-7. *Changing the drag image*

Dragging Between Windows

As I mentioned at the beginning of the chapter, there are separate events raised on the source element and on the target element. It is possible that these elements can be in different browser windows or even different applications. The process, however, works the same way.

To demonstrate this, open up a second instance of the Firefox browser and navigate to the Checkers application. You should see two browser windows each showing the checker board. Select a checker on one window and drag it to a square in the second window. You'll notice that you can only drop it on squares relative to its original location in the first window. When you drop it, the piece is moved to the drop location but is removed from the second window, not the image you initially selected.

The key to cross-window dragging is the dataTransfer object. This is provided in the dragenter, dragover, and dragleave events on the target object. It doesn't really matter where the drag initiated, this information is placed in the dataTransfer object and provided to any window that supports these events. When the drop event received this information, it removed the img element at the location specified in the dataTransfer object. Because the drop event was processed on the second window, the img element was removed from the second window.

The drag and dragend events are raised on the source element. Whatever logic was written on these event handlers is executed in the first window. Notice that the selected img element was muted during the drag but went back to normal when the drop was executed. This is because the dragend event fired on the source element clears the selected attribute.

When you control both sides of the operation as you do here, you can decide what data needs to be transferred and implement both sets of event handlers. In many cases, you can control only one side of the process. For example, a user could drag a file from Windows Explorer onto your web page. The dragstart, drag, and dragend events (or their equivalents) are raised in the Windows Explorer application, which you can't control. However, the dragenter, dragover, dragleave, and drop events are all fired on your web page. You can decide if you will accept the drop based on the element it is being dropped on and the contents of the dataTransfer object. You also control the process that occurs when the drop is completed.

Summary

In this chapter I explained all of the events that are raised as part of the DnD API and which elements they are raised on. The source element receives the following events:

- dragstart – when the element is selected and the mouse is moved
- drag – called continuously while the mouse is moved
- dragend – when the mouse button is released

The following events are raised on the target element:

- dragenter – when the mouse first enters the target's space
- dragover – continuously while the mouse is moved and over the target
- dragleave – when the mouse leaves the target's space
- drop – when the mouse button is released

The dataTransfer object is used to pass information about the source element. This is provided in all of the event handlers. It is used especially by the drop event handler to perform the necessary processing. This also enables dragging across applications.

The dragover event handler sets the dropEffect, which controls the cursor that is used. Setting this to "None" will cause the "not allowed" cursor to be used, signaling that the source cannot be dropped there.

To provide some visual feedback, the dragstart and dragend event handlers should modify the source element to indicate that it is selected and being dragged. Likewise, the dragenter and dragleave event handers should highlight the target element. This will provide an easy way for the user to see where the selected element will be dropped.

The sample application that you created implemented some complex rules for determining which elements could be dragged and where they could be dropped.

■ ■ ■

Chapter 4 – Sample Content

Listing A-1 specifies the initial HTML content used for the exercises in Chapter 4. This is available from the downloaded source in the `Default_content.cshtml` file. I'm including it here in case you want to see it without downloading the code.

Listing A-1. Chapter 4 Sample Content

```html
<!DOCTYPE html>

<html lang="en">
    <head>
        <meta charset="utf-8" />
        <title>Chapter 4 - CSS Demo</title>
    </head>
    <body>
        <header class="intro">
            <h1>CSS Demo</h1>
            <h2>Introducing the new HTML5 features</h2>
            <h3>
                Use the new CSS3 features to build some of the most visually
                appealing web sites.
            </h3>
        </header>

        <nav>
            <ul>
                <li><a href="#feature">Feature</a></li>
                <li><a href="#other">Article</a></li>
                <li><a href="#another">Archives</a></li>
                <li><a href="http://www.apress.com" target="_blank">Apress</a></li>
            </ul>
        </nav>

        <div id="contentArea">

            <div id="mainContent">
                <section class="rounded">
                    <header>
                        <h2>Main content area</h2>
                    </header>
```

```
        <p>
            Lorem ipsum dolor sit amet, consectetur adipisicing elit,
            sed do eiusmod tempor incididunt ut labore et dolore magna
            aliqua. Ut enim ad minim veniam, quis nostrud exercitation
            ullamco laboris nisi ut.
        </p>
    </section>

    <section>
        <article class="featuredContent">
            <a id="feature"></a>
            <header>
                <h3>Featured Article</h3>
            </header>

            <div class="rotateContainer" >
                <p>This is really cool...</p>
                <img class="rotate" id="phone"
                    src="images/phonebooth.jpg"
                    alt="phonebooth" />
                <p>
                    Lorem ipsum dolor sit amet, consectetur adipisicing
                    elit, sed do eiusmod tempor incididunt ut labore et
                    dolore magna aliqua. Ut enim ad minim veniam, quis
                    nostrud exercitation ullamco laboris nisi ut.
                </p>
                <p>
                    Lorem ipsum dolor sit amet, consectetur adipisicing
                    elit, sed do eiusmod tempor incididunt ut labore et
                    dolore magna aliqua. Ut enim ad minim veniam, quis
                    nostrud exercitation ullamco laboris nisi ut.
                </p>
                <p>
                    Lorem ipsum dolor sit amet, consectetur adipisicing
                    elit, sed do eiusmod tempor incididunt ut labore et
                    dolore magna aliqua. Ut enim ad minim veniam, quis
                    nostrud exercitation ullamco laboris nisi ut.
                </p>
            </div>
        </article>

        <article class="otherContent">
            <a id="other"></a>
            <header>
                <h3>Rounded Borders</h3>
            </header>

            <div>
                <p>Details about rounded corners</p>
                <p>
                    One of the most common features that you'll hear
                    about is the use of rounded corners and we'll cover
```

```
                that here. Also, by configuring the div size and
                radius properly you can also make circular divs
            </p>
            <p>
                Lorem ipsum dolor sit amet, consectetur adipisicing
                elit, sed do eiusmod tempor incididunt ut labore et
                dolore magna aliqua. Ut enim ad minim veniam, quis
                nostrud exercitation ullamco laboris nisi ut.
            </p>
        </div>
    </article>

    <article class="otherContent">
        <a id="another"></a>
        <header>
            <h3>Another Interesting Article</h3>
        </header>

        <div>
            <p>More things to say...</p>
            <p>
                Lorem ipsum dolor sit amet, consectetur adipiscing
                elit. Proin luctus tincidunt justo nec tempor.
                Aliquam erat volutpat. Fusce facilisis ullamcorper
                consequat. Vestibulum non sapien lectus. Nam mi
                augue, posuere at tempus vel, dignissim vitae nulla.
                Nullam at quam eu sapien mattis ultrices. Quisque
                quis leo mi, at lobortis dolor. Nullam scelerisque
                facilisis placerat. Fusce a augue erat, malesuada
                euismod dui. Duis iaculis risus id felis volutpat
                elementum. Fusce blandit iaculis quam a cursus.
                Cras varius tincidunt cursus. Morbi justo eros,
                adipiscing ac placerat sed, posuere et mi.
                Suspendisse vulputate viverra aliquet. Duis non
                enim a nibh consequat mollis ac tempor lorem.
                Phasellus elit leo, semper eu luctus et, suscipit
                at lacus. In hac habitasse platea dictumst. Duis
                dignissim justo sit amet nulla pulvinar sodales.
            </p>
        </div>
    </article>
</section>
</div>

<aside id="sidebar">
    <h3>Other Titles</h3>
    <div id="moon"></div>
    <p>
        Check out some of the other titles available from Apress.
    </p>
    <section id="titles">
        <article class="book">
```

```
<header>
    <a href="http://www.apress.com/9781430240747"
        target="_blank">
        <img src="images\office365.png"
            alt="Pro Office 365"/>
    </a>
</header>
<p>
    Pro Office 365 Development is a practical, hands-on
    guide to building cloud-based solutions using the
    Office 365 platform.
</p>
</article>

<article class="book">
    <header>
        <a href="http://www.apress.com/9781430235781"
            target="_blank">
            <img src="images\access2010.png"
                alt="Pro Access 2010"/>
        </a>
    </header>
    <p>
        Pro Access 2010 Development is a fundamental resource
        for developing business applications that take
        advantage of the features of Access 2010. You'll learn
        how to build database applications, create Web-based
        databases, develop macros and VBA tools for Access
        applications, integrate Access with SharePoint, and
        much more.
    </p>
</article>

<article class="book">
    <header>
        <a href="http://www.apress.com/9781430228295"
            target="_blank">
            <img src="images\sharepoint_pm.png"
                alt="Pro Project Management w/SharePoint 2010"/>
        </a>
    </header>
    <p>
        The intention of this book is to provide a working
        case study that you can follow to create a complete
        PMIS (project management information system) with
        SharePoint Server's out-of-the-box functionality.
    </p>
</article>

<article class="book">
    <header>
        <a href="http://www.apress.com/9781430229049"
            target="_blank">
```

```
                <img src="images\office_workflow.png"
                        alt="Office 2010 Workflow"/>
            </a>
        </header>
        <p>
            Workflow is the glue that binds information worker
            processes, users, and artifacts–without it,
            information workers are just islands of data and
            potential. Office 2010 Workflow walks you through
            implementing workflow solutions.
        </p>
    </article>

    <article class="book">
        <header>
            <a href="http://www.apress.com/9781430224853"
                target="_blank">
                <img src="images\beginning_wf.png"
                        alt="Beginning WF"/>
            </a>
        </header>
        <p>
            Indexed by feature so you can find answers easily
            and written in an accessible style, Beginning WF
            shows how Microsoft's Workflow Foundation (WF)
            technology can be used in a wide variety of
            applications.
        </p>
    </article>
</section>
</aside>
</div>

<footer>
    <p>
        Last updated <time datetime="2012-05-12T20:32:22+05:00">
            May 12th 2012</time>
        by <a href="http://www.thecreativepeople.com"
                target="_blank">Mark J. Collins</a>
    </p>
</footer>

</body>
</html>
```

■ ■ ■

Chapter 4 – Completed Style

Listing B-1 shows the completed style element from the Chapter 4 project. I've explained this in pieces but am including it here if you want to see it all together.

Listing B-1. Chapter 4 completed style element

```
<style>
    /* Basic tag settings */
    body
    {
        margin: 0 auto;
        width: 940px;
        font: 13px/22px Helvetica, Arial, sans-serif;
        background: #f0f0f0;
    }

    h2
    {
        font-size: 18px;
        line-height: 5px;
        padding: 2px 0;
    }

    h3
    {
        font-size: 12px;
        line-height: 5px;
        padding: 2px 0;
    }

    h1, h2, h3
    {
        text-align: left;
    }

    p
    {
        padding-bottom: 2px;
    }
```

```css
.book
{
    padding: 5px;
}

/* Content sections */
.featuredContent
{
    background-color: #ffffff;
    border: 2px solid #6699cc;
    padding: 15px 15px 15px 15px;
}

.otherContent
{
    background-color: #c0c0c0;
    border: 1px solid #999999;
    padding: 15px 15px 15px 15px;
}

aside
{
    background-color: #6699cc;
    padding: 5px 5px 5px 5px;
}

footer
{
    margin-top: 12px;
    text-align:center;
    background-color: #ddd;
}

footer p
{
    padding-top: 10px;
}

/* Navigation Section */
nav
{
    left: 0;
    background-color: #003366;
}

nav ul
{
    margin: 0;
    list-style: none;
}
```

```css
nav ul li
{
    float: left;
}

nav ul li a
{
    display: block;
    margin-right: 20px;
    width: 140px;
    font-size: 14px;
    line-height: 28px;
    text-align: center;
    padding-bottom: 2px;
    text-decoration: none;
    color: #cccccc;
}

nav ul li a:hover
{
    color: #fff;
}

/* Rounded borders */
.rounded
{
    border: 1px solid;
    border-color:#999999;
    border-radius:25px;
    padding: 24px;
}

aside
{
    border: 1px solid #999999;
    border-radius:12px;
}

/* Make the radius half of the height */
nav
{
    height: 30px;
    border-radius:15px;
}

footer
{
    height: 50px;
    border-radius:25px;
}
```

```css
/* Gradients */
.intro
{
    border: 1px solid #999999;
    text-align:left;
    margin-top: 6px;
    padding-left: 15px;
    border-radius:25px;
    background-image: -webkit-linear-gradient(45deg, #ffffff, #6699cc);
    background-image: linear-gradient(45deg, #ffffff, #6699cc);
}

/* Setup a table for the content and sidebar */
#contentArea
{
    display: table;
}

#mainContent
{
    display: table-cell;
    padding-right: 2px;
}

aside
{
    display: table-cell;
    width: 280px;
}

/* Setup multiple columns for the articles */
article div
{
    text-align:justify;
    padding:6px;

    -webkit-column-count: 2;
    column-count: 2;

    -webkit-column-gap: 20px;
    column-gap: 20px;
}

/* Add the box shadow */
article img
{
    margin: 10px 0;
    box-shadow: 3px 3px 12px #222;
}
```

```css
.book img
{
    margin: 10px 0;
    display: block;
    box-shadow: 2px 2px 5px #444;
    margin-left: auto;
    margin-right: auto;
}

aside
{
    box-shadow: 3px 3px 3px #aaaaaa;
}

/* Stripe the title list */
#titles article:nth-child(2n+1)
{
    background: #c0c0c0;
    border: 1px solid #6699cc;
    border-radius: 10px;
}

#titles article:nth-child(2n+0)
{
    background: #6699cc;
    border: 1px solid #c0c0c0;
    border-radius: 10px;
}

/* Transforms - not supported yet */
.rotateContainer
{
    -webkit-perspective: 600px;
}

.rotate
{

    -webkit-transform-style: preserve-3d;
}

/* Animate the moon phases */
@@-webkit-keyframes moonPhases
{
0%    {background-image:url("images/moon1.png");}
12%   {background-image:url("images/moon2.png");}
25%   {background-image:url("images/moon3.png");}
37%   {background-image:url("images/moon4.png");}
50%   {background-image:url("images/moon5.png");}
62%   {background-image:url("images/moon6.png");}
75%   {background-image:url("images/moon7.png");}
```

```
87%    {background-image:url("images/moon8.png");}
100%   {background-image:url("images/moon1.png");}
}

@@keyframes moonPhases
{
0%    {background-image:url("images/moon1.png");}
12%   {background-image:url("images/moon2.png");}
25%   {background-image:url("images/moon3.png");}
37%   {background-image:url("images/moon4.png");}
50%   {background-image:url("images/moon5.png");}
62%   {background-image:url("images/moon6.png");}
75%   {background-image:url("images/moon7.png");}
87%   {background-image:url("images/moon8.png");}
100%   {background-image:url("images/moon1.png");}
}

#moon
{
    width:115px;
    height:115px;
    background-image: url("images/moon1.png");
    background-repeat: no-repeat;
    -webkit-animation-name:moonPhases;
    -webkit-animation-duration:4s;
    -webkit-animation-delay:3s;
    -webkit-animation-iteration-count:10;
    animation-name:moonPhases;
    animation-duration:4s;
    animation-delay:3s;
    animation-iteration-count:10;
}

</style>
```

■ ■ ■

Chapter 14 – Final Code

Listing C-1 specifies the final code for the project in Chapter 14. This is available from the downloaded source in the Index.cshtml file. I'm including it here in case you want to see it without downloading the code.

Listing C-1. Chapter 14 Final Code

```
@{
    Layout = null;
}

<!DOCTYPE html>

<html>
<head>
    <meta name="viewport" content="width=device-width" />
    <title>Chapter 14 - Checkers</title>
    <style type="text/css" >
        .board
        {
            width: 400px;
            height: 400px;
        }
        .bblack
        {
            background-color: #b93030;
            border-color: #b93030;
            border-width: 1px;
            border-style: solid;
            width: 48px;
            height: 48px;
            float: left;
            margin: 0px;
            padding: 0px;
        }
        .bwhite
        {
            background-color: #f7f7f7;
            border-color: #b93030;
            border-width: 1px;
            border-style: solid;
```

```
                width: 48px;
                height: 48px;
                float: left;
                margin: 0px;
                padding: 0px;
            }
            .piece
            {
                margin-left: 4px;
                margin-top: 4px;
            }
            .bblack.drop
            {
                opacity: 0.5;
            }
            .piece.selected
            {
                opacity: 0.5;
            }
        </style>
</head>
<body>
    <div class="board">
@for (int y = 0; y<8; y++)
{
    for (int x = 0; x<8; x++)
    {
        string id = x.ToString() + y.ToString();
        string css;
        if ((x + y) % 2 == 0)
        {
            css = "bwhite";
        }
        else
        {
            css = "bblack";
        }
        <text>
        <div id="@id" class="@css" draggable="false">
            @if ((x + y) % 2 != 0 && y != 3 && y != 4)
            {
                string imgSrc;
                string pid;
                if (y < 3)
                {
                    imgSrc = "Images/WhitePiece.png";
                    pid = "w"+id;
                }
```

```
                else
                {
                    imgSrc = "Images/BlackPiece.png";
                    pid = "b"+id;
                }
                <text>
                <img id="@pid" src="@imgSrc" draggable="true" class="piece" >
                </text>
            }
        </div>
        </text>
    }
}
    </div>
    <script type="text/javascript">
        // Get all the black squares
        var squares = document.querySelectorAll('.bblack');
        var i = 0;
        while (i < squares.length) {
            var s = squares[i++];
            // Add the event listeners
            s.addEventListener('dragover', dragOver, false);
            s.addEventListener('drop', drop, false);
            s.addEventListener('dragenter', dragEnter, false);
            s.addEventListener('dragleave', dragLeave, false);
        }

        i = 0;
        var pieces = document.querySelectorAll('img');
        while (i < pieces.length) {
            var p = pieces[i++];
            // Add the event listeners
            p.addEventListener('dragstart', dragStart, false);
            p.addEventListener('dragend', dragEnd, false);
        }

        // Handle the dragover event
        function dragOver(e) {
            if (e.preventDefault) {
                e.preventDefault();
            }

            // Get the img element that is being dragged
            var dragID = e.dataTransfer.getData("text/plain");
            var dragPiece = document.getElementById(dragID);

            if (dragPiece &&
                e.target.tagName === "DIV" &&
                isValidMove(dragPiece, e.target, false)) {
                e.dataTransfer.dropEffect = "move";
            }
```

```
        else {
            e.dataTransfer.dropEffect = "none";
        }
    }

    function dragStart(e) {
        if (e.target.draggable) {
            e.dataTransfer.effectAllowed = "move";
            e.dataTransfer.setData("text/plain", e.target.id);

            e.target.classList.add("selected");

            var dragIcon = document.createElement("img");
            dragIcon.src = "Images/smiley.jpg";
            e.dataTransfer.setDragImage(dragIcon, 0, 0);
        }
    }

    function drop(e) {
        // Prevent the event from being raised on the parent element
        if (e.stopPropagation) {
            e.stopPropagation();
        }

        // Stop the browsers default action
        if (e.preventDefault) {
            e.preventDefault();
        }

        // Get the img element that is being dragged
        var droppedID = e.dataTransfer.getData("text/plain");
        var droppedPiece = document.getElementById(droppedID);

        if (droppedPiece &&
            e.target.tagName === "DIV" &&
            isValidMove(droppedPiece, e.target, true)) {

            // Create a new img on the target location
            var newPiece = document.createElement("img");
            newPiece.src = droppedPiece.src;
            newPiece.id = droppedPiece.id.substr(0, 1) + e.target.id;
            if (droppedPiece.draggable){
                newPiece.draggable = true;
                newPiece.classList.add("jumpOnly");
            }
            newPiece.classList.add("piece");
            newPiece.addEventListener("dragstart", dragStart, false);
            newPiece.addEventListener("dragend", dragEnd, false);
            e.target.appendChild(newPiece);

            // Remove the previous image
            droppedPiece.parentNode.removeChild(droppedPiece);
```

```
        // Remove the drop effect from the target element
        e.target.classList.remove('drop');

        // See if the piece needs to be promoted
        kingMe(newPiece);
    }
}

function dragEnd(e) {
    e.target.classList.remove("selected");
}

function dragEnter(e) {
    // Get the img element that is being dragged
    var dragID = e.dataTransfer.getData("text/plain");
    var dragPiece = document.getElementById(dragID);

    if (dragPiece &&
        e.target.tagName === "DIV" &&
        isValidMove(dragPiece, e.target, false)) {
        e.target.classList.add('drop');
    }
}

function dragLeave(e) {
    e.target.classList.remove("drop");
}

function isValidMove(source, target, drop) {
    // Get the piece prefix and location
    var startPos = source.id.substr(1, 2);
    var prefix = source.id.substr(0, 1);

    // Get the drop location
    var endPos = target.id;

    // You can't drop on the existing location
    if (startPos === endPos) {
        return false;
    }

    // You can't drop on occupied square
    if (target.childElementCount != 0) {
        return false;
    }

    var jumpOnly = false;
    if (source.classList.contains("jumpOnly")) {
        jumpOnly = true;
    }
```

```
        // Compute the x and y coordinates
        var xStart = parseInt(startPos.substr(0, 1));
        var yStart = parseInt(startPos.substr(1, 1));
        var xEnd = parseInt(endPos.substr(0, 1));
        var yEnd = parseInt(endPos.substr(1, 1));

        switch (prefix) {
            // For white pieces...
            case "w":
                if (yEnd <= yStart)
                    return false; // Can't move backwards
                break;

            // For black pieces...
            case "b":
                if (yEnd >= yStart)
                    return false; // Can't move backwards
                break;
        }

        // These rule apply to all pieces
        if (yStart === yEnd || xStart === xEnd)
            return false; // Move must be diagonal
        if (Math.abs(yEnd - yStart) > 2 || Math.abs(xEnd - xStart) > 2)
            return false; // Can't move more than two spaces
        if (Math.abs(xEnd - xStart) === 1 && jumpOnly)
            return false; // Only jumps are allowed

        var jumped = false;
        // If moving two spaces, find the square that is jumped
        if (Math.abs(xEnd - xStart) === 2) {
            var pos = ((xStart + xEnd) / 2).toString() +
                      ((yStart + yEnd) / 2).toString();
            var div = document.getElementById(pos);
            if (div.childElementCount === 0)
                return false;  // Can't jump an empty square
            var img = div.children[0];
            if (img.id.substr(0, 1).toLowerCase() === prefix.toLowerCase())
                return false; // Can't jump a piece of the same color

            // If this function is called from the drop event
            // Remove the jumped piece
            if (drop) {
                div.removeChild(img);
                jumped = true;
            }
        }

        // Set the draggable attributes so the next player can take a turn.
        if (drop) {
            enableNextPlayer(source);
```

```javascript
        // If we jumped a piece, we're allowed to go again
        if (jumped) {
            source.draggable = true;
            source.classList.add("jumpOnly");
        }
    }

    return true;
}

function kingMe(piece) {

    // If we're already a king, just return
    if (piece.id.substr(0, 1) === "W" || piece.id.substr(0, 1) === "B")
        return;

    var newPiece;

    // If this is a white piece on the 7th row
    if (piece.id.substr(0, 1) === "w" && piece.id.substr(2, 1) === "7") {
        newPiece = document.createElement("img");
        newPiece.src = "Images/WhiteKing.png";
        newPiece.id = "W"+piece.id.substr(1, 2);
    }

    // If this is a black piece on the 0th row
    if (piece.id.substr(0, 1) === "b" && piece.id.substr(2, 1) === "0") {
        var newPiece = document.createElement("img");
        newPiece.src = "Images/BlackKing.png";
        newPiece.id = "B" + piece.id.substr(1, 2);
    }

    // If a new piece was created, set its properties and events
    if (newPiece) {
        newPiece.draggable = true;
        newPiece.classList.add("piece");

        newPiece.addEventListener('dragstart', dragStart, false);
        newPiece.addEventListener('dragend', dragEnd, false);

        var parent = piece.parentNode;
        parent.removeChild(piece);
        parent.appendChild(newPiece);
    }
}

function enableNextPlayer(piece) {

    // Get all of the pieces
    var pieces = document.querySelectorAll('img');
```

```
            i = 0;
            while (i < pieces.length) {
                var p = pieces[i++];

                // If this is the same color that just moved, disable dragging
                if (p.id.substr(0, 1).toUpperCase() ===
                    piece.id.substr(0, 1).toUpperCase()) {
                    p.draggable = false;
                }
                    // Otherwise, enable dragging
                else {
                    p.draggable = true;
                }

                p.classList.remove("jumpOnly");
            }
        }

    </script>
</body>
</html>
```

Index

▓ U

▓ V

▓ W, X, Y, Z

Lightning Source UK Ltd.
Milton Keynes UK
UKOW010311021012

199897UK00004B/3/P